LANDSCAPE AESTHETICS

Landscape Aesthetics

TOWARD AN ENGAGED ECOLOGY

Alberto L. Siani

Columbia University Press
New York

Columbia University Press
Publishers Since 1893
New York   Chichester, West Sussex
cup.columbia.edu
Copyright © 2024 Columbia University Press
All rights reserved

Library of Congress Cataloging-in-Publication Data
Names: Siani, Alberto L., 1983- author.
Title: Landscape aesthetics : toward an engaged ecology / Alberto L. Siani.
Description: New York : Columbia University Press, 2024. |
Includes bibliographical references and index.
Identifiers: LCCN 2023057162 (print) | LCCN 2023057163 (ebook) |
ISBN 9780231213660 (hardback) | ISBN 9780231213677 (trade paperback) |
ISBN 9780231559966 (ebook)
Subjects: LCSH: Landscapes—Philosophy. | Aesthetics. | Social ecology.
Classification: LCC BH301.L3 S565 2024 (print) | LCC BH301.L3 (ebook) |
DDC 304.201—dc23/eng/20240126
LC record available at https://lccn.loc.gov/2023057162
LC ebook record available at https://lccn.loc.gov/2023057163

Cover design: Elliott S. Cairns
Cover image: Peter Henry Emerson, *The Old Order and The New*, 1886.
Digital image courtesy of Getty's Open Content Program.

For Alfonso Kemal,
May he be fully present in the landscapes of the future.

The activities of the fox, the dog, and the thrush may at least stand as reminders and symbols of that unity of experience which we so fractionize when work is labor, and thought withdraws us from the world. The live animal is fully present, all there, in all of its actions: in its wary glances, its sharp sniffings, its abrupt cocking of ears. All senses are equally on the *qui vive*. As you watch, you see motion merging into sense and sense into motion—constituting that animal grace so hard for man to rival. What the live creature retains from the past and what it expects from the future operate as directions in the present.

—JOHN DEWEY, *ART AS EXPERIENCE*

CONTENTS

ACKNOWLEDGMENTS   xiii

LIST OF ILLUSTRATIONS   xv

PREFACE   xix

Prologue
Where Are Landscapes?   1

1. Instead of a definition, looking for a place   1
2. The risks of knowledge and the spaces of philosophy: A Kantian topology   3
3. Habitats, aesthetics, cultures   9

Chapter One
A Game of Landscapes: Methodological, Linguistic, and Conceptual Rules   14

1. A pragmatist setting   14
2. Landscape, environment, territory   17
3. Performing landscapes, moving borders   22
4. "Like the dog and the flea"   28

Chapter Two
Landscape and Aesthetics 33

1. A double marginality 33
2. Paradoxes of isolationism 37
3. Dewey's re-legitimation of aesthetics 40
4. Landscape as experience 45
5. Which aesthetics for which landscape? Which landscape for which aesthetics? 52
6. The substantiality of aesthetics and the plurality of landscape 54

Chapter Three
Patterns of Encounter I: Aesthetic Matters 62

1. Interpretation 63
   1.1. Nature and art: Deflating differences 64
   1.2. For a consistently pragmatist interpretive framework 69

2. Art 72
   2.1. Art in landscapes, landscapes in art: From painting to experiencing and back 73
   2.2. Painting, mapping, gardening, writing 78

Chapter Four
Patterns of Encounter II: Landscape Matters 83

1. Temporalizations of space and spatializations of time 84
   1.1. Experience, knowledge, and appreciation 84
   1.2. History, identity, and palimpsests 86
   1.3. Loss of innocence, ideology, and critique 87
   1.4. Climate change, infrastructure, and ecologies of scale 89
   1.5. Anthropocene, cultural ecologies, and ephemerality 91

2. Pre- and post-: Modernism and environmentalism 95
   2.1. Landscapes and modernity 95
   2.2. From environmentalism to postenvironmentalism: Wind turbines and the role of aesthetics 97
   2.3. "Beyond the modern landscape" 100

CONTENTS

3. Justice and politics 103
   3.1. Breaking ground: The European Landscape Convention 103
   3.2. Participation and the insiders/outsiders dilemma 106
   3.3. Local versus global and the Eurocentrism charge 107
   3.4. Migration and settledness, displacements and lockdowns 109
   3.5. A very provisional upshot 111

4. Education 112
   4.1. Landscape education: Not just a pastime 112
   4.2. "An entirely different game": Wittgenstein and enskilment 114
   4.3. Aesthetic education: Skills for our time 117

5. Interdisciplinary perspectives 120

Chapter Five
Building Common Ground:
Landscape Character and Its Assessment 123

1. Reasons and limits of objectivism in landscape character assessment 124
2. The narrowness of experience and the disappearance of aesthetics 128
3. A pragmatist alternative 132
4. Beyond subjects and objects: Reframing the twofold perspective challenge 134

Chapter Six
Lived Landscapes: Three Sketches 138

1. Valleriana: A Tuscan reverie 139
2. Heaven over Münsterland 148
3. *Hüzün* and a promise of immanence: Coda in Istanbul 153

Conclusion 161

NOTES 167

BIBLIOGRAPHY 205

INDEX 215

ACKNOWLEDGMENTS

I have discussed many of the issues in this book in a number of venues and have received valuable feedback from the audiences. The students of my undergraduate and graduate courses on aesthetics and landscape and on Dewey at the University of Pisa between 2021 and 2023 provided many stimulating observations and questions. Paolo D'Angelo, Alfredo Ferrarin, Ivan Gaskell, and Yuriko Saito greatly helped me with their suggestions on the book idea and proposal. A first draft of the manuscript benefited from the insightful critique of three anonymous reviewers, and the introduction was carefully read and commented on by Elena Romagnoli. At Columbia University Press, Wendy Lochner provided vision and encouragement, Marisa Lastres and Lowell Frye kind and unfailing support. As always, my wife, Çiğdem Oğuz, assisted me with illuminating conversations, focused advice, and so much more. My heartfelt thanks go to all of them.

ILLUSTRATIONS

FIGURE 0.1   View of the departmental library's garden from my office on an early spring morning, Pisa, Italy   2
FIGURE 0.2   Königsberg (former Prussia) before its bombing in 1944   4
FIGURE 0.3   Today's Kaliningrad, Russia, with Kant's Island and the cathedral where he is buried in the foreground   5
FIGURE 0.4   Frontispiece of Francis Bacon's *Novum Organum* (1652)   6
FIGURE 0.5   Flag of the city of Kaliningrad today   8
FIGURE 0.6   A rose, Kant's example of free natural beauty   10
FIGURE 0.7   Cueva de las Manos, Argentina (the painted hands are dated to around 7,000 years ago)   12
FIGURE 1.1   Aerial view of the barrage in Eiderstedt, North Frisia, Germany   15
FIGURE 1.2   Balconies in the "Angeli" (Angels) neighborhood, Caltanissetta (Sicily, Italy)   19
FIGURE 1.3   Dolly Sods Wilderness near Davis, West Virginia   24
FIGURE 1.4   Rural landscape in Nauviale, Aveyron, France   24
FIGURE 1.5   Café in Baarle-Nassau, the Netherlands, with the border between the Netherlands and Belgium marked on the ground   27
FIGURE 1.6   *Wittgenstein's Cabin 11*, from the series Wittgenstein's Cabin, by Spanish visual artist Dionisio González   30
FIGURE 2.1   Hidden threats of classical scenic views, in the Bavarian Alps, Berchtesgaden, Germany   34
FIGURE 2.2   Artificial lake of Campo, close to Pisa, Italy   36

ILLUSTRATIONS

FIGURE 2.3 Filters-enhanced postcard view titled *The Orange Skies at Ladram Bay* (England) 39
FIGURE 2.4 Pueblo Indian pottery, from Hano pueblo in northeastern Arizona 44
FIGURE 2.5 Mountains, wooden bench swing with wicker hammocks, and a bamboo footbridge in a paddy field at sunset during the monsoon, Vang Vieng, Laos 46
FIGURE 2.6 *Landscape and Bamboo* by Tani Bunchō 50
FIGURE 2.7 *Landscape with Windmills and Christ as Good Shepherd* by Lucas Gassel 55
FIGURE 2.8 *Market Outside Tripoli's Walls, Castle and Cemetery on the Right* 59
FIGURE 2.9 *Landscape with Two Peasant Girls and a Rainbow* by Konstantin Somov 60
FIGURE 3.1 Sign to the entrance of the Nature Center in Blacklick Woods Metro Park, Ohio 63
FIGURE 3.2 View of Husband Hill on Mars 67
FIGURE 3.3 Tree of Jesse, Wells Cathedral, England 71
FIGURE 3.4 Giorgione's *The Tempest* 74
FIGURE 3.5 *Mont Sainte-Victoire* by Paul Cézanne 75
FIGURE 3.6 *Bathers, Mont Sainte-Victoire in the Background* by Paul Cézanne 75
FIGURE 3.7 *The Great Alachua-Savana* by William Bartram 79
FIGURE 3.8 The grandiose, violin-shaped plan for the garden of the Borbone Royal Palace in Caserta, Italy, by architect Luigi Vanvitelli, inaugurated 1774 81
FIGURE 3.9 Guerrilla gardening in Berlin, Germany 81
FIGURE 4.1 Archaeological-agricultural landscape around the ancient city of Troy (today Hisarlık, Turkey) 87
FIGURE 4.2 Detail of Alan Sonfist's land artwork *Time Landscape*, New York City 89
FIGURE 4.3 Layers of rubbish from a former landfill 92
FIGURE 4.4 *The Harvesters*, by Pieter Bruegel the Elder 94
FIGURE 4.5 Windmill and wind turbine, Eaucourt-sur-Somme, France 99
FIGURE 4.6 Earthrise from the Lunar Reconnaissance Orbiter above Compton Crater 102
FIGURE 4.7 Longjing tea district, Hangzhou, China 108

ILLUSTRATIONS

FIGURE 4.8   Garden of contemplation, Canadian Museum of Human Rights, Winnipeg, Canada   110
FIGURE 4.9   *Surf-swimming, Hawaii*, by G. T. Bettany   113
FIGURE 4.10 Landscape and interdisciplinarity   121
FIGURE 5.1   The process of landscape character assessment   130
FIGURE 6.1   Pontito, the remotest and least populated of the *castella* of Valleriana, Italy   141
FIGURE 6.2   Preparation of *necci*, the chestnut-flour flatbreads typical from Valleriana, Italy   145
FIGURE 6.3   The three Anabaptists' cages on St. Lambert's Church tower, Münster, Germany   149
FIGURE 6.4   *Münsterlander Parklandschaft* with the moated Burg Kakesbeck, Germany   150
FIGURE 6.5   Savage urbanization in Istanbul, Turkey   155
FIGURE 6.6   Istanbul from the ferry, with the bridge connecting Europe and Asia   159

PREFACE

It was mainly two nonacademic reasons that prompted me, in 2021, to start working on what would become this book. The most important and wonderful reason was the birth of my son, Alfonso Kemal. The other reason, less impactful on a personal level but dramatic on a global scale, was the enduring COVID-19 pandemic, with the changes and restrictions it brought to daily life, which were particularly severe in Italy and with a newborn. Both circumstances generated in me an intense concern for the importance of lived spaces, (re)learning to orient oneself in the world, and sustainability. This, in turn, quickly led to a deeply felt need to open up new horizons in my research and academic work, in which the issues addressed in this book had until then played an almost entirely irrelevant role. As I began to systematize what I was learning, it became clear that, whatever the original reasons and the links with my previous research, the new topics inevitably revolved around a discourse of crisis, or more precisely, of several crises. Although I had little sympathy for this expression in a philosophical context, it was almost natural for me to accept it as the background for my new research. Writing this book meant finding ways to philosophically mediate the input given by this sense of destabilization, translating abused crisis discourses into more negotiable and fruitful terms.

Stating that the main input for this book is a discourse of several crises may sound pretentious. How can something as harmless and disengaged as landscapes and aesthetics have to do with crises, itself a hyperinflated term? The unease will not be dispelled but perhaps increased once I specify which crises I mean. There are three of them, and they can be presented by decreasing generality. The first crisis is the environmental one, in its broadest sense, as a sum of well-known issues such as climate change, global warming, sea-level rise, deforestation and desertification, pollution, and loss of biodiversity, with the attending impacts on human beings, from natural catastrophes to climate-induced mass migrations, displacements, and so on. The second one is the crisis in the humanities, another broad, often confused concept that entails declining (or at least not growing, especially if compared with STEM disciplines) numbers of students, professors, programs, and departments; the restructuring of the academic profession according to criteria that often do not fit the humanities; generalized doubts about their individual and social relevance and legitimacy. The third one is the crisis of aesthetics within recent landscape studies, where it tends to be marginalized and viewed with suspicion. These three topics are too broad, as well as too loosely interconnected, to be reasonably investigated together in one book. While the input for the book comes from all of them, here I only address the last in a direct way, as announced by the title. However, it is my hope that the discussion of landscape and aesthetics can contribute to the discourses on the first two as well, although in a more indirect way. Before going into the subject of the book itself, I would like to give a few reasons for this hope, not least to circumscribe, if not eliminate, the impression of pretension.

It is a triviality (a bitter one, though) to say that the environmental crisis, with its many facets and implications, is one of the greatest challenges of our time, if not the greatest. Understandably, this makes it one of the most attended to topics of our time, both from a strictly scientific point of view and from a broader one, including political action, public activism, individual habits, economic choices, all the way to media and artistic representation, fashion, food.... Humanities, to touch upon the second crisis, have consequently developed, in the last fifty years, a growing interest for environmental matters. As a matter of fact, a brand-new autonomous field of study—namely, "environmental humanities"—emerged and established itself within the last couple of decades. Environmental humanities have their own university programs and research groups, journals, and conventions based at dozens of universities and centers around the world. Environmental humanities combine themes, disciplines, and methods that are characteristic of humanistic forms of knowledge with topical environmental problems, also in an applied sense. They are hence structurally multi- and interdisciplinary, and they aspire, beside their topic-specific environmental goals, to reaffirm the importance and practical viability of humanities as well as to overcome the boundaries between different forms of knowledge and traditions. They also act as an ambitious attempt to integrate diverse cultural backgrounds as well as a global point of view and local ones.

Environmental humanities thematize the environment in an intentionally broad and abstract sense, from a primary reference to wild, uncontaminated nature to a more and more widespread interest in anthropized, urban, and everyday environments. They do so from the equally broad perspective of humanities, including all humanistic forms of knowledge, however conceived. It is almost as if the lemma "environmental humanities" tried to programmatically reunite two general abstract terms that are, or are normally conceived of as, opposed to or at least different from each other: on one side, the environment; on the other, the human. Environmental humanities, I am suggesting, display from their very name an essential dualism whose reconciliation is, broadly stated, their aim. This dualistic stance is understandable based on the genealogy of environmental humanities, born in a context in which *both* the environment and the human *and* the environment and the humanities were thought of as dichotomies to be reconciled. Accordingly, on the one hand, the environment is conceived of as the space enveloping or containing humans, postulating some ultimate difference between them as well as the structural threat posed by the latter for the former. On the other hand, the environment is the theoretical and practical monopoly of natural sciences, a relatively stable, objective, measurable set of nonhuman (and noncultural) hard facts and quantitative relationships: humanities have little or nothing to say about it.

Based on these starting assumptions, the task of environmental humanities was, and is, about throwing bridges and tearing down boundaries between terms conceived of as essentially different. Needless to say, this task was, and is, of the highest importance. At the same time, in part through the contribution of environmental humanities themselves, some reasons for dissatisfaction, or at least for acknowledging that task's partiality and looking for an alternative angle, have emerged. To put it a bit emphatically, the rationale behind the birth of environmental humanities was to have the most global, inclusive, and broadest possible basis to address the double crisis of the environment and the humanities: a huge collective effort to mobilize all possible resources at hand to fight the ultimate battle ahead. Hence the use of such abstract umbrella concepts such as environment and humanities and of a dualistic, clear-cut approach. Such an approach rightly accounts for a crisis rooted in that very dualism and tries to overcome it, yet can only do so up to a certain extent, beyond which it just perpetuates the dualism itself. This persisting dualism and indefinitely postponed reconciliation are distinctive, I believe, not just of environmental humanities but of much of the way we think of both the environment and the human / the humanities. Indeed, it is apparently more natural, and in some cases necessary, to begin with dualisms and to set their reconciliation as a task. It looks less commonsensical to try to think in a nondualistic way from the very beginning, yet there is a point at which to keep pursuing reconciliation means indefinitely keeping it at bay. To bring forward the goals of this mobilization in a fresh and effective way, we need a more fine-grained, less universalistic, less abstract discourse.

The intersection of landscapes and aesthetics is the way through which I suggest we try to think from a point that is already beyond the dualism without, of course, disavowing the legacy of environmental humanities. Here, however, we encounter the third crisis mentioned at the beginning: that of aesthetics within the current landscape discourse and practice. Aesthetics was traditionally an integral part of the landscape discourse and practice, so it may be surprising to see how little relevance it has in today's: indeed, one has a feeling of outright rejection toward aesthetics. As we will see, there are good reasons for this. And yet, once again, what generates the crisis is an unresolved dualism. The aesthetics that was an integral part of the traditional landscape discourse aimed at essential separation and distinction between the aesthetically valuable and the ordinary, non- or antiaesthetic reality. Such separation was rooted in and confirmed a worldview and an ideology that have become unduly reductive and ultimately unacceptable for us. At the same time, rejecting aesthetics as such within the landscape discourse (i.e., exasperating the dualism) perpetuates traditional prejudices or ideologies and leads to new forms of reductionism and exclusion. The marginality of aesthetics in landscape discourse is the flipside of the marginality of landscape in aesthetics. Such marginality is partly due to the privilege of artistic beauty over natural beauty in traditional aesthetics: landscapes are, in a traditional framework, interesting for aesthetics only insofar as they are "art"—that is, valuable painted ones, or natural ones so beautiful that they look like art. Throwing a bridge over the mutual neglect and suspicion, I will argue, on the contrary, that landscapes are *as such*, independent of their beauty, important to aesthetics somehow even more than art and that this acknowledgment requires a perspective shift in aesthetics itself: a shift, to anticipate, toward an engaged, continuistic, holistic, anti-exceptionalist, and pragmatist conception.

Working through, and then against, the immediate appearance of complicit disengagement associated with both landscapes and aesthetics, the book proposes a joint reframing of both terms and reclaims the full, indispensable value of their engagement together and beyond traditionally more "activist" disciplines, terms, and oppositional couples. Compared to environmental humanities, on the one hand, the reference is not to the humanities in their full breadth but, in a more targeted and modest way, to aesthetics. This does not mean renouncing other themes and concepts belonging to humanistic forms of knowledge but rather trying to give them a more precise direction, in a way that will hopefully become clear in the course of the argument as I explain how I understand aesthetics. On the other hand, the reference is not to the environment as a universal objective container, semantically already strongly connoted within the crisis discourse concerning it, but to landscape as the space concretely lived and experienced by humans in ways that are ever different and hence necessarily conceived of in a plural, nonabstract way. Thus, beside and beyond the oneness and universality of environment as an overarching abstract concept, I suggest we put at the center the plurality of single concrete landscapes. The concept of landscape hence becomes the focal point of intersecting nondualistic approaches to the crisis discourses presented at the outset and revolving at different distances from that focal point. Landscapes can do so, I claim, because they are already situated beyond dualisms, thus allowing perspective shifts in those discourses. Landscapes are the intersection of the environment and the human, the thing and its image, the place and the people, natural sciences (or STEM) and the humanities, enjoyment and utilization, subjective and objective standpoints, form and function, nature and culture, globalism and localism, different cultures, and so on.

By merging landscapes and aesthetics, my main aim, to give it a provisional formulation, is to trace a principle of sense and order in the irreducible plurality and contingency of concretely lived and experienced spaces. This aim will be pursued based on the double presupposition that humans and the spaces they inhabit are not to be conceived of as mutually independent and external to each other and that we do not need to struggle to bring a humanistic perspective into the discourse around this aim because framing it without concepts and themes associated with the humanities simply does not make sense. This double presupposition is not, I want to stress, the result of wishful thinking but established through the very use of the term *landscape*, including in ordinary contexts. At least in this sense, then, this term already puts us beyond dualism, and the point becomes reflecting this perspective shift in the crisis discourses, whereby aesthetics will lead the path. This leads to reconceiving both landscapes and aesthetics no longer as two separate independent domains, coming together only on exceptional occasions (as traditional aesthetics does) or to be kept well apart to avoid ideological intrusions (as today's "critical" landscape discourse does). Landscapes and aesthetics, this book claims, intersect at their very core, always and not just in some exceptional circumstances. Aesthetics becomes nondispensable but in fact path-leading in thematizing lived and experienced spaces as such, and landscapes become core embodiments of the meaning and functioning of a nondualistic aesthetics.

Landscapes, I argue, are specific configurations of the concrete units of sense we experience, institute, and inhabit. Our experience "with" our surrounding environment is multifaceted and multilayered and risks to be confusingly haphazard. When a sense of order, completion, and unity steps in and gives it structure and purpose, then we can relate to and communicate meanings: we no longer have "just" a surrounding environment, but we inhabit a landscape. The aesthetic is nowhere to be isolated but everywhere in this process: it enables a methodological move from the abstract generality of environments to the concrete plurality of landscapes. Aesthetics is what gives perspective, sense, and order to an otherwise irremediably fragmented discourse, and in doing so it takes a new face and function itself. Landscapes are not just ways of contemplating the world as "beautiful" but of being in it, engaging it, and inhabiting it in multiple ways that make sense for us in their empirical plurality, preventing conceptual and essential generalizations and clear-cut borders. The combination of landscape and aesthetics named in the title of this book does not stand, therefore, for the attempt to bring together two mutually independent concepts but for the attempt to illuminate their structural conceptual intersection: saying something about landscapes means saying something about aesthetics, and vice versa. This intersection, in turn, configurates itself as the core matrix of an engaged ecology, which, while not thematized as such by the book, constitutes its ultimate horizon and destination as expressed by the subtitle. In building up the core matrix together with its main "regional" implications, my view on negotiating the terms of the current crisis and transitioning toward an engaged ecology delineates itself.

Let me sum up what I have said so far. The book's underlying concern is about the environmental crisis and the crisis in the humanities. On this background, the question then is how humanities can meaningfully contribute to addressing the environmental crisis, thus concretely displaying their ability to be effective and topical. The attempt to bring the environment and the humanities together presupposes the immediate, structurally dualistic configuration that is characteristic of environmental humanities. While certainly not denying their importance, I am ultimately not satisfied with the persisting dualism inherent in their very denomination. Looking for an alternative guiding thread that could present itself as already nondualistic and hence able to turn the tables of the underlying crisis discourses, landscape stands out. Starting with landscape instead of with the environment adds substance to the relative crisis discourse *and* makes the humanities' contribution indispensable, all in one go. While the environment works as a maximally abstract and universal umbrella concept, landscapes only exist in the plurality of their singular configurations, making it difficult, and in fact impossible, to talk about them in an essentialist way. This is where I resort to a pragmatist approach, led and structured by aesthetics, itself holistically reconceived in order to avoid the isolationist and exceptionalist threads that have basically driven it out of the landscape discourse.

The book then thematizes landscape as a key concept at the intersection of several crises and, on this background, attempts to establish through a pragmatist-aesthetic strategy its full potential not only in a theoretical sense but also through some concrete instances of its practical way of functioning, thus outlining a core matrix, both theoretical and practical, of an engaged ecology. With some approximation, the prologue and first two chapters mainly cover the theoretical part, the last two chapters are of a more applied nature, with the two middle chapters bridging them by outlining some broad patterns of interaction between a philosophical approach and critical, contemporary landscape-related issues. Although I have generally strived for inclusion rather than hyperspecialization, the more theoretical chapters might be more accessible to a philosophical readership and more challenging (although possibly more original) for a nonphilosophical, landscape-oriented one, and vice versa. The interweaving of exquisitely philosophical topics and concepts, confrontation with landscape literature including its technical aspects, and broader societal concerns is, I think, a strong point of originality of this book—but, whatever the merits of this interweaving, it also posits peculiar difficulties and constraints. For this I can only ask for the patience of readers who have backgrounds, a patience that would already be welcome here as I provide some details on the chapters.

In the prologue, consistent with the rejection of essentialisms that is in my opinion necessary to tackle landscapes, I do not begin, as is often the case in philosophy, by asking "what are landscapes?" (i.e., with a matter of definition) but by asking "where are landscapes?" (i.e., with a matter of topology). The searched location of landscapes is both the empirical and the philosophical one, which I bring together by outlining a theory of habitats based on Immanuel Kant. Habitats, in this context, are the spaces of empirical contingency where humans cannot hope to establish necessary and universal laws but at most a provisional, a posteriori order of familiarity. The latter, while lacking the certainties of Kantian a priori, can still hopefully be stable enough to allow not only survival but also a meaningful interchange with the space and the time we happen to inhabit. The groundwork for this possibility is, according to Kant himself, an aesthetic one. Landscapes, I further claim, are to be located within such a theory of habitats; more precisely, they constitute a concrete, experienced form of appearance of habitats thus understood. Chapter 1 is dedicated to a methodological, terminological, and conceptual clarification of the linguistic game of landscapes in a nonessentialist fashion. Accordingly, first I delineate my pragmatist approach and advance, via three general features, a fundamental characterization of *landscape*, distinguishing it from the cognate concepts of *environment* and *territory*. On this basis, I then propose that landscapes are performative ways and configurations of our making sense of the world we inhabit, conjugating the contingency of nature with our need and ability to institute an inhabitable order in it. The chapter's conclusion refines this suggestion through an analogy of the suggested use of the term *landscape* and Ludwig Wittgenstein's notion of "language games." Chapter 2 is entirely devoted to aesthetics in its intersection with landscapes. It begins with the acknowledgment of the paradoxical absence or even repudiation of aesthetics in the contemporary institutional and academic discourse on landscapes. It then reclaims the centrality of aesthetics for landscapes and at the same time the necessity to frame it in an alternative way from the one repudiated in the current landscape discourse. Consequently, the chapter proceeds to outline, mostly along Deweyan lines, a holistic, antidualistic, and anti-exceptionalist aesthetics, based on which landscapes can be seen as consummated, successful, and, hence, aesthetically meaningful forms of our interaction with the world we inhabit. This also leads to reframing the general role of the aesthetic itself in our experience: no longer a beautiful, extraordinary exception to our ordinary experience, the aesthetic becomes the principle of order and meaningfulness innervating all of it. Such an aesthetic principle allows us to institute values and criteria rooted in the very core of our ordinary experience, aimed at its improvement and at any time pragmatically revisable and adjustable, thus preventing objections of relativism and affirming a convinced pluralism instead.

The following two chapters further flesh out the proposed intersection of landscape and aesthetics by presenting selected patterns of interaction between the proposed theoretical framework and some specific, though broadly framed, issues located at that intersection. The focus is first on traditionally aesthetics-related ones (chapter 3) and then on traditionally landscape-related ones (chapter 4), with the aim, however, to defuse strict disciplinary boundaries and to reinforce and develop the "landscape + aesthetics matrix" as a unitary compound in its own right. Thus, chapter 3 delves into two defining topics of aesthetics—namely, interpretation and art—insisting once again on the advantages of landscapes against or beyond the environment, on the pragmatic flexibility of the border between nature and culture, and on the co-belonging of aesthetic practices and values with seemingly nonaesthetic ones. The (only apparently) nonaesthetic side of the argument further unfolds in the broader chapter 4. This in fact pursues the landscape + aesthetics matrix in an applied sense, returning to the crisis discourse (environmental, but not only) from which I took my cue and showing how the proposed matrix can contribute to reshaping some aspects of those discourses or seeing them with fresh eyes. The discussion touches on five broad topics with several internal ramifications: temporality, modernism and environmentalism, justice and politics, education, and interdisciplinarity. I address these topics through the philosophical framework developed up to that point, yet in dialogue with a mostly nonphilosophical literature on landscape. The hope is that not only philosophy can concretely contribute from its perspective to some urgent topical issues, but the latter can, conversely, inform and give perspective to philosophy, thus helping to overcome suspicions and divides against the humanities. Given the weight of the topics considered and the ambition to develop an interdisciplinary dialogue, it should be clear that chapters 3 and 4 have the function of probing the ground and starting conversations rather than articulating detailed solutions.

A claim to detail is raised instead in chapter 5, focusing on the rather technical issue of landscape character and its assessment, with the aim to offer a critique of the current concept and practice as well as a reframing proposal, both based on the framework developed up to this point. This way the latter is put to the test of a very concrete, paradigmatic problem in landscape research and practice. The sixth and final chapter may look like an addendum, as it breaks from the main argument and has a lighter, more informal tone and topic; at least in my intentions, though, it is an integral part of the book. It consists of three "sketches" or "studies" of quite different landscapes I have directly and intensely experienced, known, and lived. The aim is to provide a unitary, meaningful, yet in no way exclusive interpretation of each of them, drawing, albeit only in a sketchy way, on the interaction of landscapes and aesthetics as I have understood it, thus showing it practically at work and ideally eliciting some "countersketches" from the reader. Chapters 5 and 6, in this way, conclude the book with the elements of detail and technicalities but also personal experience and narrative that can lend body, texture, and feeling to the landscape + aesthetics matrix.

LANDSCAPE AESTHETICS

PROLOGUE

Where Are Landscapes?

1. INSTEAD OF A DEFINITION, LOOKING FOR A PLACE

Where are landscapes situated? What is their place, empirical as well as philosophical? The first part of the question may sound weird: we all know where landscapes are. We most likely think either of some famous scenic view, the kind mentioned in travel guides or road signs, or of some personally valued one, not necessarily famous but relevant for our memory, taste, or some specific experience we had there. In any case, we would normally be able to indicate the position of a landscape or take someone there. If we arrive to the intended position and come upon some significant change in the scene, we may say something like: "This is not what I meant," or even: "The landscape I meant does not exist anymore." In a similar circumstance, a travel guide may strike that specific place off or refer to it in the past tense. Thus, a landscape is not just (in) some place, however delimited or recognized. It also has to do with the objects within it and with their arrangement. This already complicates the empirical search for the landscape's place. But even if the place, the objects within it, and their arrangement do not materially change, they are obviously different at different times or seasons, in different weather conditions, and so on. If I take someone to see a mountain area with snow in the winter and then again in the summer with green-yellowish meadows, am I taking them to see the same landscape? Besides, should not places respond to at least a few criteria in order to answer the "where" question and qualify as landscapes? I may prompt my inquirer to just look outside my office window and see a piece of landscape there, and they may be disappointed in finding just a nice but not extraordinary view, even though I attach some aesthetic or sentimental value to it. Or I could show the inquirer some beautiful piece of coast, with white sand, a turquoise sea, a tranquil wharf with painted wooden boats, and my inquirer may reply that it is surely a pleasant view, but it is nothing special as a landscape. A further major complication is that landscapes can also be (in) paintings or photographs, in which case we should point the inquirer toward a museum, an exhibition, a framed picture, or even a laptop or phone screen. If the inquirer comes from a significantly different path of life, culture, or educational background, our divergences may become irreconcilable, beginning with the very fact that a term for *landscape* might be absent in their language. Even when confronted with someone with a similar background, subjective elements such as mood, disposition, imagination, knowledge, and memories play an essential but elusive role in identifying landscapes' places. Several further complications may be added, leading to the conclusion that finding the empirical place of landscapes is not, after all, such a menial business.

FIGURE 0.1. View of the departmental library's garden from my office on an early spring morning, Pisa, Italy. Photo by author.

Moving on to a more abstract level, we can then ask ourselves what the philosophical place of landscapes is. To which area of philosophy does their investigation belong, which philosophers have dealt with them, and in what contexts? Here too we may feel some disappointment: landscapes per se are not a traditional topic for philosophy.[1] As for the area of philosophy, landscapes are likely to be most interesting for aesthetics, but political philosophy, ethics, philosophy of language, ontology, epistemology, and the like may offer a peculiar angle on them as well. From this point of view, however, landscapes seem to be a rather marginal, not well-defined topic in philosophy. In this book, I make a claim not just for the philosophical interest of landscapes but also for their centrality both in philosophy and in our nonphilosophical experience. For the moment, anyway, I delve into the issue of their philosophical whereabouts in an attempt to trace if not an exact location then at least their surroundings. Instead of starting with landscapes as such, I circumscribe the place of this research by working out a topology of philosophical spaces, and I do so along Kantian lines.

2. THE RISKS OF KNOWLEDGE AND THE SPACES OF PHILOSOPHY: A KANTIAN TOPOLOGY

Immanuel Kant, probably the most influential philosopher in the modern Western tradition, supposedly never ventured beyond his hometown of Königsberg, a port city in (then) Germany, now called Kaliningrad, in Russia.[2] He had no time for traveling to other places, so the story goes, because he wanted to learn as much as he could about other places.[3] Kant, the philosopher of pure reason and rational cosmopolitanism, was an avid reader of travel literature and was knowledgeable about local empirical details, physical characters, customs, stories, and so on. In addition to lecturing on logic, metaphysics, and other typically philosophical subjects, he also taught physical geography and anthropology. Spatial references and geographical images hold a significant presence in Kant's work, with the most well-known example being the "land of truth," which "is an island, and enclosed in unalterable boundaries by nature itself. It is the land of truth (a charming name), surrounded by a broad and stormy ocean, the true seat of illusion, where many a fog bank and rapidly melting iceberg pretend to be new lands and, ceaselessly deceiving with empty hopes the voyager looking around for new discoveries, entwine him in adventures from which he can never escape and yet also never bring to an end."⁴ Truth versus illusion: Kant's island-of-truth image may seem way too sharply dualistic to leave any significant place for a concept as blurred as that of landscape. Yet, in his project of critically mapping the limits and possibilities of human knowledge, Kant is not only concerned with preventing illusion from looking like truth (the dangers of following the ocean's fogs and icebergs—that is, the dangers of dogmatism) but also with preventing an excessive fear of illusion from paralyzing human theoretical and practical enterprises in the space of their legitimacy (the dangers of renouncing trips for fear of getting lost in the ocean—that is, the dangers of skepticism).⁵

In setting up a philosophical framework to deal with these two inherent risks of human knowledge, Kant introduces a systematic, although

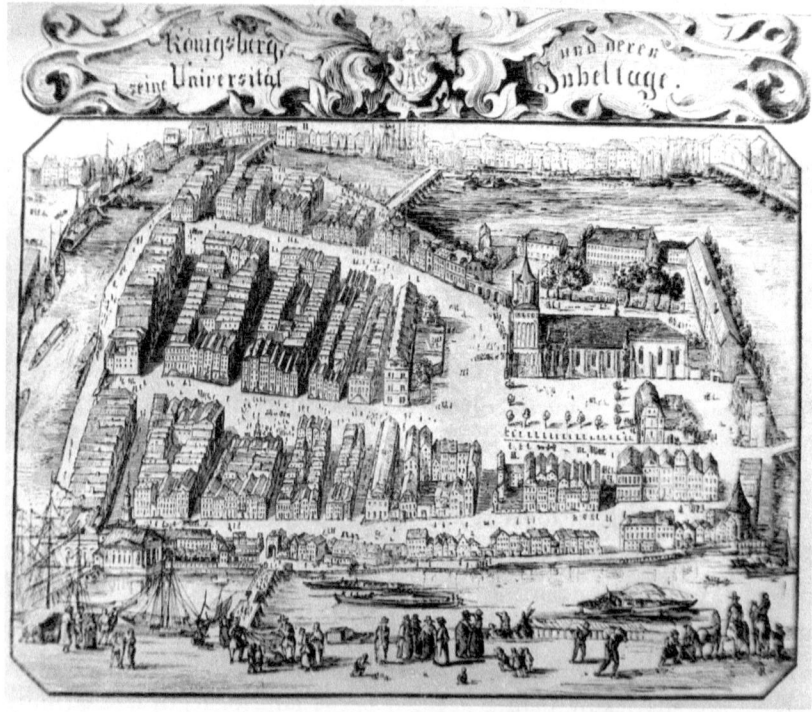

FIGURE 0.2. Königsberg (former Prussia) before its bombing in 1944. The map shows the rectangular Kneiphof island (today known as Kant's Island), with the cathedral on the right. Kneiphof was also the seat of the University of Königsberg, where Kant taught his entire life. Reprinted from Wikimedia Commons, https://commons.wikimedia.org/wiki/File:K%C3%B6nigsberg_244.jpg.

FIGURE 0.3. Today's Kaliningrad, Russia, with Kant's Island and the cathedral where he is buried in the foreground. Photo by A. Savin, May 2017. Reprinted from Wikimedia Commons, https://commons.wikimedia.org/wiki/File:Kaliningrad_05-2017_img10_aerial_view.jpg.

not always consistent, taxonomy of philosophical spaces in the second paragraph of the introduction to his third "Critique," the *Critique of the Power of Judgment*, titled *On the Domain [Gebiet] of Philosophy in General*.[6] The most generic and undefined space is the "field" (*Feld*), that is, the space of "concepts, insofar as they are related to objects, regardless of whether a cognition of the latter is possible or not."[7] Then "the part of this field within which cognition is possible for us is a territory [*Boden*] (*territorium*) for these concepts and the requisite faculty of cognition."[8] Furthermore, "the part of the territory in which these are legislative is the domain [*Gebiet*] (*ditio*) of these concepts and of the corresponding faculty of cognition."[9] Thus, the most general space or field is divided into a space of the unknowable and a space of the knowable. Within the latter—that is, the territory—we can identify a space called domain, in which concepts and faculties have legislative power (i.e., the space of a priori knowledge), and a space in which concepts are merely empirical, therefore not legislative and necessary but contingent. To these latter concepts Kant attributes "no domain (only their habitat [*Aufenthalt*], *domicilium*), because they are, to

FIGURE 0.4. Frontispiece of Francis Bacon's *Novum Organum* (1652), with a galleon passing the Pillars of Hercules, a possible source for Kant's navigation metaphors. The Latin motto under the galleon translates as "Many will pass and knowledge will be increased." Kant's own motto for his *Critique of Pure Reason* is a quote from Bacon (it begins with the famous *de nobis ipsis silemus*, that is, "about ourselves we shall say nothing"). Illustration republished in Maria Wakely and Graham Rees, "Folios Fit for King," *Huntington Library Quarterly*, vol. 68, no. 3 (2005): 489. Reprinted from Wikimedia Commons, https://commons.wikimedia.org/wiki/File:Instauratio_Magna_1620.jpg.

be sure, lawfully generated, but are not legislative, rather the rules grounded on them are empirical, hence contingent."[10] The space of our possible certain knowledge has precise boundaries and inner divisions, and so does philosophy: "Our cognitive faculty as a whole has two domains, that of the concepts of nature and that of the concept of freedom; for it is *a priori* legislative through both. Philosophy is also divided accordingly into the theoretical and the practical."[11] For our purposes, we are leaving aside the philosophical "proper"—that is, the domain and the a priori—and investigating the empirical, contingent spaces called habitats instead. If the field is the space of most general possibility, the territory is the space of what is possible for humans and the domain of what is necessary, then the habitat is the space of contingency: of what is there in a certain way but could be or could have been different.[12]

Now, if theoretical and practical philosophy address the two domains of nature and freedom, respectively, we may say that aesthetics (and what Kant calls teleology) addresses habitats. The space of habitats, to be sure, is unlike that of domains not organized according to the iron objective rules of legislative concepts. This, however, does not mean that habitats are governed by absolute chaos, with no hope of orientation for human beings. On the contrary, Kant's goal is precisely to trace a leading thread allowing us to inhabit the space outside our a priori legislative faculties. So the issue is about instituting a meaningful order and web of connections in a contingent realm that may deny any hope of ordering. In the latter case, humans would only be able to fumble around in the darkness of a literally inhumane chaos. We are left with a hope: the hope that our freedom does not remain a noumenon, a pure a priori construct, but is effective in the empirical world, the potentially absolute contingency of which, we hope, will not confirm the doubts of radical skepticism but will let the possibility of a humanly accessible sense be construed. As a matter of fact, "what may I hope?" is the question moving Kant's *Critique of the Power of Judgment*. This question cannot strive for objectivity, exhausted in Kant's first two *Critiques*, but for what human subjectivity can realistically aim to achieve outside the domains of objectivity.[13] The search for an answer to this question opens up an uncertain, dimly lit space at the intersection of the two strongly illuminated domains of nature and freedom. It is, more precisely, the space of the presence of freedom in nature, a presence we cannot objectively ascertain, but for which we can have some subjective grounds—that is, some hopes. The principle regulating and substantiating these (realistic) hopes is what Kant calls "purposiveness" (*Zweckmäßigkeit*), acting as a nonobjective umbrella rule allowing us to conjecture and search for a sense in the contingent empirical manifold.[14] Following this principle, we can orient ourselves in the territory of experience and establish a habitat in it. The latter, as opposed to a domain, is a space we can inhabit but over which we cannot impose an a priori, objective legislation: a sort of intermediate space halfway between the domain of the pure universal a priori and the possibility (which we may call Humean) of a completely arbitrary, recalcitrant world. It is delimited on one side by the temptation of dogmatism and on the other by the risk of radical skepticism. If we fell prey to either of them, we would not be able to orient ourselves in the world, and even less to inhabit it: in the former case, because we would keep attempting to build sky-rising towers without having adequate material and projects, in a Babelish chaos of constant collapses, in the latter case because no place would look safe enough to establish a living.[15]

Since it is neither organized a priori nor completely contingent and external to human freedom, the space of habitats is not, in any sense, a "given" space but is a space constituted only through our theoretical and practical activity of orientation, mapping, communication, and construction. What is more, because this is the space concretely moved through and inhabited by humans, the human being (and the being human) itself is constituted in the act of definition and construction of this space. Before and independently of this act, we may have a priori forms and concepts, but while delimiting the space of human possibilities and defining the necessary and

FIGURE 0.5. Flag of the city of Kaliningrad today: navigation remains the leading theme. Image by И. Д. Бакрымов, Э. И. Григо, and С. А. Колеватов, April 2011. Reprinted from Wikimedia Commons, https://commons.wikimedia.org/wiki/File:Flag_of_Kaliningrad.svg.

universal laws structuring it, such forms and concepts do not offer any indication on how to empirically move in it, arrange it, inhabit it.[16] Of course, the latter indications can be nothing more than empirical and provisional concepts, but without them we would be utterly lost in a hostile, or at best indifferent, space: "The third *Critique* . . . also considers those parts of the territory of experience where we have not discovered universal laws and where the most we can hope for are empirical concepts or vague notions. These are local habitats where order is 'contingent.' . . . Habitats exhibit . . . the order of familiarity of where we happen to be."[17]

3. HABITATS, AESTHETICS, CULTURES

The groundwork for the possibility of this "order of familiarity" and thus for the legitimacy of the hope not only to find a place in it but also to be able to modify, communicate, and inhabit it is, for Kant, an aesthetic one.[18] In pure aesthetic judgments (or judgments of taste, having to do primarily with the beautiful and secondarily with the sublime), we are confronted with the fact of the claim to a universal consensus, which, however, lacks any objective and conceptual basis.[19] If I call a rose beautiful, I cannot base this judgment on any objective property of the rose or on any concept from which I can deduce its beauty, yet I expect other subjects to share my evaluation, otherwise it would just be the expression of a wholly subjective preference (as would be a statement regarding the flavor of the ice cream I would like to eat now). Calling an object beautiful, rather than saying something about that object, expresses a subjective feeling of pleasure stemming from the ability to evaluate things in a way that can be shared and, ideally, approved by fellow human beings, even without being able to bring any object-related evidence in support of that evaluation. The beautiful is at the same time the archetype and the epiphenomenon of the human capacity to orient oneself *as if* there were objective indications or rules that do not, as such, apply to the contingent concreteness of the space called "habitat" and of the experience we make of it every time.

Therefore, the beautiful takes on a paradigmatic role in the search for stability in the instability, of the universal in the individual instance, and of the necessary in the contingent: it bears testimony to the possibility of actualizing our freedom in the realm of nature. This also means that, despite its singularity, subjectivity, and lack of determinate concepts, the judgment

FIGURE 0.6. A rose, Kant's example of free natural beauty. Photo by Stan Shebs, May 2005. Reprinted from Wikimedia Commons, https://commons.wikimedia.org/wiki/File:Rosa_rubiginosa_1.jpg.

of taste is not a mere individual reaction to a punctual feeling; on the contrary, its very possibility is grounded upon the claim to a universal consensus. Taste and beauty burst open the private limitations of individual feeling, which would otherwise be the only motive of orientation in the empirical world.[20] They therefore provide legitimacy to the hope of attributing meaning to the facts and objects within it, thus establishing their communicability: "The predicate 'beautiful' is a mere placeholder for a more considered assessment that needs to be made in conjunction with those who experience the world like us. It invokes a human communicability without appealing to ready concepts. . . . Kant regards [this] as the core function of the imagination, namely, to project a figurative meaning on things."[21] The capacity to evaluate the beautiful does not only manifest the possibility of mapping the territory of the absolutely contingent but also of building a sufficiently stable habitat within it. Even where our concepts are not enough to legislate in a necessary and objective way, we can still discern, institute, and communicate meanings, thereby finding and giving the space we find ourselves in an order or familiarity that is realistically not recalcitrant to our freedom.

Admittedly, for Kant such space is not a philosophically central—indeed, not even a properly philosophical—one. Philosophy only reaches as far as our a priori concepts can apply, thus only the two domains of nature and freedom and at most the attempt to bridge the gap between them through an a priori principle—that is, purposiveness. Even this attempt is presented in a somewhat puzzled and embarrassed way, as an adventure into a fictional, nonextended space, almost a nonplace with the only function to provide a passage between the only two properly philosophical ones.[22] Nevertheless, this deviation undeniably ends up changing the aim and the nature of the journey. Having established the possibility of a bridge between the two domains, the issue becomes more and more the bridge itself, which becomes the philosophically central, although only partially controllable, space, in Kant himself and in the philosophy after him, so much so that we can "regard Kant's habitat as a local sphere that is useful as an initial point of reference for the understanding of human historical life."[23] From a liminal, dubious quasi-nonplace, habitats end up being the space of the already concretely reconciled dualism: not just the space of physical being, not just the space of the moral "ought to be," but the space of the "familiar," of consensus, of horizontal human interaction, and of contingent order and regularity. A space that is human construction in which the human being constructs itself, yet not in the sense of domination but of openness to the contingent, the nonhuman, the other.

We may call it the space of "culture" as long as we do not mean it as a dichotomy versus nature but as inclusive of the environment in which we find ourselves to live, experience, and act—that is, as our habitat. There is of course a contingency, and therefore an irreducible plurality in finding ourselves in a specific habitat rather than in another, and in this habitat being shaped in a certain way rather than in another. And yet, equally irreducibly, there is the awareness of a relationship of co-implication, or even of the impossibility to neatly distinguish (if not in a pragmatic and provisional, not essentialist and clear-cut sense) between my identity as a human

FIGURE 0.7. Cueva de las Manos, Argentina (the painted hands are dated to around 7,000 years ago): instituting spaces of culture. Photo by Mariano, August 2005. Reprinted from Wikimedia Commons, https://commons.wikimedia.org/wiki/File:SantaCruz-CuevaManos-P2210651b.jpg.

being and the conformation of the habitat where I happen to be. I am not suggesting a reductionist position based on which humans are the product of their environment or vice versa. I am saying that we try to build habitats as fitting us, and in doing so we build ourselves as fitting them.[24] In this relationship of co-implication, we attribute and institute meanings and regularities, communicate them, expect the others' consensus on certain conditions, and accept that others expect the same of us too. The habitat is then at least in part what we make of it, and we are at least in part what the habitat makes of us: the space in which we find ourselves to build our habitat, as provisional as it can be, is instituted by and dependent on our practices and on the care we take, and vice versa.

Both the dimension of radical contingency and that of inevitable co-implication find an emblematic expression in the aesthetic judgment. This is characterized both by the absence of preordained concepts, interests, goals, and so on (hence, by contingent, undisciplinable singularity) and by the necessity and universality of the consensus it demands (hence, by our capacity and disposition to cross the narrow borders of our individualities to enter and contribute to an ample, shared space). In our natural drive to establish and inhabit a habitat, we accept a game with certain rules that we can make sense of and that we can communicate and modify, spurred by a hope that is essential for our (meaningful) existence and the possibility of which is granted by our capacity to see and communicate aesthetically, in a sense that we will have to better explain.[25] The game we play is that of "culture" as a local habitat or domicile with changing borders, constituting—without locking us in it—a horizon in which we can orient ourselves within the limits of our possibilities. Returning to the starting question of this chapter, we have hardly gained any insight into a possible definition of landscapes. Yet I believe we have come closer to their philosophical place. Landscapes, I claim, belong to such a theory of habitats. In fact, in the next chapters, I articulate and defend the stronger thesis that landscapes are the concrete, experienced, lived presence of habitats thus understood—or at least a central, emblematic configuration of such presence.

Chapter One

A GAME OF LANDSCAPES

Methodological, Linguistic, and Conceptual Rules

1. A PRAGMATIST SETTING

The prologue, instead of directly trying to grasp the essence or delineate a concept of landscape, looked for its philosophical place. Landscapes, I argued, philosophically belong to a theory of habitats, as I have outlined it in Kant's wake. If habitats are the spaces of contingent yet familiar order, instituted by our need and ability to meaningfully situate ourselves in the world, then we need to place landscapes in the context of this ordering, indeed, as an emblematic and condensed shape. To develop this suggestion, let us begin with some terminological remarks. Originally, the word *landscape* meant a bordered territory ("land") that has somehow been "created" or "made" ("scape," see the Dutch: *-schap*; German: *-schaft*, from *schaffen*; English: *-ship*). It later took the meaning of "scenery," both natural and artistic: interestingly, *landscape* in the sense of natural scenery derives from *landscape* in the sense of a painted one and not the other way around. *Landscape* is also a "made land" in the sense of an organized one, with reference to the people materially creating, reclaiming, and inhabiting a territory, or administering it, their culture, politics, and so on. Also, *landscape* can be the visual appearance of the "typological" identity of a territory (such as in "Mediterranean" or "desertic" landscape).[1] Clearly, from its very inception, *landscape* is an intrinsically polysemic term. This is not because of some historical confusion. The polysemy is, on the contrary, the accurate

A GAME OF LANDSCAPES

FIGURE 1.1. Aerial view of the barrage in Eiderstedt, North Frisia, Germany. Preventing the sea from overtaking the settlements through diking was only possible through strong cooperation, which led Eiderstedt to adopt a special form of self-government early on, granting the county a high degree of independence and freedom expressed in its administrative status of "landscape," a perfect example of the "territorial" or "substantive" meaning of landscape, as discussed, for example, by Kenneth Olwig. Photo by Ra Boe / Wikipedia, May 2012. Reprinted from Wikimedia Commons, https://commons.wikimedia.org/wiki/File:Luftaufnahmen_Nordseekueste_2012-05-by-RaBoe-355.jpg.

reflection of a conceptual openness and dynamism. The term puts together an apparently exclusively natural, nonhuman material (the land) and an apparently exclusive human prerogative (creating, making, shaping). Rather than resulting in chaos or even an oxymoron, this combination points to the shapes that a fusion of human prerogative and nonhuman material can take. This fusion can be taken to be, I suggest, the underlying common root of the various semantic dimensions or families covered by the term *landscape*. And it is, of course, its inherently dynamic and polysemic conceptual raison d'être.

Regarding this situation, one possible starting strategy is to attempt to reduce and discipline the semantical spectrum of the landscape by unraveling its underlying essence. Defining *landscape* is, from this perspective, a matter of isolating its univocal core essence. The latter will then serve as a criterion to assess proper and improper uses of the term. While the promise of terminological and conceptual clarity is appealing, there are also fundamental downsides to this strategy. First, disagreement and divergence on the very essence of landscape are not only predominant and possibly growing in the literature but, as we saw already, implicit in the etymology of the term. Such disagreement hardly looks like a contingent definitory problem and seems instead inherent to the whole idea of landscape from the very beginning. Second, the very absence of the term in several languages suggests that the idea of landscape is so culturally conditioned and connoted that it would not make much sense to try to tie it to a single, objective essence. It would be, at the very least, strange to suppose that a term found only in few languages and polysemic even in those could point us toward a transcendental, objective essence. Third, and most important, this essentialist strategy would risk impoverishing the wealth of associations, meanings, references, media of transmission, and cultural embodiments connected to the term *landscape*. A good part of the literature underscores, in fact, the importance of retaining the semantic plurality.[2] Admittedly, this is often done not based on an examined conceptual choice but rather as a positive acceptance of a given state of affairs. However, even from a philosophical point of view, rather than committing to the search for a single true essence, it seems more sensible to accept the irreducibility of the semantic plurality and to try to investigate the resemblances between the different contexts in which the term is used as well as between the different uses themselves. This is not only more in line with the Kantian foundation deployed in the previous chapter, which renounced an a priori, "legislative" approach to this topic, but also with the applied, pluralistic, and interdisciplinary orientation of this book. Therefore, as opposed to the essentialist strategy, I employ a pragmatist-Wittgensteinian one.[3]

My general claim is that the wide semantical range of the word *landscape* corresponds to (but does not overlap with) the philosophical openness, flexibility, and vagueness of Kant's notion of habitat, as interpreted in the previous chapter. Based on this correspondence, I think it is possible to identify three main features that seem to be transversal to different uses of *landscape* and can hence be considered "family resemblances."[4] Just like Kant's habitat, landscape (1) does not refer to something given, whether empirically or a priori. It points toward a dynamic, always changing, sense-making process—that is, the human activity of inhabiting, mapping, and shaping the world. At the same time, however, it also excludes full manipulation, or creation through, or dependence on, human hands. And (2) it expresses, or embodies, the absence of fundamental dualisms between subject and object, freedom and nature, *res cogitans* and *res extensa*. More precisely, "landscape" points to a priority of the relationship over the related terms: it does not refer to the coming together of two previously mutually independent terms but rather to their togetherness. It does not call for the abolition of dualism, but it rather enounces a nondualistic state of affairs that, as we will see, calls for continuous differentiations and adjustments. Finally, (3) points 1 and 2 rely on the ineliminable aesthetic dimension implicit in the use of the word *landscape*. I jointly develop the first two points in this chapter, whereas the whole next chapter is devoted to the third point.

2. LANDSCAPE, ENVIRONMENT, TERRITORY

To develop these three general features, in addition to the etymological clarification sketched in the previous section, we also need to preliminarily discuss the semantic differences between *landscape* and two commonly associated terms, often used as synonyms: *environment* and *territory*. Let us take the Cambridge Dictionary. *Environment*, in the usage relevant for us and often overlapping with *landscape*, is defined as "the air, water, and land in or on which people, animals, and plants live." The definition is starkly dualistic. Environment has the connotations of something thoroughly independent of us and merely "enveloping" us: we can certainly relate to it and act on it (and vice versa), but it would exist without us. Semantically, the environment is indifferent to our existence (or, for that matter, to the existence of any sentient being). *Territory*, on the other hand, refers to a space delimited or meaningful *only* with regard to the existence of humans or other sentient beings, again in a dualistic way. It is defined as "(an area of) land, or sometimes sea, that is considered as belonging to or connected with a particular country or person," or as "an area that an animal or person tries to control or thinks belongs to them." In this regard, *environment* and *territory* are semantically opposed, even when they materially overlap. The same portion of space can be referred to both as an environment and as a territory. In the first case, we are mostly interested in its "natural," "objective" properties; in the second one, in its relation (political or other) to a sentient being. In both cases, we tend to think (or, at the very least, we are semantically allowed to think) in dualistic terms: the space considered as environment or territory, and its inhabitants are conceived of as mutually independent entities.[5] The term *landscape*, on the contrary, implies at a basic level the interdependence of a certain space and a human subject and is defined as "a large area of countryside, especially in relation to its appearance," or as "a view or picture of the countryside, or the art of making such pictures." A certain portion of space, conceived of as landscape, is neither an object that can be considered independently of a human subject nor a mere function of the latter.

Let us try to gain some conceptual depth by commenting on the distinction proposed by the Italian philosopher Rosario Assunto in a short paper titled "Paesaggio, ambiente, territorio: Un tentativo di precisazione concettuale" (Landscape, environment, territory: An attempt at conceptual clarification). Assunto begins by making a distinction between territory and environment. The former has an almost exclusively spatial and quantitative-extensive, rather than qualitative-intensive, connotation. The latter has two main meanings: a biological one, referring to the physical living conditions of a certain space, and a historical-cultural one, referring to its economy, traditions, morals, religion, politics, arts, and so on. Environment includes territory, but not the other way around: there can be no environment without territory; however, an environment involves further definitional features besides the ones defining a territory. Briefly, an environment is the sum of the territory plus its life, history, culture. *Landscape* is a more complex yet more concrete term. Assunto defines it as the "'form' that the environment ('function' or 'content') . . . lends to the territory as the 'matter' of which it makes use—or, to be more precise: 'landscape' is the 'form' in which the synthetic a priori unity (in the Kantian sense: not a 'unification' of separately received data, but a necessary 'unity' conditioning their presenting themselves in the consciousness) of the 'matter (territory)' and the 'content-or-function (environment)' is expressed."[6] In simpler terms, "no territory and no environment makes itself known to us as such, because indeed 'territory' and 'environment' are conditions which we can only attain through an effort of abstraction from the concreteness of the landscape that we live in, experience, and know as territory and environment in their indissoluble unity."[7] Put otherwise, *territory* and *environment*, separately taken, are abstract terms. We never only experience a territory or an environment; we only experience their indissoluble unity—that is, the concreteness of the

FIGURE 1.2. Balconies in the "Angeli" (Angels) neighborhood, the oldest core, partly of Arab origin, of the city of Caltanissetta (Sicily, Italy), Assunto's birthplace. Photo by OppidumNissenae, April 2022. Reprinted from Wikimedia Commons, https://commons.wikimedia.org/wiki/File:Quartiere_Angeli_Caltanissetta_16.jpg.

landscape. To be sure, we can—and in many contexts we have to—refer to environments or territories, but we should be aware that these are only abstractions. The actual reality we encounter, experience, study, and can act upon is that of the landscape.

In this way, Assunto overturns the common, naive understanding of the relationship between the three terms. It would seem natural to think of territory and environment as the most concrete terms, pointing to hard facts, whereas landscape would seem to point toward a more abstract, impalpable relationship. On the contrary, in Assunto's footsteps, we only make experiences of landscapes, and turn to talking of territories and environments when we need abstract concepts. Landscape is the unity and form providing the ground and the meaning for the abstraction of material (territory) and content/function (environment). I argue that, while Assunto's antidualistic and concrete-aiming conceptual attempt is seemingly modest in its scope as it "only" tries to mediate between the matter versus content/function dualism, it actually predates and provides a broad and solid conceptual ground to many later calls for a dynamic, holistic, antidualistic conception of landscape, as in the first two points I raised at the end of the previous section.[8] Emphasizing the concreteness of landscape and its priority over territory and environment implies, first, putting forward the need for a dynamic understanding of landscape. Landscape is not a "given" but a process in which a certain space takes (and changes) shape, allowing, only on this basis, the "static" abstractions of matter and content/function. Second, the dynamic character implied in the term should point our attention to the ontological priority of the relational unity over the related terms. While landscape has been and should be conceived of as bridging the gap between dualisms, such as matter and form, object and subject, body and mind, nature and culture, we should not be misled into thinking that landscape has the power to unify independently, separately existing terms. On the contrary, as Assunto's reversion clarifies, unity comes first and every isolation of the two terms of each dualism is an abstraction with a specific purpose and should not be essentialized.

This is in line with, or anticipates, much of the contemporary nonphilosophical and sometimes apparently mutually exclusive orientations of research about landscape, to which I return in the next chapters. According to such orientations, landscape is a process, practice, and performance rather than a static fact; it enables the temporalization and historization of space; it is a relational concept and not the product of a Cartesian divide; it intertwines perceiving and acting; it erodes the difference with the self; it renounces ocularcentrism without giving up the importance of visuality; it pushes the boundaries between nature and culture; and it rejects a puristic limitation to few extraordinary preservation-worthy places.[9] Indeed, Assunto's clarification is also in line with the pragmatist approach I adopted. Assunto does not offer an essentialist or normative definition of landscape. He does not tell us what a landscape is or should look like. He offers the reasons why we use that specific term without prescribing, in that essay, any essence-based limitations on its use. Landscape is first and foremost a way of referring to the concrete space we live in, experience, and know.[10]

We may even say, taking a step beyond Assunto, that the employment of the term *landscape*, in its most general sense, expresses our response to the space we inhabit in a temporally, spatially, and culturally unified way.[11] Or even better: our need to give a name to the unifying, meaningful background on which the isolation and identification of punctual stimuli and responses is possible is what underlies our use of the word *landscape*.[12] Now, an immediate objection may be that the word *landscape* is seldom, if ever, used in this complex philosophical sense. I would like to resist this objection by pointing out, first, that many contemporary definitions of *landscape* seem to be out of touch with more common or traditional uses and, second, by arguing that this complex philosophical sense is what underlies the broad spectrum of such more common/traditional uses. The latter are therefore derivative with respect to a concept that is too complex to be reduced to any single one of them. What is more, reductionist attempts are in fact detrimental to the richness, both theoretical and applicative, of the concept. Different cultures have different understandings and practices of the relational, dynamic, antidualistic background unifying the different aspects of our inhabiting the world. But even within any given culture, different individuals, different times, or different contexts require different understandings and practices—hence the variety of contexts in which we can meaningfully and appropriately use the word *landscape* without falling prey to the abstractions and genericness of *territory* and *environment*. Consistently with the pragmatist approach pursued here, it should be clear that I am not trying to formulate *a* correct definition based on which certain uses should be ruled out as wrong or imprecise. On the contrary, I believe that most if not all of them are meaningful and that exactly because of this we should not easily rule some of them out but rather find, as I am doing here, a broader, encompassing meaning of *landscape*, capable of making sense of and keeping together such disparate uses but also capable of acknowledging their differences.

At the same time, I should clarify that I am not putting forward an "anything goes" conception of landscape. I am not saying that we are simply responding to different ways of being in and inhabiting the world by using this term in different ways, and that all of them are correct. This would be problematic, not only because of the intrinsic relativism, with the dangerous practical implications of an "anything goes" approach to landscape.[13] It would also imply an essentialist division of language and world, based on which we simply use the word *landscape* to reflect or express, in a plurality of contexts, a certain way of positioning ourselves in the world, as if such a position would be a given object to describe and *landscape* the sign or description for it. What I am claiming is rather that our use of the word *landscape* does not simply reflect or express but institutes (or at least contributes to institute) the way we position ourselves in the world, inhabit it, experience it. Not only the different contexts in which we use the word institute different ways of inhabiting the world (of instituting our "habitat," to go back to Kant), but the very fact that certain languages have a term for *landscape* whereas others do not institute different ways of doing that. We can now return to the three encompassing features outlined with reference to Kant's habitats at the end of the previous section: the next section brings together the first two—namely, the nongivenness of landscapes and their antidualistic character.

3. PERFORMING LANDSCAPES, MOVING BORDERS

"All that can be established with any certainty is that, like place, landscape is a vague concept and in reality has fuzzy edges. And yet we know what we mean and can spot when the term is being stretched, used metaphorically or misapplied."[14] When are we using this vague concept appropriately? When are we stretching it, using it metaphorically, or misapplying it? It is easy to answer the first question.[15] As for the others, we may be said to be stretching it when applied, for example, to a video game scenery, to be using it metaphorically in front of a table laden with appetizing foods, and to be misapplying it with reference to a water bottle. To be sure, there are some "fuzzy" cases, such as talks of Mars's landscape, or of "urban landscape," or even more so of "digital landscape," yet normally we know what we mean, and we do not need conceptual or philosophical clarifications.[16] On closer inspection, however, this situation, while not uncommon in our linguistic practices, is at least to some extent surprising. How can a term with such fuzzy edges, eluding a precise definition, and used among others to refer to a certain (beautiful) space or scene, to the way we see it, to its artistic representation, to a "region, rural jurisdiction or system of rural spaces," be clear in its meaning and in its limits as well as in its material application?[17] Paradoxically enough, it is so because of the peculiarly complex language-game we play with this word.

When we use the word *landscape*, we do not mean to offer a description of a place. We do not want to describe or point to the objects found within it, nor its boundaries, nor its objective characteristics, whether physical, cultural, or any other kind. We are instead "building" a habitat and at the same time the experience of it by putting certain things there and leaving others out, highlighting some and leaving others in the shadow. Most of all, in doing so we are making a home by saying that a certain space is legible and interesting to communicate, that it makes sense. Indeed, this "sense" is something that we institute when we designate that space as a landscape; that is, based on the Kantian groundwork established in the previous chapter, we practice our freedom in the world and at the same time we acknowledge our freedom as wired in it, whereby practicing and acknowledging would not be possible without each other.[18] In doing so, we overcome the dualism of nature and freedom. When we (appropriately) use the term *landscape*, we perform and at the same time we express a repositioning of ourselves in the world. While not describing anything, landscapes say much about the various, ever-changing configurations of the way we see, imagine, and inhabit the world. Just think of the two main paradigms of *wilderness* in the United States versus *cultural* or *rural* in Europe and the historical, cultural, geographical, or socioeconomical differences they suggest.[19] At the same time, the very fact that the word *landscape* can correctly refer both to a wilderness and to an intensely cultured area implies, first, that we can speak of landscapes whether or not they contain human artifacts since the human presence is already embedded in the very use of the term and does not require a material affirmation, and, second, that we need a concept of landscape broad and flexible enough to explain the possibility of such a divergence in the ordinary use. The concept of landscape is therefore a particularly powerful and yet incredibly elusive instance of the human ability to inhabit a space of radical contingency and to build sufficiently stable domiciles within it. "Landscape is about wholes":[20] true, but in the sense that, through this concept, humans express and communicate their ability to find and institute webs of meanings amid the otherwise full-blown contingency of the world. The "wholes" we identify through the utterance of the word are the counterpart of the human ability and need to find and institute order in contingency and thus to experience meaningful unities instead of irredeemably disjoined and unrelated particulars.[21]

Let us recall Kant, however. His habitats are something other than domains: they are not the spaces of a dominating, legislating, all-powerful

FIGURE 1.3. Dolly Sods Wilderness near Davis, West Virginia: an "American" paradigm? Photo by Nicolas Raymond, October 2016. Reprinted from Wikimedia Commons, https://commons.wikimedia.org/wiki/File:Dolly_Sods_Twilight_Trail.jpg.

FIGURE 1.4. Rural landscape in Nauviale, Aveyron, France: a "European" paradigm? Photo by Krzysztof Golik, May 2020. Reprinted from Wikimedia Commons, https://commons.wikimedia.org/wiki/File:Rural_landscape_in_Aveyron.jpg.

(and, possibly, ultimately tautological) reason but those of the hope to make sense of a contingent reality and be at home in it. Landscapes as an eminent instance of Kantian habitats fully retain this sense of contingency and otherness, whether they are "natural" or "cultural." That is, both their matter (Assunto's territory) and the way they are arranged and functionalized (Assunto's environment) are not fully under our control and power. This aspect has been particularly stressed in the recent literature on landscape, partly because of its obvious practical implications. It reminds us that the space we inhabit is not fully available and disposable for humans and that its contingency or otherness is not just the playground for our appetites or interests.[22] While this may sound like an almost trivial environmentalist claim, I believe the philosophical argument laid out herein adds to it an important dose of conceptual depth, detail, and practical cogency. This is why I dwell on this point a bit longer.

Landscapes, I argue, are performative configurations of our making sense of the world we inhabit.[23] They are performative in the double sense that our sense-searching and sense-making activity performs them by instituting specific "units of sense" and that they sensibly express and put before our eyes our sense-making activity by embodying and letting us experience and encounter it. They are particularly emblematic instances of "habitats" in that they conjugate the contingency of nature with our need and ability of instituting an inhabitable order in it. They cannot be reduced to either nature or freedom. We do not dominate or legislate on them, but we are not hopelessly lost or let down in front of them. They are spaces of familiar, contingent, provisional order. They are more meaningful than unrelated, unpatterned natural objects, and more arbitrary than products of our unconstrained freedom. In other words, they are not impermeable to our sense-making need and capacity, but they are not fully transparent to it either. If they were either fully impermeable or fully transparent, they simply would not exist as such. Better said, the language-games associated with them can only be played in a both non-impermeable and non-transparent space, as delineated in the previous chapter. Hence, the demand for full transparency—that is, for a fully anthropized, dominated, available, and disposable space—clearly destroys the possibility of landscapes and anything associated with them. But there is more. This demand ultimately undermines itself: a fully transparent world would be a world of empty tautologies, where the domain of our freedom would be uncontested only because it is entirely self-referential (Kant's dogmatism). On the other hand, in a fully human-impermeable world, we would have only despairing chaos and no possibility of tracing/instituting a sense (Kant's skepticism).

Landscapes, as emblematic instances or "condensations" of habitats, remind us that we live where nature and freedom, resistance and transparency to sense-making, and passivity and activity meet. Properly speaking, as we saw, they are not the encounter of otherwise independent and separate dimensions but rather, as I go on to claim, "units of sense" that are ontologically and epistemically prior to the possibility of separation and isolation. We may hence concur with a recurring trend of contemporary literature on landscapes as well as one of its few entirely shared—possibly because it is often stereotyped—philosophical references: the concept of landscape runs (or should run) contrary to the foundational modern dualism—namely, the Cartesian distinction between *res cogitans* and *res extensa*.[24] However, this is not because that dualism is invalid or dangerous per se, and an unqualified unity with nature would be a safe haven of peace, universal respect, and harmony. Such unexamined, nonphilosophical stance would simply reproduce a dualistic, fragmented worldview resulting in antiscientific positions, anachronistic calls for premodern patterns, and populistic environmentalism.[25] On the contrary, based on the philosophical argument laid out herein, landscapes and values associated with them may be presented and defended in a nondualistic fashion. Landscapes are units of sense, patterns of the human ability and need to be situated in a meaningful, inhabitable space. They do not just bring nature and culture together: they *are* instantiations of the continuity between them.

This continuity, therefore, does not imply a simplistic—almost mystical—unity between the human being and the whole of nature and the impossibility to draw borders and distinctions. The point is, instead, that we are always situated within this continuity, that this continuity is the "human being" and the "being human." We can, we need to, and we do draw borders and distinctions all the time. They, including the Cartesian dualism, are essential for us to map, make sense of, and inhabit the world, yet they should not be essentialized but taken pragmatically instead. Separating *res cogitans* from *res extensa*, for example, means drawing a pragmatic border, which is necessary in a certain context to explore reality and come up with scientific and philosophical innovations.[26] As such, there is nothing philosophically or morally wrong with it. Yet we should not take this separation as an essential, precisely defined objective fact of our world. Borders can and need to be redrawn and relocated all the time, as needs change and worldviews shift.[27] In fact, in my discussion of landscapes, I rely on what has been called the ambivalence and paradox of borders: "Borders are about claims to land, but as soon as you draw one you limit yourself. Every border is also an act of denial, an acknowledgment of another's rights. By contrast, the claim to want no borders, much prized by corporate executives and anticapitalist activists alike, is a claim to the whole world. Borders have a far more ambivalent and complex relationship to territory; they combine both arrogance and modesty, both demand and denial."[28] Landscapes are extremely good media for thematizing and performing both this continuity and the continuous metamorphoses, relocations, and adjustments taking place within it, enabling us to experience and reckon with our ways of drawing borders and meanings.[29] For these reasons, despite their ephemerality and elusiveness, landscapes are incredible witnesses to the power of humankind and to its fragility, of particular importance in the recently, still controversially, inaugurated Anthropocene epoch.[30]

FIGURE 1.5. Café in Baarle-Nassau, the Netherlands, with the border between Netherlands and Belgium marked on the ground. Photo by Jérôme, September 2001. Reprinted from Wikimedia Commons, "https://en.m.wikipedia.org/wiki/File:Baarle-Nassau_fronti%C3%A8re_caf%C3%A9.jpg.

4. "LIKE THE DOG AND THE FLEA"

I have connected the first two general features of landscapes as presented in section 1—namely, the nongivenness (point 1) and the antidualistic character (point 2)—under the common heading of performativity and pragmatic mobility of borders. To finish laying the ground for finally addressing point 3 about aesthetics and thus providing a unified picture of the way I understand landscapes, I want to offer a focused discussion of "language-game" (*Sprachspiel*) and "form of life" (*Lebensform*) in Ludwig Wittgenstein, guided by the idea of landscape as developed so far.[31] This adds a further layer of complexity to the pragmatist approach adopted herein as well as some clarity. In Wittgenstein's "Remarks on Frazer's *The Golden Bough*," we find the following comment:

> It could have been no insignificant reason—that is, no *reason* at all—for which certain races of man came to venerate the oak tree other than that they and the oak were united in a community of life, so that they came into being not by choice, but jointly, like the dog and the flea (were fleas to develop a ritual, it would relate to the dog). One might say, it was not their union (of oak trees and humans) that occasioned these rites, but, in a certain sense, their separation. . . . For the awakening of intellect goes along with the separation from the original *soil*, the original ground of life. (The origin of *choice*.) (The form of the awakening mind is veneration.)[32]

I think what Wittgenstein writes here regarding myths and rites may very well be applied to the conception of landscapes I am advancing. Looking for reasons to explain *why* humans choose, institute, recognize, or appreciate certain landscapes instead of others can easily put us off track if we are not clear about the kind of reasons we are looking for.[33] Unity comes first, I claim: humans come into being in and together with certain environmental elements or features not by choice but jointly. It is not (only) such archetypal unity with them that generates certain practices and attitudes (especially, but not only, aesthetic ones) toward them but rather our separation from them.[34] We are at first one thing with the space in which we come into being: we are like fleas to their dog. Developing a distance (both physical and mental, and both phylogenetic and ontogenetic) from our original soil or ground of life goes along with the awakening of a more reflective, contemplative, and intellectual attitude, based on which we choose, institute, or recognize landscapes and at the same time begin to appreciate them aesthetically, venerate them, and so on.

This does not mean that we can only relate to the landscapes as the places where we came into being or in which we grew up. Indeed, part of the process of distancing ourselves is the development of a language, which is what in turn allows us to institute and relate to other, different landscapes. I am hinting, of course, to Wittgenstein's notion of language-game, which he introduced after his encounter with Sir James George Frazer.[35] Language, for Wittgenstein, does not have a meaning through its referring to given objects but rather through its enabling and performing actions or practices—that is, through its use.[36] The term *language-game* is therefore meant to express the interwovenness of linguistic and nonlinguistic practices: "The word 'language-*game*' is used here to emphasize the fact that the *speaking* of language is part of an activity, or of a form of life," and "to imagine a language means to imagine a form of life."[37] To be able to play certain language-games, we need to be acquainted with (or be part of) a certain form of life or culture.[38] This, of course, also applies to landscapes. What is crucial, however, is that "the notion of language-game not only serves to embed language in other activities, it conversely captures how language-use enables, entwines, and entails nonlinguistic actions."[39] In Wittgenstein's words: "I shall also call the whole, consisting of language and the activities into which it is woven, a 'language-game.'"[40] Not only language-games grow out of forms of life: the opposite is also true.

Language-games, therefore, are not at all purely about language: they are about "wholes" constituted of language and actions. The notion itself makes any dualism or correspondentism of language versus object and self versus world meaningless. The very difference between linguistic and nonlinguistic and between linguistic game and form of life refers to more "discrete" or more "dense" ways of that interaction with the environment, in which the human biocultural niche is constructed.[41] Language-games are growingly complex practices, refinements of our ways of acting and situating ourselves in the world: "Language . . . is a refinement, 'in the beginning was the deed.'"[42] In other words, language is part of "the *environment* of a way of acting."[43] Just as the interweaving of language-game and form of life refers neither to an absolute and essential determinacy nor to a universal contingency or manipulability, so too landscapes are the preexisting concrete

FIGURE 1.6. *Wittgenstein's Cabin 11*, from the series Wittgenstein's Cabin, by Spanish visual artist Dionisio González. A (more-than-linguistic) game on Wittgenstein's famous self-planned, secluded hut on the shore of lake Eidsvatnet in Skjolden, Norway. Image courtesy of the artist, https://www.dionisio gonzalez.es/.

unity: not, of course, of the existing subjects or objects (dogs and fleas) connected in a relationship that can take the form of landscape among others but of the abstract dualisms of nature/freedom, biology/culture, determinacy/contingency, which are revealed as possibilities in and of landscapes. Only because of their nondualistic origin, then, can landscapes be understood as one of the possible forms of mediation and recovery of the unity with the Wittgensteinian original soil after the experience—individual and collective, historical and psychological—of separation.

This opens up a view that is pluralist and concrete at the same time. Wittgenstein's philosophical remarks are aimed at "describing" and "putting before us" the actual use of language and offering a "surveyable representation [*übersichtliche Darstellung*]" of our "deficient grammar."[44] Philosophy can only pragmatically, and never in a dogmatic-essentialist way, "establish an order in our knowledge of the use of language: an order for a particular purpose, one out of many possible orders, not *the* order."[45] Given the endless number of possible specific purposes and orders, it is clear that "there is not a single philosophical method, though there are indeed methods, different therapies, as it were."[46] In this sense, as already remarked at the end of the prologue, Wittgensteinian language-games share a lot with Kantian habitats, and, according to my thesis, landscapes are eminent, condensed forms of the latter. Therefore, not only landscapes are a peculiar and complex kind of language-game, but the two notions are mutually illuminating. After all, Wittgenstein himself states in the preface to his *Philosophical Investigations*: "The best that I could write would never be more than philosophical remarks; my thoughts soon grew feeble if I tried to force them along a single track against their natural direction. —And this was, of course, connected with the very nature of the investigation. For it compels us to travel criss-cross in every direction over a wide field of thought. —The philosophical remarks in this book are, as it were, a number of sketches of *landscapes* which were made in the course of these long and meandering journeyings."[47] If philosophical remarks about language-games are similar to sketches of landscapes, then may we assimilate language-games to landscapes? Indeed, both are rooted in our ability and need to institute meanings that enable us to inhabit the world: they are "refinements" of deeds. Both presuppose at least a minimal degree of separation from our original ground: they include attitudes and practices of "veneration," wonder, interrogation, imagination, appreciation, and knowledge that are only possible once we are at least partially "awakened" (once the flea has separated itself from the dog's skin). Both are ways of gathering objects together, each time following one out of many possible orders (and never *the* order) that we can then reconstruct and describe.[48] Both are units of sense, in which dualisms (between language and nonlanguage, nature and culture, self and world . . .) are only possible as pragmatic tools for analyzing and drawing/redrawing borders that are always provisional, never based on an eternal transcendental essence. Both are indeed, at least to some extent, something we enjoy doing or having.

This last point in particular, but in fact all of them, have to do with something I have been postponing and hinting at all along—namely, the aesthetic dimension presented as the third common feature at the end of the first section of this chapter. I now turn to it not only because it has historically always been a fundamental aspect connected with most theories and practices of landscape but also because aesthetics is an integral part—in fact, the systematic keystone—of the view I advance. This was already clear in the prologue on Kant, but it becomes even more so in the light of the pragmatist, antidualistic orientation of this chapter. In it I have stressed the elements of conceptual openness, dynamism, and pluralism inherent in "landscape performances": landscapes have to do with precarious, ever-changing attempts at sense-giving according to ever-changing purposes, and they function like Wittgensteinian language-games, embedded in ever-changing forms of life. The following discussion of landscapes and aesthetics act as a counterbalance to these elements, providing a backbone and a principle of order.

Chapter Two

LANDSCAPE AND AESTHETICS

1. A DOUBLE MARGINALITY

Even a rapid survey of contemporary landscape research shows a surprising fact: aesthetics, which would seem to be, and historically was, an integral constituent of the concept and practice of landscape, is largely absent or plays a secondary role. The aesthetic usage of the term was criticized by Richard Hartshorne as early as 1939 as confusion-inducing insofar as it enabled a semantic slippage from a delimited piece of land to its aspect.[1] John Jackson's pathbreaking "vernacular" attempt certified the end of the monopoly of painting and architecture over landscapes and the need for a new, broader, and more useful definition as "a composition of man-made or man-modified spaces to serve as infrastructure or background for our collective existence."[2] Kenneth Olwig and a prominent part of the literature after him have reclaimed a substantive concept, overcoming the scenic one in favor of landscape "as a nexus of community, justice, nature, and environmental equity."[3] Furthermore, contemporary literature on landscape has largely acknowledged the ambiguity, if not the outright threat, of the traditional aesthetic-scenic discourse on landscape. Laying open the rootedness of landscape as a way of seeing in the Renaissance technique of linear perspective, Denis Cosgrove has highlighted its underlying bourgeois and individualistic ideology: landscapes were ways to control and exercise power over space, serving the needs of politics, trading, military, navigation, and so on. Putting aesthetics in the foreground then means ideologically "forgetting" this fundamental historical overlay.[4] On a similar note, James Corner underscored the sentimental, escapist structure of scenic landscapes: their apparent, but in fact shrewdly designed, naturalness invites conservative nostalgia and the removal of the conflicts and privileges of the present.[5] William Mitchell spoke of a "loss of innocence" in the landscape discourse, meaning how it was finally acknowledged that its apparent harmless foundation in a supposedly universal pleasure has insidiously legitimized imperialism and exclusion under a beautiful patina.[6]

Very recent studies, too, work with definitions and across topics where aesthetics is almost absent or at best marginal: just see the section "Landscape—A Complicated Idea" in the introduction of an up-to-date standard text, the latest edition of the *Routledge Companion to Landscape Studies*, or the presentation of the main "cross-cutting themes" addressed in it: "The critique of power and hegemony," "Belonging and identity," "Everyday life," "Knowing as a body," "Process, practice and performance," "Participatory futures," "The nature-culture hybrid," and "A world in crisis."[7] What one finds plenty of instead is criticism of traditional

FIGURE 2.1. Hidden threats of classical scenic views. This breath-taking panorama is taken from Adolf Hitler's "Eagle's Nest" retreat in the Bavarian Alps, Berchtesgaden, Germany. Photo by Sandor Bordas, August 2009. Reprinted from Wikimedia Commons, https://commons.wikimedia.org/wiki/File:15.08.2009_Berchtesgaden_Kehlsteinhaus_-_panoramio.jpg.

contemplative, eye-pleasure-based landscape paradigms, and political-institutional practices aimed at singling out and protecting aesthetically and culturally extraordinary scenic landscapes. As to this last point, a privileged political interlocutor is the European Landscape Convention, which, both in its definition of landscape and cognate concepts and in the clarification of its aims and measures, basically omits any direct reference to the aesthetic sphere.[8] The list could go on, but I think these examples suffice to make my point: at the very least, one has to conclude that a large, authoritative share of the contemporary academic and institutional discourse on landscape hardly ever mentions aesthetics as an integral constituent, and in some cases it outright stigmatizes it. The neglect, to be fair, is mutual. Although natural beauty is a traditional though minoritarian topic of philosophical aesthetics, the same cannot be said for landscapes, which have historically been almost entirely ignored in this field.[9] Landscapes do not fit neatly into the traditional dichotomy of artistic versus natural beauty. Moreover, unlike art and nature, landscapes are tendentially associated with a utilitarian dimension, such as farming, dwelling, or planning, which makes it difficult to appreciate them in a disinterested, purely contemplative way, a concern that has been central to aesthetics, as we explore in the second section of this chapter. In general, due to its pronounced ambiguity and openness, landscape aesthetics, unlike environmental aesthetics, is not a unified or well-developed research field; therefore, no well-defined approaches to it can be identified.[10]

Admittedly, the reasons leading to neglect and distrust of aesthetics in landscape research, on which I say something more in the next section, are not to be easily ignored. On the other hand, though, the aesthetic dimension is deeply entrenched not only in the history of the concept of landscape but also in the contemporary ordinary discourse. In daily use, *landscape* almost inevitably contains, explicitly or implicitly, an aesthetic aspect or evaluation, whether positive or negative.[11] There seems to be a contradiction, or at least a pronounced distance, between the ordinary versus the academic/institutional use of the concept. This distance is particularly problematic if we consider the calls for democratization, shared practices, and collective deliberation that are so frequent both in the academic and in the institutional/political contemporary discourse on landscape that marginalizes aesthetics. How can the discourse on and practice of landscape

FIGURE 2.2. Artificial lake of Campo, close to Pisa, Italy, formed through mining activity for the production of bricks. After the cessation of the excavation, the lake became public and, following a partly spontaneous, partly guided renaturalization, became a small yet beloved natural area with facilities and was recovered as a habitat for several animal (mainly birds) and vegetable species. Decommissioned industrial buildings can be seen behind the trees on the right. Photo by author.

be participatory and democratic if the experts' analyses follow such a different path from the priorities of a wider public?

In this chapter, I attempt to reconcile the two perspectives, the lay, aesthetics-entailing one and the expert, aesthetics-neglecting one. I argue that both have their good reasons, and yet they remain only partial. The reconciliatory strategy I propose does not simply call for an integration of the two but rather points out that both perspectives, although diverging, refer to the same inadequate and largely outdated view of aesthetics and are therefore the two sides of the same coin. In other words, the experts' discourse leaves aesthetics out for the very reasons why aesthetics is essential to the lay discourse on landscapes. Both perspectives keep clinging to a dualistic view that is hardly beneficial to the advancement and democratization of the discourse on landscape (nor, for that matter, to aesthetics itself). Therefore, starting with a critique of the view of aesthetics common to both perspectives, I outline an alternative aesthetic conception that not only reconciles them but is also fruitful to landscape as well as to aesthetics studies.

2. PARADOXES OF ISOLATIONISM

We may call the kind of aesthetics avoided in the experts' discourse on landscape and tenaciously, if mainly unconsciously, present in the lay one "isolationist." Surprisingly enough, the putative father of isolationist aesthetics is Kant, from whom I took inspiration. He conceived of the aesthetic judgment and the aesthetic pleasure as "pure" and "disinterested": they do not (directly) contribute to our knowledge, do not have a (direct) moral value, and have to be kept free from individual preferences, desires, and inclinations. Only in this way can they claim a universal and necessary value, otherwise they would either be purely individual, philosophically irrelevant utterances of unreflected appreciation through the bare senses, or they would overlap with moral evaluations. With his disinterestedness thesis, however, Kant never meant that the aesthetic realm should be separated from real, ordinary life. In fact, as we saw in the first chapter, Kant sees aesthetics as the ground for a full engagement with the plurality of empirical forms and challenges of the world we inhabit.[12] Nevertheless, Kantian disinterestedness has often been seen as giving expression and legitimacy to the idea that the meaning or value of the aesthetic realm is misinterpreted and diminished if it is connected with the *ordinary* and should rather be placed in its being *extraordinary*. Along these lines, disinterestedness becomes distance, separation, and exception. Beauty, art, and the whole range of meaningful sensuous experiences and expressions are cut off from our ordinary interactions and practices, and relegated to few extraordinary moments or dedicated spaces. Hence, romantic aestheticism and the exaltation of genial creativity, musealization, fetishization, elitism, intellectualism, art for art's sake. The isolationist view of aesthetics seems to correspond to ordinary views and practices, where art and beauty are often seen as "different" from and higher than real life, as moments of escape, illusion, leisure, critique, and so on. We often go to a museum or to a concert as an extraordinary activity, something more valuable than our ordinary experience. In general, it is easy to conceive of authentic aesthetic pleasures as something not to be mixed with ordinary experience and higher than other forms of pleasure contained in the latter.

The isolationist view of aesthetics mostly concerns art and artworks, unlike Kant's aesthetics, for which natural, not artistic, beauty is the purest. The aesthetic contemplation of nature can generally be seen as somewhat easier, less demanding (and thus also less philosophical, hence the relative marginality) than the appreciation of complex works of art. Still, isolationism also applies to landscapes. Even in ordinary language, *landscape* designates an extraordinary place, separated and different from the usual ones. We specifically look for landscapes as something more valuable than the space we normally inhabit, and they are indicated with special marks on maps, guides, and road signs. We make extra efforts to get there, and once we are there, we feel like we are not only in a special place but also in a special time to be adequately celebrated, immortalized, and shared through photos, videos, and posts on social media. It is a time and space of excitement, wonder, meditation—all feelings or states of mind not normally associated with our daily life or activities. We may go as far as to think that only places recognized as landscapes in this exceptionalist sense are places worth experiencing and being remembered. This ordinary view has its institutional counterpart not only in such maps, guides, and road signs but also, for example, in UNESCO's mission of preservation of the "cultural and natural heritage around the world considered to be of outstanding value to humanity," clearly following an exceptionalist and isolationist aesthetic (and, more in general, cultural) paradigm, thus reinforcing the ordinary view.[13]

Finally, isolationist tenets are well rooted not only in the ordinary use and in institutional practice but also in traditional aesthetic theory. Most notably, the ocularcentrism and the obsession for the scenic character mostly associated with the aesthetic appreciation of landscapes are the legacy of the privilege traditionally accorded to sight (and, secondarily, to hearing) over the other senses in aesthetic matters. In his dialogue *Timaeus*, Plato already asserted the primacy of sight and hearing, which remained a philosophical commonplace in Western culture up to our days, convincedly shared by, among others, Kant.[14] Sight is a nobler and more theoretical sense than the others: it allows more objectivity through distance and permanence, its use does not consume its object, and it does not require "getting our hands dirty" with external objects.[15] Ocularcentrism and the obsession for the scenic can thus be seen as not just classicist but often also classist tenets of landscape aesthetics. That such tenets seem nowadays to be adopted more by the lay public at large than by experts and institutions not only does not contradict what I have been saying but actually confirms it. A

FIGURE 2.3. Isolationist beauty? Filters-enhanced postcard view titled *The Orange Skies at Ladram Bay* (England). Photo by The Narratographer, January 2016. Reprinted from Wikimedia Commons, https://commons.wikimedia.org/wiki/File:The_Orange_Skies_At_Ladram_Bay_(24166553763).jpg.

broader lay public adopts an ocularcentric, scenic-obsessed aesthetic perspective on landscapes precisely because it is consistent with the isolationist-exceptionalist aesthetic paradigm in general.[16] In other words, a nonexpert public is easily more inclined to appreciate a—however authentic or manipulated—sense of aesthetic distinction and refinement that a postcard-like landscape can offer.[17]

The aesthetic paradigm challenged by the recent academic and institutional discourse largely overlaps with the isolationist one described here. The isolationist paradigm leads to alienation from and neglect of the ordinary spaces and to the fetishization and commodification of the (supposedly) extraordinary ones. It denies value to a large, if not the largest, portion of our experience while intellectualizing the rest of it. Accordingly, the main issues of isolationist aesthetics, regarding both landscapes and artworks, are about separation: of the "true"—that is, aesthetically valuable—landscape from the ordinary, hence unworthy, hence "nonexisting" one, and of the competent judging authority from the incompetent one. Such view inclines toward a fundamentally top-down and non- (or anti-) democratic model in which decisions are mostly taken by experts or bureaucrats without taking into account different and, in particular, more "local" opinions. It also risks being oblivious to cultural and historical differences in the understanding of geographies and landscapes, leading to ethnocentric impositions or, more simply, to the marginalization of alternative points of view and emerging realities.

To sum up, I argue that the aesthetics that is rejected or neglected in the expert-institutional discourse and uncritically implied by the ordinary one coincides, to a good approximation, with the isolationist paradigm. The problem is that (rightful) challenges to this paradigm often tend to throw the baby out with the bathwater—that is, to simply set aside references to the aesthetic dimension as such instead of questioning its isolationist conception. In this way, while criticizing the latter, they end up reproducing it. With it they also reproduce some of the associated issues, such as the lack of a truly democratic, pluralistic approach, the alienation from common understandings, practices, and customs, and so on. Instead of a problematization, the result is the wholesale removal of the aesthetic dimension altogether, which, on the contrary, if more adequately theorized, could help answer legitimate, pressing desiderata. It would instead be more fruitful to question the isolationist model without dismissing or debasing the aesthetic dimension of landscapes as such.[18] To this purpose, I turn to one of the most powerful and influential critics of the isolationist model—namely, the pragmatist philosopher John Dewey.[19]

3. DEWEY'S RE-LEGITIMATION OF AESTHETICS

The main proposition of Dewey's aesthetic masterwork, *Art as Experience*, is the criticism of isolationist, dualistic aesthetic theories and the advancement of a holistic, antidualistic alternative.[20] The roots of isolationist aesthetics can be traced back to the ordinary view: "In common conception, the work of art is often identified with the building, book, painting, or statue in its existence apart from human experience."[21] This common conception is then reflected in aesthetic theory: "When artistic objects are separated from both conditions of origin and operation in experience, a wall is built around them that renders almost opaque their general significance, with which esthetic theory deals. Art is remitted to a separate realm, where it is cut off from that association with the materials and aims of every other form of human effort, undergoing, and achievement."[22] This separation is the unnatural and, as we will see, counter-evolutionary product of mutually reinforcing philosophical abstractions and social, economic, and political layouts. The task Dewey sets to aesthetics is to restore continuity: "A primary task is thus imposed upon one who undertakes to write upon the philosophy of the fine arts. This task is to restore continuity between the refined and intensified forms of experience that are works of art and the everyday events, doings, and sufferings that are universally recognized to constitute experience."[23] The fact that the focus is on artworks and not natural beauty should not mislead us into dismissing its relevance for the aesthetics of landscapes. In fact, the focus is on artworks exactly because, as we saw above, they seem to offer a better ground for isolationist aesthetics than natural beauty. Restricting the alternative approach to artworks would hence reproduce the unnatural divide postulated by isolationist aesthetics. As a matter of fact, Dewey illustrates his own constructive thread through a powerful landscape simile: "Mountain peaks do not float unsupported; they do not even just rest upon the earth. They *are* the earth in one of its manifest operations. It is the business of those who are concerned with the theory of the earth, geographers and geologists, to make this fact evident in its various implications. The theorist who would deal philosophically with fine art has a like task to accomplish."[24]

It is important to notice that, given Dewey's pragmatist ameliorism, aesthetics should oppose the isolationist paradigm not just theoretically but practically, improving not just our knowledge but also our actual experience by reconnecting the aesthetic realm to ordinary life. Thus, Dewey's criticism and his alternative proposal address not only the isolationist aesthetic theory but also the material and political layout as well as individual patterns of experience, to which this responds. The widespread resistance or even hostility to "a conception of art that connects it with the activities of a live creature in its environment" brings to light both the impoverished, mutilated character of our common conception of art and the misery and stagnation of our ordinary life as such: "Only because that life is usually so stunted, aborted, slack, or heavy laden, is the idea entertained that there is some inherent antagonism between the process of normal living and creation and enjoyment of works of esthetic art."[25]

The problem, then, is not only with isolationist theories per se but with the overall context, both material and intellectual, in which they are situated and which they express. For Dewey, dismissing or debasing the value of the aesthetic dimension to avoid the problems connected with its isolationist conception would not only fail to avoid them but would actually make them worse. The aesthetic dimension is a fundamental one (if not *the* fundamental one) in human life, for reasons that will bring us back, in the next section, to the landscape discourse. For now, let us notice that, although landscapes do not feature prominently in Dewey's aesthetics, the concept of environment is a central one.[26] Its structural link to aesthetic theory is made explicit from the very beginning: "Fortunately a theory of the place of the esthetic in experience does not have to lose itself in minute details when it starts with experience in its elemental form. Broad outlines suffice. The first great consideration is that life goes on in an environment; not merely *in* it but because of it, through interaction with it."[27] The relationship between creature and environment is not one of instrumentality and exteriority, it is life itself: "No creature lives merely under its skin; its subcutaneous organs are means of connection with what lies beyond its bodily frame, and to which, in order to live, it must adjust itself, by accommodation and defense but also by conquest. At every moment, the living creature is exposed to dangers from its surroundings, and at every moment, it must draw upon something in its surroundings to satisfy its needs. The career and destiny of a living being are bound up with its interchanges with its environment, not externally but in the most intimate way."[28] "No creature lives merely under its skin" obviously also applies to that peculiar creature that is the human being. Our relationship to the environment is not exterior and dualistic: the environment is part of us just as much as we are part of it. There is simply no "us" without intimate interactions with the environment, therefore any philosophical theory needs to begin by avoiding essentialist dualisms of human being versus the world, subject versus object, and similar. This undermines the purely representational and subjectivist theories of experience: in fact, "experience is the result, the sign, and the reward of that interaction of organism and environment which, when it is carried to the full, is a transformation of interaction into participation and communication."[29]

Here is where aesthetics comes in. Human beings are bound to their environment as much as any other living thing, yet they are able to transform their interactions into self-aware, participated, communicable exchanges. This happens when we have experiences in the "full" sense of the word—that is, when we reach "inner harmony [which is] attained only when, by some means, terms are made with the environment."[30] Our ongoing interactions are a mix of activity and passivity, struggle and resistance, effort and relaxation. When we manage to turn this contingent mix into a balanced rhythm, we attain what Dewey calls "consummation"— that is, a full experience, a condition of, always transient, equilibrium: "In the process of living, attainment of a period of equilibrium is at the same time the initiation of a new relation to the environment, one that brings with it potency of new adjustments to be made through struggle. The time of consummation is also one of beginning anew."[31] The aesthetic realm has its roots in the very midst of our normal experience, not in some place removed from and elevated above it. The very word *consummation* implies a continuity, not a break.

This also undercuts any form of intellectualism with its related dualisms: "Since sense-organs with their connected motor apparatus are the means of this participation, any and every derogation of them, whether practical or theoretical, is at once effect and cause of a narrowed and dulled life-experience. Oppositions of mind and body, soul and matter, spirit and flesh all have their origin, fundamentally, in fear of what life may bring forth. They are marks of contraction and withdrawal."[32] Dualisms, isolationism, and antisensualism are brought by a fear of not being in control, of being exposed to the potentially destructive contingency of life, which puts us in the same condition as any other creature. Instead of accepting life in its fullness, including its uncontrollable aspects, and trying to discover traces and coordinates to establish at least provisional, realistic habitats (recall Kant), the isolationist attitude pathologically—and, as I hinted, counter-evolutionarily—denies whatever it cannot dominate or legislate over (again, recall Kant). In doing so, under the pretense of acknowledging the specific, distinctive nobleness of being human, it basically prevents mapping human experience as an organic, holistic unity of creature-like groundwork and human-specific towering heights. On the other hand, "full recognition . . . of the continuity of the organs, needs and basic impulses of the human creature with his animal forbears, implies no necessary reduction of man to the level of the brutes. On the contrary, it makes possible the drawing of a ground-plan of human experience upon which is erected the superstructure of man's marvelous and distinguishing experience."[33]

There is no qualitative break or demarcation line between animal flesh and senses and the specifically human "marvelous and distinguishing experience" as well as between what is "useful" to us as animal creatures and what is aesthetically valuable.³⁴ In fact, denying this continuity means a mortification of the richness and variety of human life and experiences and leads to an obtuse solipsistic withdrawal from the world and other creatures: "It is mere ignorance that leads then to the supposition that connection of art and esthetic perception with experience signifies a lowering of their significance and dignity. Experience in the degree in which it *is* experience is heightened vitality. Instead of signifying being shut up within one's own private feelings and sensations, it signifies active and alert commerce with the world; at its height it signifies complete interpenetration of self and the world of objects and events."³⁵ Again, in Kantian terms, denying the continuity means falling prey to dogmatism and skepticism (which are, as we saw, the two sides of the same coin) and renouncing any hope to truly dwell and experience the habitat as a space of contingency and to institute/communicate webs of meanings within it.³⁶ Embracing experience does not mean settling for the unqualified chaos of a world of contingency but, on the contrary, the possibility of nonstatic sense

FIGURE 2.4. Embracing continuity: Pueblo Indian pottery, from Hano pueblo in northeastern Arizona, such as the one selected by John Dewey among the illustrations for his book *Art as Experience*. Photoprint by Homer Earle Sargent Jr., 1903. Photo in Miscellaneous Items in High Demand, PPOC, Library of Congress. Reprinted from Wikimedia Commons, https://commons.wikimedia.org/wiki/File:Nampeyo,_a_noted_Tewa_Hopi_potter_of_the_Hano_pueblo_in_northeastern_Arizona,_decorating_pottery_LCCN2003653751.jpg.

and order. Briefly, all experience is embryonically and potentially art: "Instead of signifying surrender to caprice and disorder, it affords our sole demonstration of a stability that is not stagnation but is rhythmic and developing. Because experience is the fulfillment of an organism in its struggles and achievements in a world of things, it is art in germ. Even in its rudimentary forms, it contains the promise of that delightful perception which is esthetic experience."[37]

Art and aesthetic experience, then, are the marks of both the continuity and the discontinuity of the human being with respect to the rest of nature. Reducing them to exclusive marks of distinction—that is, isolating them— brings about a double impoverishment. On the one hand, the "highest," distinctive, and most delightful manifestations of the human get uprooted from their natural womb, resulting in intellectualism, elitism, and ascetism. On the other hand, ordinary functions and activities are denied any aesthetic, human-specific relevance, condemning the largest part of human beings for the largest part of their lives to a petty and mechanic materialism.[38] Briefly, aesthetic isolationism prevents the possibility of a successful, satisfying, "active and alert commerce with the world," whereas aesthetics proper should mend the ties between the human being and its environment, enhancing the capacity for interaction. Evidently, Dewey's broad, comprehensive conception of art is not the result of aestheticism. Its aim is not to aestheticize the ordinary, taken as nonaesthetic in itself, but rather to restore a fundamental holism in which the fractures typical of both commonsense and philosophical views do not and cannot exist. The aesthetic, from a separate, extraordinary dimension, becomes the true distinguishing mark of the human and of its capacity/need to place itself in the world in a meaningful way. If experience is "the result, the sign, and the reward" of our interaction with the environment, and full, consummated experience is already "art," then the aesthetic dimension is at once the heart, the central sense organ, and the nervous system of our whole experience, moving, pervading, guiding, making sense of all of our "commerce with the world."

4. LANDSCAPE AS EXPERIENCE

On this ground I want to advance the claim that landscapes, just like artworks, should be seen in Deweyan terms as expressive forms of full, consummated experience. They are, in fact, even more powerful instances of it than artworks, given how they perfectly express a successful interaction between the human organism and the environment. Landscapes are, then, an emblematic shape of the human capacity not to "surrender to caprice and disorder," and to institute "a stability that is not stagnation but is rhythmic and developing."[39] From this perspective, evidently, the landscape discourse should indeed renounce disinterestedness, ocularcentrism, and the obsession for the scenic-extraordinary but cannot dispense of aesthetics altogether, which on the contrary emerges as an integral constituent.[40] Thus, Dewey's holistic and pragmatist approach provides the sought-after ground to reconcile landscape and aesthetics as well as the experts' and the lay discourse on landscape. Bringing—or, rather, keeping—a structural aesthetic dimension in the landscape discourse does not, on this ground, mean isolating landscapes as extraordinary places to be delimited and spared from the ugliness and oppression of our ordinary life.[41] They are not (just) the material of postcards and selfies; they are expressions of successful, meaningful interactions with our environment, units of sense embodying the

FIGURE 2.5. Provisional successful interactions with the environment: mountains, wooden bench swing with wicker hammocks, and a bamboo footbridge in a paddy field at sunset during the monsoon, Vang Vieng, Laos. Photo by Basile Morin, June 2020. Reprinted from Wikimedia Commons, https://commons.wikimedia.org/wiki/File:Wooden_bench_swing_and_wicker_hammocks_on_a_bamboo_footbridge_in_a_paddy_field_at_sunset_during_the_monsoon,_Vang_Vieng,_Laos.jpg.

harmony attained when "terms are made with the environment." They are experienced, lived configurations of a rhythmic, always-developing order resulting from our "active and alert commerce with the world [which] at its height it signifies complete interpenetration of self and the world of objects and events."[42] As such, their existence is not predicated on our ability or willingness to distance ourselves from our ordinary experience but, on the contrary, on that to embrace it to the fullest, instituting it with new worldviews and meanings that break the solitary shell of private feelings and sensations, opening up to participation and communication with our fellow human beings.[43]

What Dewey says about art can be rightfully applied to landscapes as well:

> Every art communicates because it expresses. It enables us to share vividly and deeply in meanings to which we had been dumb, or for which we had but the ear that permits what is said to pass through in transit to overt action. For communication is not announcing things, even if they are said with the emphasis of great sonority. Communication is the process of creating participation, of making common what had been isolated and singular; and part of the miracle it achieves is that, in being communicated, the conveyance of meaning gives body and definiteness to the experience of the one who utters as well as to that of those who listen.[44]

Landscapes express the presence or, better, the continuous performance of a provisional order of meanings, and in doing so they enable its communication. Both expression and communication are not about emphatic scenes or sights but about the process through which isolated objects are gathered in a meaningful, shareable way, embodied for everyone to experience it. One may object that the last sentence quoted hardly seems to be applicable to landscapes unless they are artistic ones (paintings, photographs, installations . . .). It does not seem to make much sense to say that landscapes impact the experience of both the utterer and the listener, as is the case in artworks. Here too, though, I think there is something to be gained for the landscape discourse. The point is that aesthetic holism does not only concern the creative moment but also the reception or fruition or, more precisely, that, on the basis of aesthetic holism, this distinction can be functionally and heuristically made but loses all sense if essentialized. For Dewey, as a matter of fact, art is not to be identified with the artistic object but rather with the experiential process set in motion by ideation through creation, all the way to fruition. As we saw, while "in common conception, the work of art is often identified with the building, book, painting, or statue in its existence apart from human experience," "the actual work of art is what the product does with and in experience."[45] Art is, indeed, experience.

The thesis of the processual, performative, expressive, and communicative character of art/experience can be extended to landscapes. Let us compare Dewey again:

> The real work of art is the building up of an integral experience out of the interaction of organic and environmental conditions and energies.... The act of expression that constitutes a work of art is a construction in time, not an instantaneous emission. And this statement signifies a great deal more than that it takes time for the painter to transfer his imaginative conception to canvass and for the sculptor to complete his chipping of marble. It means that the expression of the self in and through a medium, constituting the work of art, is *itself* a prolonged interaction of something issuing from the self with objective conditions, a process in which both of them acquire a form and order they did not at first possess.[46]

In this quote, I believe, "work of art" could be replaced with "landscape" without any loss of meaning. Certainly, the "work" required for art is quite different from the one required for landscapes. In the former case, we need paint, canvas, marble, and the like. In the latter case, we do indeed use tools and materials, if we are talking about planned, architectural, or cultural landscapes. But even the experience of a wilderness as a landscape, in which no tools or materials are involved, has the same fundamental structure, although with an immaterial scaffolding: construction in time, transferring or projection of imagination and meanings onto a medium, prolonged interaction between self and objective conditions, and a resulting new order for both. The parallel between landscapes and artworks is, I believe, emphatically sealed by the sentence immediately following the last quote: "Even the Almighty took seven days to create the heaven and the earth, and, if the record were complete, we should also learn that it was only at the end of that period that he was aware of just what He set out to do with the raw material of chaos that confronted Him."[47] What is an artistic creation for God can very well be seen as a landscape for us: in both cases, the aesthetic element is not just a superimposed plus of beauty and pleasantness but the very dynamic principle structuring any actualization of order and sense out of "the raw material of chaos." Even in God's mind, order and sense are not a plan *before* the aesthetic process is set in motion: they are the "consummation" of a performative experience that with the same move creates and experiences them.

To the parallel between landscapes and artworks one might further object that in the case of wilderness the space *before* its experience as a landscape and the one *after* it are objectively the same since no manipulation intervened, but this objection is a weak one. First, many artworks are the product of a process in which no material manipulation by the artist intervenes (obvious examples are Marcel Duchamp's *Bicycle Wheel* or Andy Warhol's *Brillo Box*). Second, even concerning more traditional artworks, the creating and the perceiving selves do not undergo any objective, verifiable change. There is instead an important difference between artworks and landscapes, but if anything, it paradoxically shows, I believe, that Dewey's general aesthetic conception seems to fit the latter even better than the former. The difference is that artworks have, in different degrees and ways, a certain finality about them: there is, in the large majority of cases, a point in which a painting, a sculpture, a symphony, or a movie are considered "completed" by their maker and, consequently, by their receivers. This is not the case for landscapes, where talking of completion does not seem to make much sense. Therefore, if anything, landscapes respond at least as well as, and probably better than, artworks to the aforementioned claim "that the expression of the self in and through a medium, ... is *itself* a prolonged interaction of something issuing from the self with objective conditions, a process in which both of them acquire a form and order they did not at first possess."[48] Or, we may say, based on Dewey's aesthetics, landscapes prompt us to rethink even our relationship with artworks by questioning their appearance of finality.[49] The central point is that, on the one hand, Dewey's aesthetics provides powerful conceptual tools to question the idea of a stable, punctual, "final" character of landscapes, an idea underlying much of the traditional aesthetics of landscapes, starting with the conceptual slippage between landscape as a piece of land and landscape as its pictorial, bidimensional representation. On the other hand, it does so without having to dismiss the aesthetic dimension of landscapes but, on the contrary, by imposing its presence at the center of the stage.

Connecting the landscape discourse with the aesthetically substantiated and oriented conception of experience presented here leads to a reassessment of the spatiotemporal framework regarding both. We may think of landscape as a primarily spatial concept or construct, an intuition that the ineliminable connection with visuality seems to undergird. If landscapes have to do with images, paintings, perspectives, sceneries, then their temporal dimension seems to be quite irrelevant to, or in fact obstructing, their understanding and even their appreciation. However, just as the priority (or exclusiveness) of the visual has been questioned, the same happened with that of spatiality. Dewey's aesthetics allows to address this challenge without relapsing in a new dualism. Even if the landscape was only visual, seeing is for him more than a punctual act of recognition: "To see, to perceive, is more than to recognize. It does not identify something present in terms of a past disconnected from it. The past is carried into the present so as to expand and deepen the content of the latter. There is illustrated the translation of bare continuity of external time into the vital order and

FIGURE 2.6. *Landscape and Bamboo* by Tani Bunchō (1804): time, rhythm, growth. Reprinted from Wikimedia Commons, https://commons.wikimedia.org/wiki/File:'Landscape_and_Bamboo'_by_Tani _Buncho,_Honolulu_Museum_of_Art,_13165.1-3.jpg.

organization of experience."⁵⁰ This is because, as we saw, experience is a continuous, rhythmic process rather than a series of punctual, momentary events. Time is integral, not exterior to the aesthetic structuring and organization of experience: "Time ceases to be either the endless and uniform flow or the succession of instantaneous points which some philosophers have asserted it to be. It, too, is the organized and organizing medium of the rhythmic ebb and flow of expectant impulse, forward and retracted movement, resistance and suspense, with fulfillment and consummation."⁵¹ The fulfillment of experience is the mind's growth, which in turn becomes the ground for further growth, following a rhythm of change and pause. Time is precisely the underlying structure of this rhythm: "Time as organization in change is growth, and growth signifies that a varied series of change enters upon intervals of pause and rest; of completions that become the initial points of new processes of development. Like the soil, [the] mind is fertilized while it lies fallow, until a new burst of bloom ensues."⁵²

The image of maturation is then used in direct connection with a landscape simile, further clarifying this view of time: "When a flash of lightning illumines a dark landscape, there is a momentary recognition of objects. But the recognition is not itself a mere point in time. It is the focal culmination of long, slow processes of maturation. It is the manifestation of the continuity of an ordered temporal experience in a sudden discrete instant of climax. It is as meaningless in isolation as would be the drama of Hamlet were it confined to a single line or word with no context."⁵³ Imagine having had no experiences at all of landscapes and lightnings. In this case the situation described would be literally meaningless for us: we would have absolutely no clue about what is going on, or about how to react to it, just as it would happen if we were confronted with a single line or word of *Hamlet*.⁵⁴ It is only because of a long preceding process of experience that we can "recognize" what is going on. As in the case of God's creation and contemplation, in this case too it is the aesthetic principle giving order, continuity, and meaning to otherwise unrelated events. Aesthetically organized time becomes the underlying structure of our meaningful positioning in the world and interaction with the environment.⁵⁵ Put it this way: not only we can reconcile aesthetics and the landscape discourse, but the former becomes in fact essential to the latter, and vice versa.

5. WHICH AESTHETICS FOR WHICH LANDSCAPE? WHICH LANDSCAPE FOR WHICH AESTHETICS?

Aesthetics as understood here is not a special discipline focused on the investigation of a special part of our experience, such as the beautiful, art or the arts, the sublime, taste, aesthetic pleasure or emotions, and so on. To be sure, such topics are not excluded either, but they do not constitute an essentially separated realm of our experience. The aesthetics at issue here understands the aesthetic element as spread throughout and innervating all our experience.[56] Experience, in turn, is not something "of" or "about" a separate, independently existing objective realm. The human being is not a disembodied subject (a *res cogitans*) existing in front of a material realm to be experienced (*res extensa*). Experience is instead interaction, correspondence, and exchange with the environment. Briefly, it is experience "with," not experience "of." I rely here on Giovanni Matteucci's recently proposed redefinition of the aesthetic, which "is not really a 'what,' but rather a 'how,' a modal index. It is the modality in which the interaction between organism and environment takes place that qualifies, if anything, the experience as aesthetic, and not single elements, contents, or acts belonging either to the organism or to the environment."[57] Further, "the aesthetic designates a form of an organism-environment interaction so integrated that it generates a sort of full 'collusion.' In other words, it is a kind of practices in which the organism and the environment are coupled and mutually supportive in a holistic experiential configuration."[58] Now, "in this framework, the distinction between experience-of and experience-with, which has been traditionally neglected, is crucial."[59] Indeed, "we may sum this point up by saying that in the experience-of, 'of' marks a distance that may generate distinction and abstraction, while in the experience-with, 'with' marks a relationship that is always mutually supportive and material. The first one is inclined to generalization and hence risks being inefficacious in practice, while the second one is ineludibly topologically bound and hence it possesses a whole efficacy which yet is valid only for that specific moment."[60] What Dewey called interaction and commerce is here qualified as a reciprocity of organism and environment that is aesthetic insofar as it "requires collusion, participation in a correspondence... between players who are looking for reciprocal agreement, and hence, a common expressivity."[61]

Here Matteucci's proposal seems particularly suitable for thematizing the structural link between aesthetics and landscapes. The aesthetically expressive "is precisely the experiential field as a whole, not its components as isolated and thematizable entities."[62] Think of how landscapes have to do with wholes, with gathering objects together according to a pragmatically intended principle of order. We can now enounce the deeper meaning of this statement. The principle of order does not simply concern an exterior harmony between the objects *of* our experience but rather the way we make experience *with* them. It does not (primarily) have to do with the beauty (or the sublime, or the picturesque) of objects, or of the way they are arranged together. It has to do with the complex, ever-changing rules of the game we play in our collusion with the environment, a collusion in which the aesthetic element cuts in, not as a special form or quality but as a new role of the ordinary: "The aesthetic property is the non-aesthetic property itself that takes on a different role: we no longer have experience of it, but we experience with it."[63] The aesthetic, as presented here, is what takes us from the monolithic abstraction of the environment to the plural concreteness of landscapes. Conversely, the removal of aesthetics from the landscape discourse is at the same time a consequence of and an input for the monodirectional reduction of concrete landscapes to the abstraction of the environment. Landscapes, therefore, are neither objective places "out there" waiting to be discovered nor just subjective ideas or images in our mind waiting to be realized in the external world. They point instead to the impossibility of reducing our experience, also in its most extraordinary achievements, to the activity of a separate, disembodied mind that is only exteriorly and dualistically related to the objective world. This irreducibility, already signaled by Dewey's "no creature lives merely under its skin," has been in recent years requalified, as Matteucci reminds us, through the "extended mind model, that precisely underlines how mental vectors are distributed in the environment (as scaffoldings) rather than confined inside the organism."[64] According to this model, we may say that our mind is in the landscapes just as much as landscapes are in our mind or even, going back to my interpretation of Kantian habitats, that we exist in the landscapes just as much as they exist in us.

It is necessary, at this point, to address an objection about which I have already hinted in the previous chapter: that of relativism. If after all landscapes are not special or extraordinary places endowed with some particular, object-based qualities or forms but are instead perceptible configurations of our ever-changing collusion with the environment, and there are no aesthetic properties but rather aesthetic roles, then the "anything goes" stance seems to be hardly avoidable. If this were the case, then any space at any time for any experiencing individual could be called a landscape in the sense of a successful moment of consummation of our experience, and there would be no way to establish some minimal categories or coordinates for a meaningful discourse or practice of landscapes. I resist this objection in two steps: in the next section, which concludes this chapter, I suggest that my framework is in fact not relativist but pluralist and pragmatist, and I sketch some important implications. In the next chapter, then, I turn to two topics that are traditionally central to aesthetics—that is, interpretation and art—concretely showing how the proposed pluralist yet antirelativistic framework can be reflected in them while completing my picture of the relationship between aesthetics and landscapes.

6. THE SUBSTANTIALITY OF AESTHETICS AND THE PLURALITY OF LANDSCAPE

Claiming that there are no distinct, objective, essential categories does not mean relativistically denying the possibility of criteria, borders, and systems of values as such. It only means that the latter should be interpreted pragmatically—that is, not as designations of essential properties but as dynamic, purpose-guided clusters of preferences.[65] Landscapes have to do with (ordered) wholes; these wholes are expressive units of sense brought together through our collusion with the environment; the game we play is a different one each time, but some (at least loose) systems of preferences and principles of order or harmony coalesce historically and culturally around the values, beliefs, traditions of different habitats and communities of people. Let us compare this with Cosgrove:

> Landscape is a connecting term, a *Zusammenhang*. Much of its appeal to ecologists, architects, planners and others concerned with society and the design of environments lies in landscape's capacity to combine incommensurate or even dialectically opposed elements: process and form, nature

LANDSCAPE AND AESTHETICS

and culture, land and life. Landscape conveys the idea that their combination is—or should be—balanced and harmonious, and that harmony is visible geographically. Balance and harmony carry positive moral weight, so that a disordered or formless landscape seems something of a contradiction. Scenic values thus come to act as a moral barometer of successful community: human, natural or in combination.[66]

Thus, landscapes express, embody, and institute different ways of experiencing and dwelling. The basic claim that landscapes are tied to principles of order does not mean *prescribing this or that order*, or even just *prescribing that an order (whatever order) be*. It just means explicating and describing the language game we play when we speak of landscapes.[67] It makes sense to speak of landscapes because we need and are able to look for some order and sense in the contingency of the world, thus establishing habitats

FIGURE 2.7. Substantive landscape 1: *Landscape with Windmills and Christ as Good Shepherd* by Lucas Gassel (1560–1570, Metropolitan Museum of Art, New York City). Purchase, Howard A. Fox Gift, Chester Dale Bequest, by exchange; A. Hyatt Mayor Purchase Fund, Marjorie Phelps Starr Bequest, 1999. Reprinted from Wikimedia Commons, https://commons.wikimedia.org/wiki/File:Landscape_with _Windmills_and_Christ_as_Good_Shepherd_MET_DP875197.jpg.

in it. A disordered landscape is indeed an oxymoron, yet the order or sense we look for in landscapes massively varies historically, geographically, and culturally. What is more, our very relation to and awareness of this order or sense follows massively different shapes and patterns. Let us recall Wittgenstein: our relationship to place can go from the immediate one of the fleas with the dogs to different forms of "awakening" (veneration, rituals, imagination, artistic representation, scientific and philosophical knowledge . . .) that normally coexist.

The view I am advocating, then, is not relativistic but pluralistic. Not anything goes, and for two main reasons. The first is that landscapes always have a material side that orients our practices and determines the space of our interactions and exchanges, although without setting insurmountable limits to them. Landscapes are not the passive playground of our arbitrary wills; to put it more technically, they present us with "affordances."[68] Clearly, different landscapes "afford" different experiential and practical possibilities, already undercutting full-blown relativism. Second, also from the point of view of our agency, evaluations always remain possible, although not necessarily easy and certainly not taking place on the basis of eternal transcendental criteria.[69] Accordingly, practices and arrangements that simply destroy principles of order without constructively contributing to our collusive interaction with the environment are to be evaluated negatively. In Deweyan terms, they diminish and mutilate the full potential (successful consummation) of our experience, undermining the continuous development of our capacity to position ourselves in our environment and inhabit it.

From this point of view, we can pick up again the main questions asked by the isolationist paradigm with an intent of dualistic separation: "Which landscapes are true/valuable?" and "which authorities are competent to evaluate?" this time though with an intent of integration, inclusion, and dialogue (also through competition).[70] At each moment and in each context, the landscape discourse needs to be composed of different voices, partly agreeing, partly competing, but all of them ideally adding to that capacity. Obviously, conflicts can and will ensue. Different stakeholders (or the same stakeholders in different contexts) will have different positions, beliefs, and preferences. How are we to judge them when it comes to the necessity of a deliberation? Again: different voices are to be heard and weighed, reasons are to be exchanged, aims to be defined, compromises to be made—in short, all the democratic procedures are to be set in motion. Admittedly, this may sound too generic or even utopic. This is necessarily so insofar as the view I am advancing is not only pluralistic but also renounces the idea that there is an essentialist definition of landscapes from which decisions can be expertly deduced.[71] In other words, the philosophical approach itself participates in this discourse without however having any claim to exact prescriptive competence. Once again, though, this does not mean relapsing into a relativistic or indifferent perspective. What prevents it is exactly the assertion of the structural bond of aesthetics (as understood here) and landscapes. To quote Matteucci again: "The aesthetic turns out to be a primitive (underivable) manifestation of an extended mind as the analogical competence (the knowing-how) that an individual must possess in order to emerge from within the interaction with the surrounding environment."[72] Thus, while a plurality of voices and perspectives is necessary, the advancement and continuous adjustment of the landscape discourse also make certain competences necessary. In judging the relative value of those plural voices, the focus should be on the aesthetic as the pervasive dimension based on which we can successfully thematize landscapes and act on/with/within/for them. Clearly, then, I am talking about a very varied, and possibly not standard, set of competences, which is not the exclusive privilege of certain groups but aims at overcoming the traditional boundaries and hierarchies of experts versus nonexperts, insiders versus outsiders, science versus folklore, economy versus beauty, preservation versus development, and so on.[73]

The suggested joint abandonment of the isolationist perspective on landscapes and, together, on aesthetics has significant consequences, some of which I would like to stress. I suggest that detaching the concept of landscape from the totalizing embrace of the beautiful as of something extraordinary involves the realization that the modern scenic conception of landscape is the tip of the iceberg of a larger story. That conception brings to the fore, in a concentrated form, the issue of our meaningful institution of and relationship with our habitats. This is both the merit and the limit of that—let us call it modernist—conception. The merit, because it imposes the thematization, philosophical and non, of a topic so broad and pervading that it was hardly thematized as such. The limit, because it suggests, or at least it lends itself to suggest, that only certain, strictly selected ways of that institution and relationship are meaningful.

Within that paradigm, only certain voices can be heard—namely, the ones capable of formulating a contemplative, disinterested, nonutilitarian view. All the other forms of that institution and relationship might have been vital in other respects, but they could not fall under the "landscape" heading. I do not think, as some of the contemporary critique seems to imply, that this exclusion has been, since the origin of the concept of landscape, the intentional result of a consciously adopted modernist, bourgeois, imperialistic ideology, although of course discourses that today reproduce that mechanism of exclusion may be branded as intentionally ideological.[74] Instead, I think that the "modern" discourse on landscapes was, with all its limits, a way to bring forward an issue of universal interest yet of difficult thematization, and that this could happen, in its first formulations, only in a way that, from our point of view today, is evidently partial and unsatisfactory as well as unfair.

This is also the groundwork on which I would address the controversy regarding "landscape civilizations"—that is, the idea, most notably brought forward by Augustin Berque—that even though humans have always had a relationship with their environment and different ways to thematize it, there are only

> few civilizations in which the environment has been the object of explicit landscape imagery: that is to say, civilizations whose vocabulary includes a word for "landscape," and whose pictorial repertoire includes a genre in which the depiction of the environment is elevated to a theme in its own right, denoted by the term "landscape." Surprising though it may seem to us, there have in fact been only two civilizations in the history of mankind which have (to any extent) evolved an aesthetic of the landscape as such: that of China and that of Europe, together with their respective spheres of influence.[75]

While I cannot enter the controversy here, I would argue that Berque may or may not be right about what I have called landscape as "the tip of the iceberg," but that does not cover the whole story. Indeed, landscape as explicitly named and thematized is limited to a few contexts—namely, the ones in which the scenic-pictorial-disinterested depiction of the environment (what Berque calls "an aesthetic of the landscape") has been developed. However, I believe that concluding, from here, that only (modern)

FIGURE 2.8. Substantive landscape 2: *Market Outside Tripoli's Walls, Castle and Cemetery on the Right*. Photo from Charles Wellington Furlong, *The Gateway to the Sahara: Observations and Experiences in Tripoli* (New York: Charles Scribner's Sons, 1909), 50. Reprinted from Wikimedia Commons, https://commons.wikimedia.org/wiki/File:The_gateway_to_the_Sahara;_observations_and_experiences_in_Tripoli_(1909)_(14784520292).jpg.

Europe and China have thematized landscape in a way that is different and more concrete than "mere" environment would be too simplistic. Put otherwise, once we conceive of both aesthetics and landscape, as I suggest in this chapter, in an inclusive and antidualistic way and as having to do not so much with specific artistic forms or viewpoints but rather with a modality of habitats and experience, then we have good reasons to expand our consideration beyond "explicit" landscape civilizations.

This proposed expansion concerns not only civilizations but also people (or groups, or classes of people). As I mention in the previous chapter, in classic examples, from Petrarch to Wilde and Cézanne, peasants or shepherds are uninterested in or puzzled by the artists' or thinkers' passion for landscapes, and the latter in turn react with surprise or scorn at the ignorance of the former. As I suggest above, this is partly the case because peasants and shepherds lack the necessary distance to appreciate and evaluate the landscape, or even to perceive it as something different from the strictly utilitarian. This is, however, only part of the reason. The other part is that the framework in which landscape was thematized was—necessarily—too narrow and elitist to include the peasants' and shepherds' points of view. What I am suggesting is that Petrarch's shepherds' or Cézanne's peasants' neglect of the beauty of their landscape was indeed connected *with their own view* of landscape, even though it was not, and could not be, thematized as such. In other words, their neglect of the aesthetic-contemplative landscape was not just a negation of landscape but a different, excluded way of thematizing it. In our own age, the aim is to include more and more such voices into the landscape discourse and practice.

This, however, cannot just happen by way of unqualified additions ("the more the merrier") to the scenic-exceptionalist view, in which case we would just have a hodgepodge of actually incompatible and partial views. What we need is to develop a framework that may be inclusive enough to embrace a broad participation in the discourse as well as a serious, unprejudiced weighing of different opinions, including those that so far have been left out. Rather than remaining prisoners of a dualistic approach in which, to simplify a bit, we are forced to choose between the presence of the aesthetic in an exclusionary way and the rejection of it for the sake of unqualified inclusion, we have to broaden the spectrum of the discourse beyond the

FIGURE 2.9. Substantive landscape 3: *Landscape with Two Peasant Girls and a Rainbow* by Konstantin Somov (Russia, 1918, private collection). Reprinted from Wikimedia Commons, https://commons.wikimedia.org/wiki/File:Konstantin_Somov_-_landscape-with-two-peasant-girls-and-a-rainbow.jpg.

restricted canon of the landscape-aesthetic-visual while retaining the possibility of operating based on criteria and principles of order, however minimalistic and flexible.[76] Within this broader spectrum, the point of view of the peasant or the shepherd must no longer feature in a merely negative form—that is, as ignorance and neglect of the "true" discourse—but should instead play a positive and proactive role of its own. This is clearly not something that can be established at once and built on a top-down dynamic; it is a difficult and long process of adjustment to which multiple perspectives, disciplines, and practices must contribute, including technology and the new media, with their increasing accessibility (which arouses other concerns itself). This is the challenge; at the same time, to paraphrase Kant, this is what we can hope to achieve based on the current directions and needs of landscape research. To this aim, as I have shown, the inclusion of an adequate aesthetic framework is indispensable. In the next two chapters, I further flesh out the proposed intersection of landscape and aesthetics by presenting selected patterns of interaction between my proposed framework and some specific, though broadly framed issues located at that intersection, focusing first on traditionally aesthetics-related ones (chapter 3) and then on traditionally landscape-related ones (chapter 4), with a view to overcoming traditional boundaries.

Chapter Three

PATTERNS OF ENCOUNTER I
Aesthetic Matters

I started off on a philosophical path into landscape, moved by a many-sided crisis discourse and a many-sided dissatisfaction with the predominant ways of framing and addressing it. I summarized that crisis discourse under three main headings: (1) environmental crisis, (2) legitimacy crisis of the humanities, and philosophy in particular, and (3) crisis of aesthetics within landscape studies. My dissatisfaction was both with the humanities being denied a substantial role in addressing the environmental crisis and with "environmental humanities" as an answer to such neglect. I hence turned to the concept of landscape, in the belief that it can provide better answers, or at least put us on a better track. However, I felt a new dissatisfaction, this time at the neglect of aesthetics within the landscape discourse. In the previous chapters, I attempted to bring together these threads, showing how reconceptualizing landscapes can bring us to reconceptualize aesthetics and vice versa, and anticipating some reasons why, in my opinion, this joint reconceptualization can be of help in engaging the environmental crisis, suggesting a prominent role of the philosophical-aesthetic approach and thus also addressing the legitimacy issue of the humanities.[1] It is now necessary to identify some patterns of the contribution that the intersection of aesthetics and landscape can offer, beginning with two traditional and central topics in aesthetics—namely, interpretation and art—and soliciting them from this original angle.

PATTERNS OF ENCOUNTER I

1. INTERPRETATION

Toward the end of the previous chapter, I underscore the pluralist and pragmatist, yet antirelativistic character of the framework I am proposing. I point out that the fact that the value of a landscape cannot be reduced to a single, stable meaning does not mean that any suggested meaning, associated each time with different reclaimed values, is as good as another. In other words, a place may be meaningful (and, hence, valuable) for different reasons to different experiencers/stakeholders. When these different meanings collide—as it typically happens, for example, with touristic or industrial development plans—we are bound to ask which one is to prevail, and each answer will obviously have different and possibly burdensome practical implications. There needs to be some general and flexible set of criteria to try to adjudicate on such questions. While here I am not directly concerned with the economical, or industrial, or historical, or political, or strategic value of landscapes, I think it is quite clear that aesthetic value is more elusive and more easily neglected—or fetishized—than others.[2]

FIGURE 3.1. "Nature Center": What does it mean to interpret landscapes? Sign to the entrance of the Nature Center in Blacklick Woods Metro Park, Ohio. Photo by Sixflashphoto, June 2018. Reprinted from Wikimedia Commons, https://commons.wikimedia.org/wiki/File:Blacklick_Woods_-_Nature_Center_Sign_1.jpg.

According to what I have been saying, this is ultimately so not because the aesthetic is confined to an impalpable ethereal realm of beauty and marvel but, conversely, because it pervades, at least in principle, each and any experience, knowledge, and practice, and hence any meaning or value we can attach to landscapes.[3] For this very reason, asking ourselves how to assess the aesthetic value of a landscape and how such value can interact and conflict with other, more objective ones is everything but an elitist, idealistic enterprise. The aesthetic can act as a principle of order but also as the ground on which to articulate always provisional and dynamic sets of criteria in the attempt to respond to the widely acknowledged and pressing problem of the meaning of habitats for the people inhabiting them as well as for outsiders. This problem in turn has serious practical implications, such as authority and decision-making, the role of the public and of institutions/experts in landscape and environmental matters, and their impact on the communities involved at different levels.[4] Since construing and explaining meanings and making sense of things is what interpretation does, what we need to address next is the issue of interpretation of/in/with landscapes.

1.1. Nature and art: Deflating differences

The issue of interpretation is a crucial one in aesthetics, whether we are dealing with artworks, with natural environments, or with landscapes.[5] Whereas the interpretation of art is an established topic, the interpretation of nature is much less so. My starting point will be Emily Brady's article *Interpreting Environments*, a fundamental work for this topic. One of the most important distinctions between aesthetic experience and enjoyment in art versus nature seems to be that, while in the first case aesthetic experience and enjoyment are somehow connected to the search for the artwork's meaning, speaking of the meaning of a natural environment does not seem to make much sense. This distinction plays a role also in Brady's discourse, although she underlines that it must be weighed against the type of environment we are interpreting.[6] However, since at least as early as Roland Barthes's famous assertion of the "death of the author," the role of the author's intention in the interpretation and appreciation of artworks has been more and more widely challenged, if not thoroughly rejected in many theories.[7] Brady herself notices this point while clinging to the classic difference between art and nature in this regard: "'Intentionalists' argue that interpretation is tied to the artist's intention, where an actual or hypothetical intention determines a correct interpretation. 'Anti-intentionalists' cite problems associated with understanding artistic intention and they argue that the artwork is more free-floating, which allows for pluralism in interpretation. More radical views hold that appreciators have a hand in constructing the work through interpretations of it. The intentional distinction is not applicable to more natural environments where humans have a minor role."[8] Unlike Brady, up to here I have been trying to deflate the aesthetic difference between artworks and landscapes: this is why hereafter I critically comment on the persistence of this difference in Brady while holding on to her general view, which I share.[9] The persistence of a structural distinction between artworks and natural environments based on the presence versus absence of intention leads, in my opinion, to some undesired consequences, which I highlight in order to lay out a consistent pragmatist framework of interpretation.

To this aim, I refer to Umberto Eco's theory of interpretation of literary texts, starting with his 1990 Tanner Lectures and the ensuing debate with Richard Rorty and Jonathan Culler.[10] After advocating, in his previous works, a broadly conceived reader's right to contribute to creating the meaning of the text, in these lectures Eco is concerned with contrasting an "anything goes" version of such right. To this aim, while still maintaining that the meaning cannot be explained in terms of the *intentio auctoris* (the intention of the author), he introduces the notion of *intentio operis* (the intention of the work) as a counterbalance to an unlimited, relativistic right of the *intentio lectoris* (the intention of the reader). Hence, the claim is that meaning coincides neither with a goal set by the author, nor with whatever the empirical reader sees in the text, but rather it needs to be conceived as an open yet not unlimited set of possibilities contained in the work itself. Rorty straightforwardly dismisses the whole idea of a meaning immanent in the text. He does so by rejecting the distinction between "interpretation" and "use": all we do when reading a text is "use" it for any purpose we like, and the issue of an alleged correspondence between our reading and an inner meaning of the text should not concern us. Finally, Culler rejects both Rorty and Eco by pointing out the constraints imposed by the given context on each textual interpretation while highlighting the potentially countless number of contexts as well as the meaningfulness of what the text does *not* say. Culler also points out the cognitive and critical value of investigating the mechanisms through which a text produces meaning.

These brief remarks already show that, despite their irreconcilable differences, none of the authors involved in the debate and covering a wide spectrum of positions in the philosophy of interpretation attaches much importance to the author's intention about the discovery of the meaning of the text. In other words, none of them believes that whatever the author thought or intended puts any substantial constraint on our interpretation. The "death of the author" in our interpretive practices seems to remove an apparently obvious difference between artistic and environmental interpretation and put them in a similar position. On this ground, I suggest deflating the difference in Brady's own discourse by pointing out fundamental similarities between her "moderate anti-intentionalism" and Eco's approach. Both authors attempt to design a middle ground between full relativism and full monism—that is, between the thesis that every interpretation is acceptable and the one that only one interpretation is true. Eco writes, for example: "I have stressed that it is difficult to say whether an interpretation is a good one, or not. I have however decided that it is possible to establish some limits beyond which it is possible to say that a given interpretation is a bad and far-fetched one. As a criterion, my quasi-Popperian stricture is perhaps too weak, but it is sufficient in order to recognize that *it is not true that everything goes*."[11] Brady, in turn, supports "critical pluralism rather than critical monism. Searching for a single, correct interpretation, being guided by just one story, would be counterproductive not only to what environments themselves demand, but also to what we should expect from ourselves as engaged participants. Critical pluralism sits between critical monism and 'anything goes,' the subjective approach of some post-modern positions. It argues for a set of interpretations that are deemed acceptable but which are not determined according to being true or false."[12]

Both authors develop this middle ground through the idea that an acceptable interpretation sits, again, somewhere in between the unlimited right of the interpreting subject and the community's established, though always conjectural, consensus. Eco writes: "[Charles Sanders] Peirce, who insisted on the conjectural element of interpretation, on the infinity of semiosis, and on the essential *fallibilism* of every interpretative conclusion, tried to establish a minimal paradigm of acceptability of an interpretation on the grounds of a consensus of the community.... What kind of guarantee can a community provide? I think it provides a factual guarantee. Our species managed to survive by making conjectures that proved to be

FIGURE 3.2. Interpretation without intention? An extreme case: View of Husband Hill on Mars. Photo by NASA, November 2005. Reprinted from Wikimedia Commons, https://commons.wikimedia.org/wiki/File:MarsPanorama.jpg.

statistically fruitful."[13] As for Brady, we read: "An interpretation must be defensible, it cannot be outlandish, irrelevant, or the whim of one person. Besides cohering with the aesthetic and non-aesthetic descriptions of the aesthetic object, the validity of interpretations must also be relativized to the background beliefs, values and cultural and historical context of interpreters. This will allow for flexibility, especially in respect of contrasting cultural meanings given to environments."[14] Hence, both for Eco and for Brady, even though it is not possible to establish a univocal and universal criterion to assess in each case which is the correct or true interpretation, it is possible to evaluate the acceptability and defensibility of any given interpretation based on some minimal fallibilist standards. Both authors clearly adopt a pragmatist strategy, according to which we should not aim to find "strong" criteria for interpretations that are "true" but, rather, "weak" ones for interpretations that are "acceptable" or "reasonable."[15] As Brady states: "Widening the scope of knowledge drawn upon does not, however, take away the problem of how we distinguish between acceptable and unacceptable interpretations of the environment. We have to pin down not those interpretations that are true, but those that are reasonable, given particular cultures and types of environments."[16] This striking similarity between the two authors also seems to further support the idea of having at least a general theoretical framework in the philosophy of interpretation to apply to both art and environment, deflating the classic, intention-based distinction.[17]

Parallel to the issue of meaning, also regarding the aim of interpretation, positions are quite varied within philosophy of art, as Brady herself notices: "In debates about interpretation in the arts, philosophers have disagreed about the proper aim of interpretation, that is, what it is that we should be doing when we interpret works of art. Some argue that the aim of interpretation is to achieve an understanding of an artwork, and this is done by reaching a correct interpretation by reference to the artist's intention. Others argue that the proper aim is to maximize enjoyable aesthetic experience, and this is achieved through a range of acceptable interpretations of the work. Still others argue that there is no single proper aim, but many."[18] But, she continues, "this issue has relevance to the environment too, where we need to ask what exactly is the point of interpreting the environment in the *aesthetic context*."[19] Once again, she opts for a middle ground between cognitivism and humanism/hedonism while still underscoring a general difference between artifacts and environments: "When no longer dealing with straightforward artefacts, ... the proper aim of interpretation is to enrich aesthetic appreciation in ways that enhance our aesthetic encounters with the environment. Interpretive activity ought to involve a variety of imaginative ways to discover meaning in our environment, ways that increase the value we find there."[20] She then further specifies that "this activity ought not be directed, however, at increasing our pleasure. Rather, we should hope for, as side effects to some extent, greater sensitivity to nature's qualities and with that, greater respect for nature."[21]

While this approach is consistent with Brady's proposed "cultural pluralism," one may wonder why the interpretive activity should not be directed at increasing our pleasure and instead produce a greater respect for nature. After all, our pleasure and our respect for nature do not seem to necessarily contradict each other: in fact, in many cases, they may be seen as corroborating each other. Brady's point is that our aesthetic pleasure should not be the only or ultimate aim of interpreting landscapes as this may lead, first, to a reductively humanistic or humanizing view of nature (and, hence, to "unreasonable" interpretations) and, second, to subjugating, manipulating, and destroying nature, seen as a fully disposable human playground rather than as a complex, independent, sophisticated organism deserving our respect. These concerns are certainly cogent, but the way they are presented leads, I think, to two undesired consequences. First, the idea that the aim of interpretation is building greater respect for nature, without further qualifications, seems to abruptly introduce an ethical concern, however legitimate, the systematic connection of which with the developed theory is unwarranted. Second, this idea implies conceiving of nature in a rather essentialistic way, as an entity endowed with an internal essence and meaning, independent of our relation to it, which is at odds with Brady's main pragmatist interpretive tenet, as formulated, for example, here: "There is no meaning internal to landscapes. We bring meaning to them or assign meaning through cultural frameworks. There is still an attempt to make sense of something, but not in terms of searching for meaning that already exists."[22] As I show in the next section, this apparent inconsistency has to do with the persistence, in Brady's discourse, of the intention-based distinction between artifacts and natural environments.

1.2. For a consistently pragmatist interpretive framework

I think it is possible to avoid inconsistencies while preserving Brady's philosophical intention, which I share. To this goal, consider Eco's answer to the issue of the aim of interpretation. Following Peirce, Eco argues in general that the issue of meaning involves some reference to a purpose. The notion of purpose marks the persistence of a realistic element in Eco's Peircean approach: "A purpose is, without any shade of doubt, and at least in the Peircean framework, connected with something which lies outside language. Maybe it has nothing to do with a transcendental subject, but it has to do with referents, with the external world, and links the idea of interpretation to the idea of interpreting according to a given meaning."[23] This realistic element is then better qualified in a nonnaive but rather conjectural sense through the association with "habit": "The Habit is a disposition to act upon the world, and this possibility to act, as well as the recognition of this possibility as a Law, requires something which is very close to a transcendental instance: a community as an intersubjective guarantee of a nonintuitive, nonnaively realistic, but rather conjectural, notion of truth."[24] The habit is hence conceived as a disposition to act, external to the interpretive process, where the latter provisionally stops and reaches the intended meaning. Reconceiving meaning via the notion of habit allows to overcome the extreme relativism, or even solipsism, of an infinite interpretive "drift," to reconnect the interpreting subject with the external world, and to make space for a conjectural notion of truth, which is not objectively, but at least intersubjectively, established.[25] "From the moment in which the community is pulled to agree with a given interpretation, there is, if not an objective, at least an *intersubjective* meaning which acquires a privilege over any other possible interpretation spelled out without the agreement of the community."[26]

Again, there are several points of contact between what Eco is saying here and Brady's overall intention. First, Eco and Brady agree that even anti-intentionalist theories of interpretation should be conceived as realistic in the sense that interpretation always entails the possibility of a reference to an object existing outside the interpretive process. Second, while Brady does not make specific reference to the concept of "habit," I maintain that the latter fits well with her idea "that the aim of interpretation ought to be one that sits easily alongside the spirit of aesthetic appreciation as an enriching encounter with the natural world."[27] Interpreting landscapes for aesthetic purposes does not aim at an endless, self-sufficient interrogation about the possible network of references of every natural object in our interpretation but at a provisionally satisfied, active disposition of interaction with and appreciation of nature, which could well be characterized as a habit, in Eco's sense. Finally, the sense-making, sense-giving, and sense-confirming role of a community of interpreters is an obvious common tenet of the two authors. For both, the community acts as a device to control the reasonableness or acceptability of interpretations, although this "communitarian" element should not be understood in a closed or authoritarian sense: interpretive communities are construed in a broad, pluralistic, historically and culturally open fashion.

Because of such closeness between Eco and Brady, I would like to suggest that some of Eco's points, although not dealing with environmental aesthetics, can corroborate Brady's discourse. First, in Eco, the pleasure we gather from interpretive acts and the respect toward the object of interpretation are not juxtaposed but rather tightly connected. This is quite evident, among others, from Eco's answer to Rorty's theorized purposelessness of literary and linguistic studies: "Rorty asked for what purposes we need to know how language works. I respectfully answer: not only because writers study language in order to write better, . . . but also because marvelling (and therefore curiosity) is the source of all knowledge, knowledge is a source of pleasure and it is simply beautiful to discover why and how a given text can produce so many good interpretations."[28] An increased respect for the object of our interpretation, be it a literary text or a landscape, can be grounded in the pleasure and sense of wonder that is intrinsic to the interpretative effort and to its discovery, and vice versa. This answer, I believe, is fully consistent with Brady's general framework, but it avoids the ad hoc introduction of an external aim, that is, of an increased respect for nature independent of our pleasure.

Second, Eco's Peircean and conjectural realism allows to think of nature as a real entity, not just as the product of our interpretation, without committing to an essentialist conception of nature as already endowed with a meaning that our interpretive acts should simply be able to discover and relate to. This is so because Eco blurs the distinction between natural objects and artifacts, which still plays a role in Brady's approach. Confronted with the assertion of a structural difference between texts and sense data from the point of view of interpretation, Eco states: "Such a distinction seems to me much too rigid. To recognize a sense datum as such we need an interpretation—as well as criterion of pertinence by which certain events are recognized as more relevant than others—and the very result of our operational habits is subject to further interpretation."[29] Hence, for Eco, consistently with his pragmatist

FIGURE 3.3. Deflating the art/nature interpretive difference: Tree of Jesse, Wells Cathedral, England. Photo by Andrewrabbott, September 2015. Reprinted from Wikimedia Commons, https://commons.wikimedia.org/wiki/File:Chancel_east_window._Tree_of_Jesse._Wells_Cathedral.jpg.

approach, each and every action entails an interpretive effort. Accordingly, when aesthetically appreciating an object, be it an artwork or a natural environment, interpretation necessarily comes into play. This idea is counterbalanced, as we saw, by the reference to the community of interpreters, which Eco conceives of as a transcendental element that, unlike the Kantian one, is configured as a somewhat paradoxical, always provisional and conjectural, a posteriori established guarantor of truth. The adoption of this consistent pragmatist framework overcomes the structural difference between artifacts and nature as objects of interpretation, avoids an essentialist conception of nature and the respect we owe to it as interpreters and aesthetic appreciators, and leaves ample room for a fruitful development of the notion of community, a central one in Brady's framework.

To summarize and conclude this discussion of interpretation: conceiving of the artist's intention as the (main) interpretive content of an artwork supports a distinction between interpretation of art and interpretation of nature. This distinction then leads to the argument that the interpretation of nature is freer and less subject to content constraints than that of art. In turn, this argument connects to the assertion of nature as a more autonomous entity than artifacts, deserving recognition and respect independent of our interpretive pleasure. In the attempt to avoid a full-blown hedonistic relativism, humanism, or solipsism, such assertion risks introducing an element of naive realism, whereas a Peircean conjectural realism, as Eco shows, would suffice to that goal. Finally, it is not out of place to remark how the very use of the term *environment* prompts one to frame the interpretive field in dualistic, essentialistic terms. On the contrary, at least some of the issues investigated can be more adequately addressed under the heading of landscape interpretation. This is because, following Assunto's distinction, landscapes are the concrete term we need to address and act upon/with, whereas environments are functional abstractions that should certainly be adopted in any context requiring it but should not be essentialized and hypostatized, including in the context of their (aesthetic) interpretation.

2. ART

The next two sections further highlight the potential of landscapes in their connection with aesthetics by addressing, after the discussion of interpretation, a related topic that is normally considered *the* paramount topic of aesthetics—namely, art—and thus concluding the more traditionally "aesthetic" part of my argument. It should not come as a surprise, given my Deweyan orientation, that artworks play quite a minor role in my discussion of art.

2.1. Art in landscapes, landscapes in art: From painting to experiencing and back

The connection with art is inherent in the concept of landscape from the very beginning. This is obviously true especially of painting: "Painting is in fact so central to the formulation and development of the idea of landscape that if we investigate the origin and history of the term, we find numerous instances when 'landscape' refers simultaneously to a view or delimited area of ground, *and* its painted representation. . . . It is understood to be both a bounded area of ground as well as a section of the earth's surface that (precisely because it can be comprehended in a single view) is susceptible to representation."[30] Even though our contemporary use of the term has become so broad and plural that it often does not seem to bear any connection with painting, "once we make the seemingly innocent choice to use the term 'landscape' (rather than land, earth, ground, [etc.]), we are inevitably and inextricably talking about paintings, or, at the very least, about conventions that are derived from, and rooted in, painterly practice."[31] At the very least and in its loosest form, the derivation from painting is present in the implication that landscape is never "only" environment but always a mediation of it through human experience.[32] Through the lens of landscape, nature is never an independently existing objective realm but always the result of a construction and representation process. There is, in short, no landscape that is free from artistic and cultural presuppositions: "There is no landscape 'out there,' landscape is always and already 'in here.'"[33] This does not mean advocating a radically subjectivist or culturalist perspective in which nature is fully reducible to an ever-different human gaze but, rather, claiming that the concept of landscape forces us to reframe the border between nature and art. As a matter of fact, as underscored, for instance, by the notion of "picturesque," the relationship between landscape and painting goes both ways: "Not only does painting precondition our understanding of landscape, but landscape also changes our understanding of painting."[34]

FIGURE 3.4. Giorgione's enigmatic *The Tempest* can be considered among the first examples of landscape painting in Europe (1506–1508, Gallerie dell'Accademia, Venice, Italy). Photo by Ismoon, February 2018. Reprinted from Wikimedia Commons, https://commons.wikimedia.org/wiki/File:6,99 Mo-Giorgione_019.jpg.

There is a continuity between landscape and painting (and, in general, between landscape and art) that is not only historical but conceptual. Even more: the relationship of derivation from painting to landscape might be reversed, and one could claim that what painting does is a derivative, more sophisticated and technical form of what landscapes do. This means, in short, to formulate an order through which objects are gathered in a meaningful, shareable way. Georg Simmel, who was close to pragmatism and can be considered the pioneer of the philosophy of landscape, expresses this through an effective metaphor:[35] "What kind of law, we need to ask further, determines this selection and composition? Whatever it is that we can take in through just one glance or from within our

FIGURE 3.5. *Mont Sainte-Victoire* by Paul Cézanne (circa 1900, Hermitage Museum, Saint Petersburg, Russia). Reproduction from art book, June 2008. Reprinted from Wikimedia Commons, https://commons.wikimedia.org/wiki/File:Cezanne_mont-sainte-victoire.jpg.

FIGURE 3.6. *Bathers, Mont Sainte-Victoire in the Background* by Paul Cézanne (1902–1906, private collection). Photo by Sotheby's. Reprinted from Wikimedia Commons, https://commons.wikimedia.org/wiki/File:Paul_Cezanne_Bathers,_Mont-Sainte-Victoire_in_the_Background.jpg.

momentary field of vision is not landscape but, at most, the raw material towards it. In the same way a row of books placed next to each other does not by itself add up to 'a library'—until and unless, and without a single book being added or removed, a certain unifying concept comes to encompass and give a form to them."[36] A unifying concept is at the same time the source of unity and a principle of order and sense. Now, whereas a unifying concept for a library can be quite straightforward, the same does not apply to landscapes because "the raw material of landscape provided by bare nature is so infinitely varied and changes from case to case. Consequently, the points of view and the forms that compose its elements into a sense-perceptual unity will also be highly variable."[37]

To provide some unity, Simmel pragmatically suggests an aesthetic approach—that is, considering landscapes in their ordinary sense and landscapes as artworks in their continuity. The order and, hence, the sense we find in a painted landscape are certainly more univocal and traceable than the ones we find in a natural landscape, yet the process through which we get there is qualitatively one and the same. Therefore, art, being a more concentrated expression of such a process, helps us understand how an order can be instituted in the apparently irreducible chaos and contingency of this raw material: "Landscape, as a work of art, comes about as the progressive continuation and cleansing of a process in which a landscape, in its ordinary sense, grows out of mere impressions of discrete objects of nature. An artist delineates one part within the chaotic stream and infiniteness of the immediately given world and conceives of and forms it as a unitary phenomenon. This now derives its meaning from within itself, having severed all threads connecting it to the world around it and having retied them into its own centre."[38] The purified, technical, sophisticated work of the painter is nothing but the refining of a procedure already at work in the perceptual experience of a natural landscape: "We follow the same procedure—only in a less developed, less fundamental degree, and in a fragmentary way unsure of its boundaries—as soon as we perceive a 'landscape' in place of a meadow, a house, a brook and passing clouds."[39] The higher, more concentrated effectiveness of the artistic in instituting and finding meanings in/through our experience with the world might therefore be seen as the main reason why the concept of landscape—though, as I argued, mainly connected with a theory of experience and habitats—was explicitly developed at its origin in the context of a contemplative, art-oriented aesthetic perspective, with the implications I have sketched above.[40]

Following up on these observations and recalling at the same time the view of experience and aesthetics delineated in the previous chapter, we can attain a more comprehensive and continuistic point of view. "Nature" or "environment" are abstractions. What we concretely perceive and relate to is *always* landscape (think of Assunto). This means, then, that our perceptual experience of the space we inhabit is connected to the aesthetic unifying force, not in an occasional, extraordinary way, but in a structural one. We *always* perceive, institute, and perform at once units of sense, not unrelated punctual facts. The latter come later: they are the product of pragmatic isolations and abstractions. The aesthetic is *always* at work, it is not an interruption of our ordinary experience, it is its very backbone. Our perception is never simply passive, it is *always* the active, potentially aesthetically guided work of severing and reconnecting the threads of the world around us. The "simple" perception of "a meadow, a house, a brook and passing clouds," its organization into a landscape, and the artistic representation of the latter in a painting, are but (individually and culturally) different degrees of articulation of our experience. This continuity covers not only the creation of the meaningful unit (whether natural or artistic) but also its effect—that is, the specific feeling that accompanies its reception and fruition, which we usually designate through aesthetic or semi-aesthetic predicates such as beautiful, sublime, sad, serene, and so on.

As a matter of fact, in line with the argument pursued here, there is only *one* act of perceptual experience, and what seem to be its ontologically and epistemically prior constituents are in fact the result of a later breakdown and abstraction: "The question has been posed wrongly were we to ask whether our unitary perception of an object or the feeling arising together with it comes first or second. There prevails, in fact, no cause-and-effect relationship between them, and, if anything, both together would count as cause and both as effect. Thus, both the unifying move which brings landscape as such into being, and the mood that a landscape projects at us and through which we comprehend it, are merely the result of a subsequent dismantling of one and the same psychic act."[41] Therefore, the landscape is constituted through our mood or experience just as much as our mood or experience is generated by it. This is, if we recall Wittgenstein, a (more-than-verbal[42]) language game, in which distinctions between language and world, saying and doing, nature and culture, seeing and feeling, are not primitive, but the results of pragmatically oriented, non-essentialist? acts of breakdown and abstraction: "For this reason, it is possible to refer to mood and the coming into being of landscape, that is, the forming of its individual parts into a whole, as one and the same act. It is as if our various psychical energies, those to do with perception and with feeling, as if each one of them, in their own tonality, were just uttering one and the same word in unison."[43] In this respect, landscapes decidedly point toward a nondualistic view of art. To qualify this point, it may be useful to delve into the interwovenness of landscape, mapping, gardening, and writing not in their opposition to the pictorial roots but as an integration.

2.2. Painting, mapping, gardening, writing

Landscapes, as a part of the contemporary literature insists, were both created *and* painted following a need for control and mastery of the human eye over the world. They responded to a visual ideology that was the mark of the bourgeois, rationalist conception of the world.[44] As such, they may be seen as a typically dualistic instrument of power and ideology, enforcing a fully anthropocentric, subjectivist, ocularcentric paradigm. But landscapes, both created and painted, were always also the playground for imagination, emotion, and utopia.[45] This coexistence, which can appear as a contradiction, is evident, for example, in William Bartram's pen-and-ink drawing of *The Great-Alachua Savana, East Florida* (circa 1765), as discussed by Rachael Z. DeLue: "A landscape produced by a multitude of operations (observing, imagining, distorting, hypothesizing, documenting, and embellishing), that compels a multitude of ways of seeing a particular terrain, that offers no single point of view or angle of vision, and that privileges no single representational mode."[46] An image like Bartram's may well communicate a feeling of chaos and inhabitability, yet it also suggests that "landscape describes the land itself but it can also refer to the myriad human activity that unfolds within and imbues the land with extra-natural systems or meanings. Landscape is not simply the context for but constitutes the very fabric of cultural, social, political, and economic formation and phenomena."[47] While a landscape independent from a human eye is only a "fantasy," such a conception of landscape as fabric may invite us to indulge this

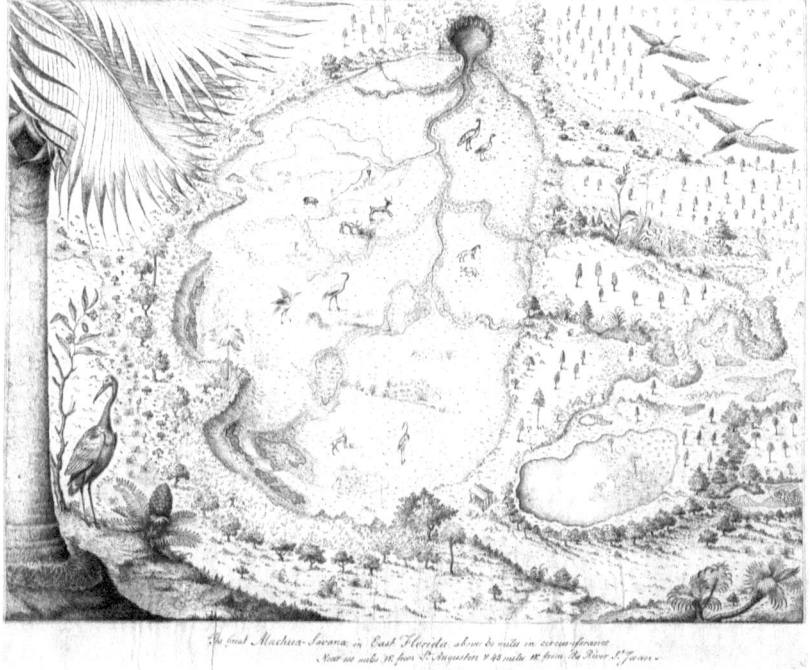

FIGURE 3.7. *The Great Alachua-Savana* by William Bartram, circa 1765. Image used with permission from the American Philosophical Society.

fantasy and to imagine what a landscape without humans would be.[48] This would mean questioning the usual subject-object paradigm, rejecting "the pictorial model of landscape," and embracing "an operational model instead, one that emphasized the processes, procedures, and instrumentalities particular to a given landscape."[49] In a way, DeLue suggests, we are invited to see things from the point of view of the landscape itself or its inhabitants: the landscape becomes the observer or theorizer.[50]

Now, this was, and is, not just a poetic endeavor. Scientifically mapping a whole new, fully unknown territory meant for Bartram also testing a range of different perspectives, "including a model of knowing that de-centered the human."[51] This attempt is even more relevant today in a context that "from animal studies, theories of the post-human, and the development of artificial intelligence to the proliferation of technologies that see and know apart from the human eye— . . . has put the vantage point of the non-human front and center once again."[52] The kind of art landscapes point to is, once again, not isolationist and for its own sake but a practice in continuity with our ordinary experience as well as with other practices, techniques, forms of knowledge, ways of interrogating, reading, ordering the world, and trying to make it our own, even when apparently fully alien, as in Bartram's case.[53] An art, in Deweyan terms, that successfully embeds and unleashes a full range of possibilities for our interaction with the environment and our response to the challenges of our own time.[54] This paradigm, evidently, does not only apply to painting. In fact, in line with current criticisms of ocularcentrism and the disembodied mind/eye, and with the corresponding calls for haptic, immersive, embodied, and enactive perspectives, the view I have been outlining favors a pluralism of artistic approaches to landscape.[55] A full, consummated experience cannot overlook the nonvisual aspects and corresponding artistic forms and the holistic character of the aesthetic.

This understanding of landscapes, art, and the aesthetic also has important implications for the relationship between art, environment, and ecology. A substantial part of the art dealing with environmental issues, including photography and land art, often favors shocking, weird, avant-garde, or disturbing approaches.[56] While the intention may be to raise the awareness of the public to important, often-neglected issues by way of a shock, the result can be an inevitably anthropocentric fetishization of certain natural forms (especially those connected with the idea of wilderness) and the preclusion of a closer, more constructive (and possibly more awareness-raising) experience of nature, which is often pictured as just distant, threatened, or hostile.[57] From this point of view, the humble and certainly less spectacular art of gardening, long neglected but on the rise again (partly due to urban gardening or, even, guerrilla gardening), cognate but also often terminologically confused with "landscaping," may have a lot to teach to environmental art, landscape architecture, and so on.[58] In gardening, we interact with nature without fear of our creativity and technology becoming hostile to it.[59] Indeed, the dualism of art and nature becomes blurred and positively pliable, and points toward a human responsibility rooted not in detachment but in multiform immersion and interaction.

Let me briefly summarize the results of this discussion of art and landscapes. What has emerged, first of all, is the need to rethink, and in fact push the boundaries characterizing much of the discourse on art. Whereas

FIGURE 3.8. Gardening 1: The grandiose, violin-shaped plan for the garden of the Borbone Royal Palace in Caserta, Italy, by architect Luigi Vanvitelli, inaugurated 1774. Engraving by Carlo Nolli, 1756. Reprinted from Wikimedia Commons, https://commons.wikimedia.org/wiki/File:Veduta_a_volo_d%E2%80%99 uccello_della_Reggia_di_Caserta.jpg.

FIGURE 3.9. Gardening 2: Guerrilla gardening in Berlin, Germany. Photo by Flittergreeze, July 2012. Reprinted from Wikimedia Commons, https://commons.wikimedia.org/wiki/File:Guerilla_Gardening _bed.jpg.

a natural landscape and a painted one may seem materially different, the word itself, being capable of designating both of them, thematizes a slippage and an instability between the two that is in fact suggestive of a deeper continuity.[60] Such deeper continuity is, indeed, our experience, which is never a purely passive reception but always also the construction and institution of an order of sense, whether by gathering natural objects (visually or materially) or by depicting them. What we call landscape as "art" or as "nature," as well as the aesthetic concepts or predicates, are breakdowns and fixations of a continuous, holistic process.[61] Second, conceived of as the dimension expressing our capacity to gather objects in a meaningful way, the aesthetic pervades and guides our whole experience, although with ever-different degrees of clarity and intensity (let us recall Dewey's "consummation"). Third, every moment or circumstance of our experience is irreducible and incommensurable. Too many factors concur in constituting it, and its outcomes are too different. This also applies to landscapes, which are, as we saw, not just "out there" like independent objects, but always (also) "in here." Therefore, in this complex sense, each landscape is unique, and landscapes in general are not a universal language.[62] Here, despite their nonverbal character, landscapes can be (and have been) compared, rather than to paintings, to literary texts with different kinds or styles—classical vernacular, sublime, monumental—and "different landscapes have different languages, presumably to be read by different publics."[63] The literary text is never just the text as such, but it is always its many possible readings and interpretations as well, as I argue at the beginning of this chapter.[64] Finally, landscapes have a lot to say about the kinds and forms of art that can help us deal with, or at the very least frame better, some extraordinarily urgent issues of our time, most notably environmental ones. The next chapter takes up a discussion of a few selected ones.

Chapter Four

PATTERNS OF ENCOUNTER II
Landscape Matters

The previous chapter has presented some patterns along which the developed framework can contribute to reframe central issues in aesthetics beyond traditional and often reductive paradigms in a way that is appealing on the background of the discourses of crisis from which the book started. In a complementary way, we now need to confront the practical and applied challenges of the environmental crisis in general and of landscape studies more specifically through the lens of the philosophical framework elaborated herein. Crisis cannot just be the starting point of philosophical reflection, casting a shade on it like an external object. Philosophy needs to be directly impacted by crisis if it aims to have an impact on it, and the present chapter also aims at outlining possible ways to achieve this mutual impact. What this chapter *cannot* aim for, on the contrary, might be summarized under two main points. The first one is qualitative: laying claim to a direct impact does not mean affirming that philosophy can hope to directly solve crises, but "only" that, in a Wittgensteinian spirit, it can help us see them in more adequate, less simplistic ways, and hence prompt nonphilosophical practices to address them more effectively. The second one is quantitative: in the limited space of a chapter, I cannot hope to touch upon all the critical issues that may legitimately be considered the most relevant to such topic. I had to make a choice, which of course may be challenged or integrated.[1] My selection has five main points, with further internal subdivisions: temporality, modernism and environmentalism, justice and politics, education, and interdisciplinarity.

1. TEMPORALIZATIONS OF SPACE AND SPATIALIZATIONS OF TIME

Both landscapes and aesthetics seem to have to do with space rather than with time, or at least more with space than with time, with this preconception being reflected both in the ordinary discourse and in the academic one. A more comprehensive, antidualistic approach like the one I put forward in the previous chapters requires not just the additional consideration of time but, in fact, thematizing experience as a spatiotemporal continuum. Even in our most punctual perceptions of objects "given" in a spatially external world, our experience is structured by temporality. The processual, continuistic temporal character of our experience, as we saw in Dewey, needs to be underscored even regarding "mere" seeing, and much more so if we are considering more complex experiential operations.[2] Much of the contemporary discourse on landscapes, partly on the grounds of its challenge to ocularcentrism, rightly insists on the centrality of this element, which I now discuss along five main axes focusing on different aspects of the omnipresence of the temporal dimension in (apparently) spatial experiences.[3]

1.1 Experience, knowledge, and appreciation

The first axis deals with time as an essential component of the experience, knowledge, and appreciation of landscapes. One may indeed claim that time is fundamental to the apprehension of space: "Time is . . . the medium of one's experience of landscape, for terrain is known most fully in the duration of spatial passage or movement, its delayed or accelerated sequences, as well as its repetitions and inaugurations. Temporality opens an essential dimension of spatial sense."[4] Now, to interpret this in the sense of a mere juxtaposition and combination of two separate elements would indeed be just as abstract as a purely spatial conception of landscapes. The point is instead that landscapes are the concrete unity of space and time: their space only makes sense if temporalized, and vice versa. The experience of a landscape takes time, both for the experience and for the landscape.

On the one hand, experience is not an exact moment of "recognition" but the consummation of a perceptual process, which in turn can give way to a new experience, and so on. On the other hand, the landscape too is a unitarily constructed whole of objects interacting not merely in space but also in time: developing, following rhythms and cycles (day and nighttime, seasons, . . .), always resulting in different arrangements. For the same reasons, our experience of/with a landscape too needs to be temporally framed and informed, lest it might deceivingly focus on a specific arrangement, treating it as a permanent whole. In fact, referring only to a specific point in time of a landscape would offer a mutilated and unrealistic knowledge of it, as referring to just one specific object within it. Admittedly, we may appreciate certain scenic landscapes because of their apparent timelessness. However, this risks to be a defective appreciation, as distant from a full authentic one as a postcard would be from the scene it actually depicts. Landscapes require an immersive, processual fruition unlike that of a simple, punctual visualization.

This is probably truer for landscapes than for artworks, at least traditional ones (without this being a denial of the continuity I have been trying to establish). Indeed, the aesthetic appreciation of a painting, or even more of a ballet, takes time, but appreciation of them does not involve the dimension of change: some physical properties of a painting may change in time, and the same ballet can be performed in different ways, but we normally refer to them as the same painting or the same ballet. This is not the case with landscapes: even an unchanging space can hardly be appreciated as the same landscape in different hours or seasons.[5] Challenging the received, reductive equation of landscapes with (pictorial) artworks also means acknowledging the centrality of change for the former, which are not just static and timeless attempts to imitate a changing reality but are "more-than-representational," thus putting into the foreground *all* the senses and the embodied, performative, affective, and complex if not outright "messy" character of our interactions with reality.[6] More-than-representational landscapes are not (just) "things" or collections of things but rather "quasi-things" or "atmospheres."[7] "It is not just a matter of understanding how we think about the landscapes that surround us but how they in turn *force us to think and feel*," a point of view prompting us, as we already saw in the previous chapter, to engage and play with a decentered, even post-humanist perspective.[8] Based on the latter, it is not with a resigned but rather with an inquiring and curious mind that we often have to take a step back and acknowledge that "the landscape has its own narrative to tell, that is not easily susceptible to our verbal discourse. We *feel* the landscape."[9] The temporality of the landscape's narrative does not coincide with our verbal discourse but is integral to our experience and appreciation.

1.2 History, identity, and palimpsests

The second temporal axis accounts for the historical-identitarian claim. Accordingly, the historicity of landscapes is not only—trivially—about their temporal development but also, and more importantly, about the mutual identification of place and community.[10] Landscapes are the very set of the history and life of people inhabiting and shaping them. Such history and life would indeed be different in different landscapes and vice versa: the landscape would be (not only materially) different if a different history had played out in them. Hence the mutual identification of landscape and communities, which does not (or at least not necessarily) imply a conservative or even explicitly exclusionary view of both terms but stands for the concrete, aesthetic relationship of our individual and collective experience and time, as maintained, for example, by Dewey.[11] If, as Dewey claimed, the success and meaningfulness of our present experience is always tied to the maturation and expansion of the past one, then the meanings embedded in landscapes are not simply "there" as static spatial properties but are accumulated throughout and performed by their history. The latter is of course to be conceived not in a linear, naively progressive sense but as the never-ending organizational work of a continuous rhythm of growth, pause, loss, new growth, and so on. In this sense, the landscape is indeed like a palimpsest to be interpreted not only according to positive and quantitative data but also as an archaeological, historical, social document.[12] This perfectly fits with the distinction presented above between abstract environment and concrete landscape. Environment is landscape minus the historically lived human experience: it can be described in purely spatial and objective terms, whereas landscape needs the historical and temporal framework. An environment can possess many spatially "good" properties, yet a community (or an individual) may prefer to inhabit an objectively less hospitable but historically more meaningful one. Lived history, collectively stipulated meanings, identity,

FIGURE 4.1. Archaeological-agricultural landscape around the ancient city of Troy (today Hisarlık, Turkey), a foundational site for European history and culture. Photo by CherryX. Reprinted from Wikimedia Commons, https://it.m.wikipedia.org/wiki/File:Landscape_around_Troy.jpg.

memory:[13] thinking of our habitats only in terms of environment might eventually leave out these integral constituents of our experience.[14]

1.3 Loss of innocence, ideology, and critique

Linking landscapes with history and identity may pose dangers, as just mentioned, and needs to be done in a critical way. Critique is indeed an important element in the current insistence on the temporal dimension of landscapes. Landscapes, at least in a rather traditional modernist (isolationist-exceptionalist) understanding, risk producing mystification and deceit. According to Corner, scenic landscapes have an "escapist understructure.... Here landscape is nothing more than an empty sign, a dead event, a deeply aestheticized experience that holds neither portent nor promise of a future. Both evil and invention are hidden, and the viewer is allowed to momentarily forget and escape from present and future difficulties, finding compensation in the recollection of earlier, 'simpler' times."[15] Besides, "because of the passage of time, landscape decontextualizes its artifactuality and takes on the appearance of something natural. Such enduring innocence may well herald great emancipating potential (as the landscape itself escapes the control and authority of its makers), but it also harbors a deceit that can be covertly appropriated by those who exercise power in society."[16] Detaching landscapes from their temporal framework, with its conflicts and resistances, may give the pleasant, reassuring appearance of natural stability, beauty, and permanence that we seek just in order to escape the hardships and conflicts of our daily life as well as of history. Such a pretense of naturality, however, clearly entails several risks: mutilation and fetishization of our experience, removal and neutralization of historical struggles, ideological naturalization of power dynamics, colonialist and imperialist nostalgia and fantasy, and so on.

The criticism of this model demands the "loss of innocence" of landscapes and necessitates, according to Mitchell, a radical shift in the very concept of landscape, "from a noun to a verb. It asks that we think of landscapes, not as an object to be seen or a text to be read, but as a process by which social and subjective identities are formed."[17] This shift clearly must be not only of a theoretical but also of a very practical nature—for example, concerning landscape design in its various forms and applications, or its artistic thematization. We need a "shift from appearances and meanings to more prosaic concerns for how things work," as well as from appearances and images to performances, tasks, and activities.[18] Both in its theoretical and in its applied dimensions, this alternative model requires the incorporation of time and complexity in thinking of landscapes. After all, instituting a landscape also means attempting to master time through space—that is, to arrange space in such a way that it can be dominated through time and look permanent through change.[19] We need a critical discourse to prevent similar power dynamics from remaining hidden under a hyper-aestheticized veil of naturality. Such an alternative paradigm needs to incorporate time not only in the sense of the dramatic turns of history but also in that of the "everyday ironies" (industrial machines in a beautiful rural landscape, homeless people in a nice city center, and similar) puncturing the veil of pretense and social convention.[20] Once again, present challenges require a holistic, anti-exceptionalist paradigm of both landscape and aesthetics.

PATTERNS OF ENCOUNTER II

FIGURE 4.2. A detail of Alan Sonfist's land artwork *Time Landscape*, New York City (1965/1978). Manhattan was originally a forest, which was fully destroyed as the city expanded. Even the green areas in present-day Manhattan have no connection to the original vegetation. *Time Landscape* consists of plants native to the area in precolonial times, which through the artwork have reclaimed a space and a time. Such "mending" of history and nature provokes a number of interrogatives and paradoxes; see the relevant chapter of Alastair Bonnett, *Unruly Places*. Art by Alan Sonfist, 1965. Reprinted from Wikimedia Commons, https://en.m.wikipedia.org/wiki/File:Timelandscapeweb.jpg.

1.4 Climate change, infrastructure, and ecologies of scale

A paradigm capable of substantially, and not just externally, incorporating the temporal dimension responds better than a primarily spatial-visual one to the needs of a world so pressingly confronted with climate change and related issues. Most likely, our way of inhabiting the world and instituting habitats will, in a more or less forcible way, have to become "lighter" and more adaptable. Once again, this implies a formidable challenge for the landscape discourse and calls for paradigm shifts. According to John Jackson, "what we need is a new definition. The one we find in most dictionaries is more than three hundred years old and was drawn up for artists."[21] What we need, instead, is first of all to fully recover the *practical, useful* character of landscape, which isolationist theories have for too long separated from its aesthetic properties.[22] One step in this direction is to draw attention, for example, to the commonality between civil engineering and landscape architecture: they "may work for different patrons, but they both reorganize space for human needs, both produce works of art in the truest sense of the word."[23] Recognizing this commonality allows, following Jackson, a redefinition of landscape as "a composition of man-made or man-modified spaces to serve as infrastructure or background for our collective existence; and if *background* seems inappropriately modest we should remember that in our modern use of the word it means that which underscores not only our identity and presence, but also our history."[24] Of course, landscape and infrastructure are different issues, yet what may look like a "reduction" of landscape to infrastructure is in fact an amplification of its meaning over and beyond the purely aesthetic one, once we consider, as Jackson does, the "historical" implication—its being not only the ground under our feet but also the road behind our backs.

Recent scholarship has ingeniously developed and applied the conceptual compound of landscape, infrastructure, incorporation of time, and ultimate focus on climate-change related issues.[25] According to Bélanger, we need a "temporal turn that puts in question the 'certainty' and 'stability' upon which the undisputed utopias of 'security' and 'safety' are predicated. Through the illusion of insurance and Newtonian predictability, mono-functional land uses and standardized infrastructures have reduced flexible alternatives and often expose large populations to mass vulnerabilities and high risks."[26] The inadequacy, or at least partiality, of this Taylorist model, with its social, economic, and political counterparts, has been revealed through climate change, which challenges rigid contours of powers and institutions and imposes the fluidity of processes over the fixity of places. Landscape, thanks to its own fluidity and "weakness," is bound to play a pioneering role in this epochal transition and decentralization of power. In the Kantian terms of the prologue of this book, landscape can be the paradigmatic representative of the meaningful contingency of habitats, challenging the still prevailing domination model of a priori domains. In cities, for example, this concretely means combining landscape and infrastructure in urban design, which at the same time addresses material problems.[27] The landscape paradigm also points toward "ecologies of scale," more and more necessitated by a growingly skeptical attitude toward the death-of-distance globalization thesis.[28] The focus is accordingly moved from the planning of specific static aims to the setting in motion of virtuous dynamics, leading to desirable directions but without the impossible obsession for control and prediction. The shift will also impact the way we map the world, which is never neutral but always informed, as we saw above, by existing power relationships and criteria for drawing boundaries. Sectional representation may become preferable to planometric one because of the higher complexity and ability to reveal deep, layered interrelationships between elements as well as the intersections of temporal dynamics (human mechanic as well as natural ecological ones).[29] If climate change is the ultimate horizon of such present and future challenges, addressing and incorporating "change" in all relevant practices and theories, thus temporally translating them, becomes imperative.

1.5 Anthropocene, cultural ecologies, and ephemerality

Going beyond the beautiful spatiality of exceptional landscapes and putting time at the center, in the sense just clarified, seems to be an important step toward the development of adequate epistemologies for the Anthropocene. I am neither interested nor competent in the discussion of the specific geological markers connected with the official acceptance and duration of the Anthropocene.[30] However, a couple of important consequences of the discussion on Anthropocene for landscapes have to be addressed: to begin with, "nature and culture [cannot] be treated any longer as distinct from one another."[31] This leads to the "rejection of what can be called the two-world hypothesis, the notion that artificial and natural terrain are categorically distinct, that landscapes that have been made are radically dissimilar to those that generate themselves."[32] The fixation on the image of past pictorialism has been replaced with a focus on the developmental nature of landscapes and their components. Anthropocene is not only about nuclear wastes but also about ideas and projects

FIGURE 4.3. Anthropocene? Layers of rubbish from a former landfill. Photo by FMichaud76, April 2021. Reprinted from Wikimedia Commons, https://commons.wikimedia.org/wiki/File:Anthropocene_layer.jpg.

"constituting a world so successfully urban that it is taken to be natural."[33] The challenge is to develop a "cultural ecology" in which the aesthetic dimension, consistent with what I have been arguing all along, is not a decorative, disinterested addition but a—if not *the*—leading thread in instituting habitats under the conditions of Anthropocene. This is not to deny, of course, the threatening and potentially catastrophic implications of Anthropocene as well as the huge, traumatic experiential and cultural adjustments it is already demanding. However, one should also, on the one hand, find new ways to institute meanings and orient oneself in the new reality and, on the other hand, resist millenarianisms that are often the product of broad popular media elaborations rather than of a sober scientific approach. At the very least, one should record a growing dissatisfaction "with the predominant view of the Anthropocene as a chilling dystopian meta-narrative" and consider the counterargument "that the 'anthro-' component of the term carries whispers of optimism" and the possibility of a resurgence of hope.[34]

An important related aspect is ephemerality. The blurring of the distinction between natural and cultural has more and more brought to the fore the untenability of the reductionist official discourse, including, at least in part, the 1972 UNESCO World Heritage Convention and imposing in a top-down and exclusionary fashion the paradigm of the tangible, permanent character of few recognized landscapes.[35] This, "in turn, is opening up new opportunities for research into local and Indigenous valuings of and attachment to ephemeral but socially meaningful places and landscapes," undergirding the "idea that place-making and place-attachment result from active, performatively mediated, interactions with socially meaningful spaces, whose configuration may be relatively fixed or fundamentally ephemeral in nature."[36] Once again, we should not interpret the more and more recognized dichotomy of ephemeral versus fixed as "simply" acknowledging the coexistence of two kinds of landscapes. In fact, only through a reductive abstraction can we isolate these two kinds. Instead, what we need to acknowledge as central is that the same place can host different and sometimes contradictory dynamics, and these very tensions can be fundamental to that place-making and place attachment. Whereas we may often privilege, both theoretically and practically, a feeling of permanence and stability, several forms of instituting "habitats" and meanings are tied to the view and treatment of certain spaces as ephemeral and short-lived: in such cases, which are likely to dramatically increase, situatedness plainly requires ephemerality and instability.

If a fundamental part of our meaningful interacting with and inhabiting our environment lies in the ability to interpret and express temporal phenomena and rhythms, then ephemerality is by no means simply the lack of a desired permanence but a sense-making form in its own right, expressing the difficult balance "of feeling temporally anchored in place and embedded within the rhythms of nature."[37] The era we live in, call it Anthropocene or not, is undoubtedly an era of "relentless and unsettling change" in which a deeper engagement with the ephemeral is needed not only to make the landscape discourse more plural, inclusive, and ubiquitous but also to thematize and respond to specific new challenges of hyperacceleration.[38] Finally, bear in mind that the framework I have been developing invites to overcome the traditional subject-object distinction in the landscape discourse. Thus, the ephemeral is not to be seen just as a characteristic of the contemplated or lived landscape but also of the

FIGURE 4.4. *The Harvesters*, by Pieter Bruegel the Elder (1565), a painting discussed by Tim Ingold in association with the concept of "taskscape." Courtesy of the Metropolitan Museum of Art, New York City. Reprinted from Wikimedia Commons, https://commons.wikimedia.org/wiki/File:Pieter_Bruegel_de_Oude_-_De_graanoogst.jpg.

experience of it (as, in fact, these are but two aspects of the same concrete unity: think of Wittgenstein). The performative, the dynamic, the transient are to be ascribed not to an independently existing object but to an experience, a practice, a linguistic game. Therefore, there is no "permanent," unchanging way of instituting, experiencing, and living landscapes, and the latter should be read from the specific perspective of each one of the experiences—incommensurable with each other—that we make every time. In this sense, I believe my framework can successfully incorporate and develop Ingold's famous explanation (or integration) of landscape through "taskscape": "*The landscape as a whole must likewise be understood as the taskscape in its embodied form*: a pattern of activities 'collapsed' into an array of features."[39] Insisting on the elements of performance, task, and activity will serve to underscore and reframe the extent of the human responsibility, fragility, and existential threat, which fixed images can hardly convey.

2. PRE- AND POST-: MODERNISM AND ENVIRONMENTALISM

Through the investigation of the temporal dimension of landscapes, the possibility of different ideal or ideological frameworks has emerged too. In this section, I develop this point regarding the intersection of landscape theory, modernism, and environmentalism.

2.1 Landscapes and modernity

Influential classics in the philosophy of landscape have insisted from the very beginning on the connection between the concept of landscape and modernity.[40] See, for example, Georg Simmel: "It is only the sensibility for that particular formation, a 'landscape,' that emerged quite late; and that is because this creation necessitated a tearing away from that unitary feeling of the whole of nature. . . . It is no surprise that, in Antiquity and the Middle Ages, there was no *awareness* of landscape, since this object as such had not yet come into being with that inner resoluteness and with its self-contained contours, which eventually came to be confirmed by the rise of landscape painting that, as it were, capitalized on this gain."[41] While premodern cultures might have had a deep feeling for nature, the specific form of the landscape is a typical product of the modern "tragedy of spirit"—that is, of the tearing away of the immediate connection between human existence and nature.[42] In modernity, nature becomes an investigable, quantifiable, disposable object for the human subject and is therefore felt as otherness. Breaking away from the immediate feeling of connection and communion, landscapes are like small, controllable portions of nature in vitro, recreating "artificial" unity where and when the natural one is lost.

Along these lines, in another classic of the philosophy of landscape, Joachim Ritter has famously asserted the compensative, sentimental nature of the concept of landscape: nature as aesthetic landscape is but the counterpart of nature as the field of inquiry and exploitation through modern science and technology.[43] More recently, Denis Cosgrove has argued that "the belief in improvement and progress generates its opposite in 'tradition,' whose poignancy bespeaks a sense of loss commonly interpreted as a sign of a more existential alienation. . . . Landscape is significant within this quintessentially modern discourse precisely because it puts into material form the matter of *dwelling*."[44] Such approaches evidently also implicitly or explicitly touch on issues of environmentalism, highlighting the ambiguity or contradiction of modernism: the idea of progress generates a feeling of loss, which then calls for a compensation that can never itself be free from that loss. The modernist contradiction is easily reflected not only in isolationist aesthetic theories, as we saw above, but also in comparable approaches to ecology and environment, epitomized by the compensative, nostalgic, exceptionalist view of landscapes. The threats implicit in such approaches are evident: if humans can decide which natural objects or configurations are worth cherishing, saving, or protecting, then clearly nature is not considered worth in itself, but only insofar as it can be enjoyed by (present-day) humans, whereby the border between "enjoying" and "exploiting" blurs.

Vis-à-vis this fundamental danger, landscape philosophy has in many cases embraced postmodernism in the form of a wholesale rejection of modernism. A good example in this sense is Luisa Bonesio's geophilosophical project, in which "the tragically modernist twentieth century" is explicitly called "a century hostile to landscape" because of its technocratic, Faustian, subjectivist, destructive nature.[45] Against the tragic modernist model, "one could say that the postmodernist comeback of local landscapes starts exactly from the checkmate of modernist rationalism, propagating nonplaces also in a very concrete sense and compelled to handle the hollowed and void spaces left behind by industrialism and the metropolitan model, and to mend a brutally lacerated, not enriched weave."[46] The modernist landscape is accordingly one in which, starting with the dystopic dream of full domination and quantification, we end up being utterly unable to make sense of the world.[47] A different, although equally eloquent, example in this respect is Kathryn Moore's "redefinition of the relationship between the senses and intelligence, . . . systematically questioning the existence of the sensory interface/mode of thinking—a disastrous idea that has haunted western civilization since the seventeenth century."[48] Within the still dominant and pervasive modernist-rationalist paradigm, falsely presenting itself under the guise of simple common sense, "the landscape is being shunted into a technological backwater" that is "up for grabs, there to be used or abused, manhandled or bulldozed."[49]

There are several reasons for distrusting the modern rationalist/Cartesian paradigm, from the point of view of both ecology and the landscape discourse, and they should not be easily dismissed.[50] There is, however, the risk that a wholesale rejection of modernism remain itself prey to modernist abstractions and lack the complexity that contemporary environmental problems require. "Pastism" is, after all, a face of modernism. Advocating, for example, for the preservation or even the return to a (premodern) normative, supposedly "normal" or healthy status would be tantamount to reproducing a typically modernist stereotype while rejecting the undeniable benefits of modernity. Indeed, the normative-environmentalist conception of ecology is a by-product of the crisis of modernism, which seems to reproduce in a specular way the basic orientation of the latter.[51]

2.2 From environmentalism to postenvironmentalism: Wind turbines and the role of aesthetics

Against the monopoly of the view just discussed, in recent years there has been a "steady paradigm shift in ecology."[52] In particular, a dynamic ecosystem model has more and more replaced the traditional linear one: while according to the latter a stable (normal) ecosystem does not change unless disturbed by some external force, the former understands ecosystems in terms of adaptive change, resilience, and unpredictability. Now, "if there are multiple possible states for any ecosystem, there can be no single 'correct' state—only those we choose to encourage or discourage. Notably, these are not questions of science, but questions of social, cultural, economic and political values—they are also questions of design."[53] This view has led to a rejection of determinism and the ideal of a natural balance or stability, and to ask *how* to change, instead of resisting change. This is in line with the already mentioned progressive "hybridization of cultural and natural ecologies," for which landscapes can take on a paradigmatic role, just as the environment did for classic environmentalism.[54] Based on the suggested distinction between environment as an abstract concept and landscape as a concrete one, it may be useful to explore the alternative paradigm of "postenvironmentalism," which is tightly connected to landscape research.[55] While environmentalism is mostly connected to a criticism (if not a rejection) of modernism, postenvironmentalism has controversially presented itself in some of its expressions as ecomodernism.[56]

Now, the ecomodernist stance in favor of a governed (if not accelerated) process of change may indeed be irredeemably optimistic or biased.[57]

However, a more complex and informed version of postenvironmentalism may instead help overcome an exceedingly restrictive, pessimistic, and ultimately sterile environmentalism: "While environmentalism had a tendency to restrict itself to nature conservation and to exempt specific landscapes from industrial development, the notion of postenvironmentalism intends to bring landscapes back into society and democracy."[58] A pragmatist and pluralist response to environmental pessimism should indeed not relapse into the ambiguities of modernism. It should, however, recognize that juxtaposing human agency as intrinsically dangerous to an idealized, normative view of pristine nature as intrinsically good risks not only reproducing some typical modernist dualisms but also being scarcely effective in bringing about the desired results, whereas a hybridization of anthropocentric and nonanthropocentric values can lead to better practices and theories.[59] From this point of view, landscape ecology can be more effective than traditional environmentalism in bringing forward "the acceptance of humans as agents of landscape change" in a qualified, pluralistically informed fashion.[60]

A concrete example is necessary here, and a powerful one is wind turbines. On the one hand, they are an endless, clean source of renewable energy. On the other hand, they arouse controversies in terms of the shape and use of landscapes (a nonrenewable resource) as well as in terms of aesthetics. Put this way, we simply have a clash that risks being ideological: if the aim is to protect the environment and preserve the landscape, then deciding pro or contra wind turbines does not seem to be possible on the ground of an authentic, democratic exchange of reasons but only of personal interest or parti pris. An alternative approach is possible (although its effectiveness needs to be tested, of course, on a case-by-case basis), and aesthetics is integral to it: "By focusing on the aesthetic qualities of the turbines, such as the clean lines, the pristine white, the elegant structure with its slim tower and vast blades, we can try out a different perspective. Perhaps instead of spoiling the landscape they draw its elements together and help to express the character of the place by making the wind more evident and bringing out the majesty of the elements in a wild environment. We can try to experience them in this light and see what happens."[61] This way we can try (in *some* cases, not as a general rule!) to be reconciled with a turbines-scattered landscape, a reconciliation taking place not only in the individual aesthetic appreciation but also in the historical-identitarian

FIGURE 4.5. Windmill and wind turbine, Eaucourt-sur-Somme, France. Photographer unknown, July 2008. Reprinted from Wikimedia Commons, https://commons.wikimedia.org/wiki/File:Eaucourt-sur-Somme_Molen_%26_Windturbine_2008.jpg.

self-awareness of the inhabitants: "While nature conservation still was completely fixed to protect ecosystems 'on the ground,' coastal inhabitants discovered the wind as part of their heritage and made it explicit as a new and renewable commodity. By way of technology . . . the coastal landscape turns out to be a truly postenvironmental landscape."[62] I want to stress that I am not suggesting that the individual or collective aesthetic projection should act as a veil to cover or make up for a certain degree of ugliness, implicit even in the effort for nature preservation. Quite the opposite, aesthetics can work to *un*veil and make explicit elements and connections contained in the landscape (in this case, the power of wind, its importance in the local imagination, identity, and consciousness, its ability to "keep the landscape together"), thus contributing to its sense-making and our ability to meaningfully inhabit it. In Deweyan terms, this would mean the consummation of an experience and the institution of a successful interaction with the environment. Clearly, this can only work based on a nondualistic, nonisolationist conception of aesthetics, whereas isolationist aesthetics would in all likelihood remain prejudicially fixed on the conservation of "natural" beauty against its utilitarian exploitation without being able to find a synthesis.

This aesthetic conception, substantiated by the concrete example of wind turbines, helps overcome the essentialist borders between nature and culture, conservation and development, global and local, and human values and natural sciences.[63] Overcoming the bias toward natural sciences, "if landscape ecology is to make an effective contribution to sustainability, then it should also work to bridge the people-nature gap, and embed its work within a broader environmental ethic—this cannot be done without truly interdisciplinary and transdisciplinary work."[64] This point is of particular importance here. Postenvironmentalism can be reclaimed as an alternative to the traditional, natural-sciences-inclined environmentalism in which the humanities, aesthetics, and the very notion of landscape are at best condemned to subservience and accessoriness. This also means not being content with the predominant (and modernist!) paradigm of natural sciences and looking instead for a more plural one in which humanities play a fundamental role under the guidance, as I argue, of aesthetics.[65] I say something on the point of interdisciplinarity and transdisciplinarity in section 5 of this chapter. Here I would like to point out that the theoretical framework I have been advancing is highly receptive of these demands, especially because of the central role it attributes to aesthetics, conceived along Deweyan lines in a concrete, pervasive, and antidualistic way. It aspires to contribute to the establishment of an ecological aesthetics, endowed with a leading orientational role also in practical matters of planning: "Planning is a vital tool for human adaptation and aesthetics help enable us to adjust to our surroundings, then adapt them to our goals."[66]

2.3 "Beyond the modern landscape"

It is aesthetics, then, that allows us, without falling prey to premodern fancies, to go *beyond the modern landscape*, as reads the title of an inspiring essay by Augustin Berque, with which, in this final part of section 2, I want to engage a dialogue. First, a brief summary of Berque's complex argument. Following the theses put forward at the beginning of this section, Berque maintains that the distinction between environment and landscape pursues a typically modern, Cartesian-Newtonian distinction pattern between facts and sensibility. The terminological and conceptual distinction corresponds yet again to a typically modern split between "our practice and our sensibility," a split that is suggestive of "the malaise of the modern condition, a condition in which facts and meaning, environment and landscape, have ceased to correspond to each other. Our civilization seems to have alienated us from our own environment," with all the attending compensatory consequences we have seen before (escapism, exoticism, relativism, etc.).[67] Berque is adamant that a regression to the premodern world is not a viable option and that the only way forward is based in modernity itself.

The idea is that "the modern split between environment (factual, physical, ecological) and landscape (sensible, phenomenal, symbolic) no longer exists."[68] Modernity became a utopia, "literally so, for it refused to acknowledge the existence of the locality, denying the qualitative particularity of real places, in the name of the quantitative laws that became ever more firmly established within Newtonian universal space," concretely leading the International Style to replace local vernacular ones.[69] The modernist utopia crumbled from within, with (postmodern) art leading ahead, from the abandonment of linear perspective all the way up to land art, which plays on both registers with the aim to bypass the rigid modern dualism. Beyond art, of course, it was the recognition of the finiteness of the ecology of our planet to end the modernist utopia. It was probably the most modernist of all enterprises to end it in a plastic way: "Man's first sight of the Earth from the Moon. In reversing the human gaze, this radical change of perspective put an end to the modern dichotomy: the factual had once more become sensible."[70] Here aesthetics shows its whole centrality: "What did the astronauts say when they saw the Earth rise above the lunar horizon? That it was beautiful, and irreplaceable."[71]

This, for Berque, is the epitome of a larger phenomenon: an aesthetically rooted and guided process of reconciliation between the space of physical laws and that of sensible meanings. Notice that this process does not simply overturn the modern unbalance of physical (environment) and meaningful (landscape). It does not attempt to establish the latter against the former, taking us back to a regressive mythical and metaphorical identification of human and natural: the human subject "can take the stage both for his own pleasure and for the sake of the beauty of the landscape, while also caring for the environment like a prudent gardener."[72]

FIGURE 4.6. "What did the astronauts say when they saw the Earth rise above the lunar horizon? That it was beautiful, and irreplaceable" (Augustin Berque). The picture shows the Earthrise from the Lunar Reconnaissance Orbiter above Compton Crater. Photo by NASA / Goddard Space Flight Center / Arizona State University, October 2015. Reprinted from Wikimedia Commons, https://commons.wikimedia.org/wiki/File:Earthrise_over_Compton_crater_-LRO_full_res.jpg.

Briefly, the modernist Newtonian-Cartesian paradigm challenged by several postmodernist landscape theorists is, according to Berque, at the origin of the notion and civilization of landscape. While the notion of landscape originated in the modern laceration of facts and meanings, with the erosion of the modern paradigm it can now perform a central function in the reconciliation of such laceration. Such reconciliation, however, does not imply the reductionist mythical triumph of meanings over facts (and of premodernism over modernism) but the formulation of a new view in which meanings are based in facts and facts are not self-sufficient but expressive of meanings. The new discourse beyond the modern landscape needs to be pluralist and pragmatist and led by a concrete, nonisolationist aesthetic stance. The challenge is about the possibility of interacting with the world in a meaningful and not destructive way, and establishing provisional (if not ephemeral) habitats in it. As we can see now, the Kantian project, while apparently irredeemably modernist, is after all not so far from our own challenge. And for Kant as for the post-moon-landing humanity, the groundwork and the beacon of hope for the reconciliation is given in aesthetic terms.

3. JUSTICE AND POLITICS

We may appreciate landscapes because they are apolitical—that is, because they provide a disinterested aesthetic enjoyment that is apparently universal insofar as it is detached from partisan interests, worldviews, and ideologies. We may, in fact, passionately yearn for the sense of release from conflicts they offer. In my opinion, only an unnecessarily hard-line militant purism would dismiss this fact or preemptively condemn such forms of enjoyment and release. At the same time, it would indeed be a naivete or, worse, an ideological imposture to reduce landscapes to escapist, harmless devices. Landscapes are and have always been political even though the nature of their being political changes across contexts and epochs.[73] This section discusses selected facets and issues of the politics of landscape in our time based on the framework developed here.

3.1 Breaking ground: The European Landscape Convention

I begin with a ground-breaking political text—namely, the European Landscape Convention (ELC), signed in Florence on October 20, 2000.[74] The ELC defines landscape as "an area, as perceived by people, whose character is the result of the action and interaction of natural and/or human factors" (Art. 1). Notice how the delimitation of landscapes is given through the perception—and, hence, the experience—of all people, without distinction. Further, notice how people's experience relates to the "character" of that area, which in turn is defined by both natural and human factors. This hints at an interdependence of collective experience and the characterization of the landscape: both terms mutually influence each other, as in the framework proposed here. The starting definition is already framed in a quite concrete, antidualistic way that is not weakened but rather reinforced by the intentional genericness, aiming at avoiding exclusion and at providing a broad enough groundwork on which to implement specific policies. This is confirmed by Article 2, setting the scope of the convention, which "applies to the entire territory of the Parties and covers natural, rural, urban and peri-urban areas. It includes land, inland water and marine areas. It concerns landscapes that might be considered outstanding as well as everyday or degraded landscapes." There is no limitation based on dualisms such as nature versus culture, habitable versus inhabitable, outstanding versus ordinary, beautiful versus ugly. As to the aims of the convention, these "are to promote landscape protection, management and planning, and to organise European co-operation on landscape issues" (Art. 3). Once more, the aims are framed in a comprehensive way, both from the point of view of the cooperative actions envisaged and of the temporal scale of the landscapes addressed: protection of the past, management of the present, and planning of the future.

The division of responsibilities (Art. 4) calls for a harmonization of the general provisions of the convention with the local policies of the parties following a principle of subsidiarity. Accordingly, every party undertakes, among others, "to recognise landscapes in law as an essential component of people's surroundings, an expression of the diversity of their shared cultural and natural heritage, and a foundation of their identity; . . . to establish procedures for the participation of the general public, local and regional authorities, and other parties . . . ; to integrate landscape into its regional and town planning policies and in its cultural, environmental, agricultural, social and economic policies, as well as in any other policies with possible direct or indirect impact on landscape" (Art. 5). Notice again the centrality of landscapes in defining the "habitat" of the people involved, by expressing, protecting, and grounding both their differences and their identities. This results in a democratic, participatory model of governance that is not restricted to political authorities but extended to the public at large and to any other stakeholder and that results in the integration of landscapes in all levels and forms of collective life. These general measures are specified with a focus on "Awareness-raising" ("Each

Party undertakes to increase awareness among the civil society, private organisations, and public authorities of the value of landscapes, their role and changes to them"), "Training and education" (at all levels and in a multidisciplinary fashion), "Identification and assessment" of the specific landscapes and their values, "Landscape quality objectives," and "Implementation" (Art. 6). The convention then proceeds to stipulate the principles of European cooperation (including a "Landscape award") and the final clauses, which I am not going to discuss here.

Independently of its specific implementations, the ELC is a fundamental text for the politics of landscape. Despite its technically being European in origin and scope (though as a Council of Europe document, not an EU document), the ELC can offer a flexible yet sound basis for landscape discourse and practice beyond Europe. The main ideas underpinning the ELC may be seen "as a way of helping to find a concept that is globally relevant. An argument can be made that the ELC's basic construct can be relevant anywhere in the world."[75] It can be argued that this is the case even when compared with the theoretically global UNESCO's World Heritage Convention (WHC).[76] The latter's "approach is neither broad nor flexible enough to encompass the plurality and fluidity of perception that dealing with landscape requires, nor to come to terms with landscape's dynamism, and with the important task of managing and leading continuing and future change. Instead, protection is the key objective for inscription into its world list, followed increasingly, it might be claimed, by national pride and the potential for touristic exploitation. The WHC convention also remains more Western-centric than the ELC."[77] It may seem problematic for the framework I have been developing that, while aesthetic evaluations and concerns feature prominently in the WHC, this is not the case for the ELC. I would argue, however, that the apparent absence of the aesthetic in the ELC in fact signifies its pervasive, unrestricted presence. Whereas the WHC is mostly interested in the "outstanding universal value" of a few places, thus implying its absence in our ordinary experience, the ELC is guided by an overall aesthetic sensitivity that is not restricted to a few peaks but rather is diluted in, and at the same time leading, its "ordinary" understanding of the place of landscapes in peoples' lives.[78] Such an overarching yet discreet sensibility is well embedded in the core defining concept of "perception," which is etymologically fundamental to aesthetics (from the ancient Greek *aisthesis*, meaning precisely "perception"). In this way, the ELC provides a seemingly simple but critical meeting point between the juxtaposed but symmetrically reductive approaches of modernist aestheticism and the contemporary neglect of aesthetics.[79] The pluralist and pragmatic approach of the ELC; its diplomatic adjustability to change; its democratic and participatory mission; its stress on the transnational and, indeed, antinationalistic character of successful landscape policies; its consistent rejection of dualistic and isolationist criteria make it a pathbreaker even when and where it lacks political effectiveness. This is why, even if I do not directly refer to it, in the rest of this section it stays in the background of my discussion of a few selected issues and concerns in the politics of landscapes (including Eurocentrism). Once again, I cannot aim at proposing specific solutions but rather at showing how the goals of advanced international conventions such as the ELC prompt us to seriously question and rethink traditional political concepts and oppositions and how this requires new and proactive theoretical frameworks.

3.2 Participation and the insiders/outsiders dilemma

In his pioneering article "Recovering the Substantive Nature of Landscapes," Kenneth Olwig suggested, based on a meticulous historical and terminological reconstruction, that the then-dominant dichotomy of landscape-scenery versus landscape-territory should be overcome, and the landscape should be conceived of "as a nexus of community, justice, nature, and environmental equity."[80] The statement of the substantive nature of landscape seems to be well reflected in the ELC's mission. The contemporary state of substantive landscapes, however, is a precarious one, at the level of both theory and practice. While participation, democracy, and justice regarding landscape politics are obviously saluted as positive universal goals, there is little agreement on how to advance them, both in the sense of what does it mean to advance them (theory) and of which concrete measures should be taken to advance them (practice).[81] Participation is clearly essential in creating more sustainable and fair landscapes *and* communities, but "there seems to be a growing recognition that any system is imperfect and perhaps this is a more useful starting point for examining participatory theory and practice. There is no ideal or single solution and the key to considering landscape issues is about trying to deal with complexity."[82]

A paradigmatic difficulty is the ambiguity of the dichotomy of insiders versus outsiders. One may assume that the insiders of a certain landscape are more involved in its protection and appreciation, whereas outsiders would rather adopt an indifferent or even exploitative view (for example, for tourism or for its resources). However, this assumption often proves wrong. Outsiders, just because they are less directly involved, may be more interested in protecting the value they attach to a certain landscape, whereas insiders might not see anything special in it and be more open to have it manipulated for short-term utilitarian reasons. On the other hand, in a case such as the above-mentioned wind-turbine diatribe, one could also argue that, on the contrary, outsiders are egoistically bent on preventing the development and protecting a static, fetishized landscape's form, whereas insiders are better equipped to plan and drive the change of a familiar landscape.[83] After all, most of today's touristic sites are the product of human manipulation and would not even exist as such if the "outsiders' argument" had prevailed in such cases. Another problematic dichotomy, stressed by Olwig himself in a later work, is the one of landscape as a common versus private good. Privatization and deregulation policies are indeed a threat to the landscape as a common good;[84] however, one should also acknowledge that private interest can act as an important counterbalance to poor, uninformed national (or nationalistic) landscape policies, which have often proved to be themselves a threat to sustainable landscapes.[85] This leads to the issue of the landscape as "local" versus "global," which I briefly address in the next section.

3.3 Local versus global and the Eurocentrism charge

A major point of uncertainty and instability is the clash between localist and globalist views of landscapes.[86] As we have seen, an important part of the contemporary landscape discourse and practice is about reclaiming the essential role of the local: local peoples, cultures, and stakeholders, regional planning, and so on can no longer be treated as passive pawns or obstacles in the modernist-globalist and Eurocentric drive for uniformity and universal control. However, the alternative to this model cannot be a unilateral withdrawal into the local and into the premodern simply because modernity is not a monolithic Western concept, and current challenges require the development of global landscape policies. Besides, the "critical conflation of 'local' with good democracy can, explicitly and implicitly, be seen to characterise much landscape literature concerned with notions of justice. Public participation does, however, not in itself make landscapes more just. There is also nothing inherently democratic about local landscapes. Landscape democracy is rather something to be always struggled towards, and not to be assumed to exist."[87]

Finally, we should also try not to essentialize the concept of Eurocentrism. Regarding, for example, landscape art in Europe and China, scholars have argued "that there is a synergy between both Eastern and Western landscape art forms, which supports the contention that an essentialist concept of Eurocentrism is in fact a mirage," and that, while international conventions may indeed be biased toward European or Western ideas, it is undeniable that also non-European states exploit landscape and heritage for nationalistic ends.[88] The arguments put forward by champions of the Eurocentrism concept are so blurred that "the question may be posed whether the 'Eurocentric' notion is in fact a straw man set up to support an argument that, at best, is hazy. It is a topic that needs vigorous debate in

FIGURE 4.7. Longjing tea district, Hangzhou, China. Photo by Niklas Dougherty, October 2017. Reprinted from Wikimedia Commons, https://commons.wikimedia.org/wiki/File:Longjing_tea_village_Hangzhou.jpg.

Asia, where it is apparent that a popular discourse focusing on an East-West split, which in reality is more imaginary than real, has taken root."[89] What we need is, rather, to have multiple discourses and negotiations on landscape change, recognizing the different values and angles of the actors involved (locals, tourists, governments . . .) without bypassing the hard questions through easy stereotypes.[90] In this regard, ideological slogans will not take us very far, whereas a sober text such as the ELC may act as a good conversation starter.

3.4 Migration and settledness, displacements and lockdowns

My last point has to do more specifically with the impact of short- and long-term catastrophes on the right to landscape. This concerns first and foremost migration. Wars, climate change, and economic needs will more and more make our time "the century of the migrant": "Displacement, placelessness, relocation and resettlement are all terms associated with migration that highlight the inherent tension between stability, mobility and a relationship with place."[91] Landscapes, as we saw, are an essential part of people's identity and feeling of belonging. Certainly, such identity and feeling can be open, and we may be adaptable to switch to different landscapes, especially if this switch is the product of a free, self-aware decision. On the other hand, uprootedness as the opposite of rootedness is often associated with an act of violence: we may be more or less violently taken away from the landscape we are rooted in, or the landscape we are rooted in may more or less violently be taken away from us. Even if our safety or health is not directly threatened, this may produce a dramatic feeling of displacement or even placelessness, further embittered by the negative values commonly associated with unsettledness and nomadism. The recognition of the urgency and scale of this problem in the century of the migrant has led to the concept of a universal "right to landscape," framed as a human right.[92] A right to landscape is different from a right to environment in that it protects not only physical safety and well-being but also cultural and psychological meanings, historical identity, and so on. Clearly, this distinction has weighty implications for the associated policies. For example, rising sea levels will more and more impose the resettlement of small island states and communities. If such resettlement "only" responds to their right to environment, then any physically safe and healthy environment will do. If, on

FIGURE 4.8. Garden of contemplation, Canadian Museum of Human Rights, Winnipeg, Canada. Photo by Bob Linsdell, February 2015. Reprinted from Wikimedia Commons, https://commons.wikimedia.org/wiki/File:Canadian_Museum_for_Human_Rights,_The_Forks,_Winnipeg_-_panoramio_(8).jpg.

the contrary, the communities' right to landscape is to be considered, then their relocation needs to provide them with conditions that minimize any alteration of their cultural references and feelings of identity. Such pressing new challenges "open a whole new realm of thinking about the ethical role of planners and designers, and the need to extend visionary and unconventional thinking to address the right to landscape. This calls for solutions that go beyond functional needs of survival and requires addressing landscape as the confluence of physical subsistence and psychological necessities, among them a right to live in dignity and freedom to define their own identity."[93] Such solutions also imply a questioning, or at the very least a reframing, of the normative character of "settledness" toward fairer and more pluralistic politics of landscape.

Not only forced displacement or change are problematic in landscape politics; stay-at-home orders are too. The obvious reference is to the less immediately violent, yet no less concerning, case of the pandemic-induced lockdowns like those enforced at different levels around the world after the COVID-19 pandemic outbreak in 2020. Here we have an extreme political measure, motivated by the need to reduce the pandemic's impact and protect the citizens' life and health, both directly and indirectly. This measure

PATTERNS OF ENCOUNTER II

does not necessarily threaten the citizens' right to the environment insofar as they are requested to confine themselves to a supposedly safe and familiar environment—namely, their homes. One may argue, though, that lockdown measures threaten the right to landscape insofar as they drastically limit the "habitat"—that is, the space for psychologically, socially, and culturally meaningful and healthy interactions. As a matter of fact, the prolonged inhibition of access to a "whole" habitat may eventually threaten the meaningfulness and quality of the domestic space too. This does not mean to deny the effectiveness or the rationale, however strong, of lockdown measures but to show, also in connection with such a recent global event, the wide reach of the concept of a right to landscape. Indeed, "during COVID, whether in lockdown or restrictions, people have become more aware of the importance of the outdoor spaces, whether it is their own garden, local or regional park and the wider landscape."[94] Such a growing awareness is evidently bound to become a more and more decisive issue in the political arena and will require a deep engagement with the theory and politics of landscapes in order to be properly addressed.[95]

3.5 A very provisional upshot

The issues raised here are evidently very far from exhausting the wide range of problems to be addressed under the heading of landscape politics and justice, a range that will in all likelihood continue to grow and change dramatically. Some important steps have been taken toward the attribution of a central political spot to landscape issues, such as the ELC. However, as I have shown, uncertainty largely prevails both on the theoretical nature of landscape-political issues and on the practical matter of how to address them. Uncertainty may feel paralyzing in politics, but I want to suggest that in this case uncertainty is not necessarily a bad thing in itself. The concept of landscape is a complex and blurred one, and any attempt to outline rigid political patterns or directions may prove unconducive or even counterproductive. Working through essentialist dichotomies (insider versus outsider, common versus private, local versus global, Eastern versus Western, settled versus nomadic . . .) may be easy, but it does not go too far. What is needed is a flexible framework enabling multiple voices to engage in a dialogue that is necessarily connoted by adaptability to change and responsivity to risk rather than by attempts to impose universal predictive patterns. Considering that landscapes are first and foremost the result of ever-changing interactions between humans and the space they inhabit, addressing the tremendous political challenges we face in this regard will require taking relationality and dynamism seriously.[96] And, of course, it will require the development of new forms of education and training in the way we institute and give meanings to our habitats. The next section is devoted to this topic.

4. EDUCATION

Environmental education is obviously an extremely pressing need of our time. Landscape education may be seen as something more restricted in scope and necessity, yet because of the concrete, aesthetic character of landscapes as opposed to nature and environment, it can in fact be framed in a more realistic (although not acquiescent) and effective way, without hiding severe conceptual and practical difficulties, which I address with reference to Wittgenstein and the notion of enskilment. At the end I lay claim to the concrete and topical value of an adequately conceived aesthetic landscape education.[97]

4.1 Landscape education: Not just a pastime

Environments require a knowledge that is largely generalizable, neutral, and relying on hard sciences but abstracted from the culture, life, and history of the place. Speaking of environmental education means framing it from the very beginning in dualistic terms, as an education to respect or protect something external to and different from us. I am certainly not denying the value of such education, yet I believe that speaking of landscape education is important not only because it covers a different area complementary to the former but also because it can be conducive to it: "Considering the locality as a place and a landscape offers better possibilities than viewing it as nature, which remains a potent but monolithic term."[98] On the contrary, knowledge of landscape and the relevant education is always local, historical, lived. In fact, it can be argued the challenges of conceptualizing education in terms of landscape rather than environment point to a level of complexity that has yet to be fully explored. Landscape education is, as has further been claimed along the lines of Deweyan pedagogy, an education that focuses on experiential and temporal continuity and on interaction.[99] It gathers

PATTERNS OF ENCOUNTER II

FIGURE 4.9. *Surf-swimming, Hawaii*, by G. T. Bettany (1888). Surfing as a form of enskilment, discussed by Wattchow and Prins. Image from George Thomas Bettany, *The World's Inhabitants; or, Mankind, Animals, and Plants; Being a Popular Account of the Races and Nations of Mankind, Past and Present, and the Animals and Plants Inhabiting the Great Continents and Principal Islands* (London: Ward, Lock & Co., 1888), 932. Reprinted from Wikimedia Commons, https://commons.wikimedia.org/wiki/File:Surf_Swimming_ _Hawaii.jpg.

material from several sources, for example, from sciences to storytelling, and from local culture to imagination. It limits itself neither to objective knowledge nor to subjective impressions, finding a place beyond this and associate dualisms and requiring participative and immersive engagement rather than just distanced theorizing, thus leading not to the acquisition of neutral skills or competences to be applied equally to any context but rather to "enskilment," as a way of learning (through) practice in place.[100] Landscape education is both super local and omni-pervasive and can pretty much be thought of as a training to orientation in interpretation, institution, and communication of habitats. Insofar as it teaches "a *way of being* in a landscape [we] call *home*," it is an education that builds continuity while changing us by making us attentive to continuity and changes in the space we inhabit and vice versa, and developing a much-needed, embodied sensitivity to the opportunities, risks, and limits of human-induced change.[101] Ultimately, landscape education is a training to become attentive to the way of being (in) a landscape that we call home.

In this last regard the intention to protect the environment and safeguard life is reflected in the literature in uncountable exhortations "to transform mindsets [and] to move from humanist to post-humanist worldviews: adopting nonanthropocentric perspectives on human interactions with nature, or dissolving this boundary entirely and letting go of the 'human as steward' image that has enthralled us for two millennia."[102] This exhortation entails an important aesthetic dimension, which takes several forms and draws on several sources, from geo-autobiography to learning how to see, from imagination to botanic knowledge, from artistic engagement to, even, neo-pagan shapeshifting.[103] While I cannot specifically dwell on them, I want to remark how they all point, in very different ways, to the importance of teaching to be more attuned to the spaces we inhabit and to learn how to embody them, even if only partially and provisionally.[104] Although learning about/with/in landscape may seem easy and enjoyable as a hobby or pastime, taking it seriously as an education is incredibly demanding and challenging. This is because, according to the antidualistic concept of landscape advanced here, being *in* a landscape means being *a* landscape. But what does this imply? How do we learn and teach this? By choosing to use the term *landscape* instead of *environment* or *nature* in relation to education, I suggest we acknowledge that this is not about learning (to be like) something else but rather developing, extending, and strengthening an existing relationship of continuity (let us recall Dewey).[105] Even so, the task at hand and its requirements are all but clarified. To move forward I propose we briefly turn to Wittgenstein.

4.2 "An entirely different game": Wittgenstein and enskilment

As we saw at the end of chapter 1, the use of a language is, for Wittgenstein, embedded in a form of life. Also, language is a refinement of more primitive reactions or deeds. Finally, the awakening of intellectual worldviews and relationships, and with it the possibility of choice, is the result of a distancing from the original soil or community of life. From this we may gather that different forms of life would be associated with different actions and reactions, whether linguistic or not. The process of communication and translation across different forms of life and their customary reactions, whether linguistic or not, can be truly challenging, and in extreme cases feel alike to attempting to learn how to play a game by relying solely on the knowledge of the rules of a different game (imagine trying to understand a baseball game when only familiar with the rules of football). One of the places in which Wittgenstein makes this abundantly clear are the "Lectures on Aesthetics," where we find, for example: "Suppose [someone] has what is called a cultured taste in painting. This is something entirely different to what was called a cultured taste in the fifteenth century. An entirely different game was played. He does something entirely different with it to what a man did then."[106] Even a cultured person in a certain age plays "an entirely different" game from an equally cultured person from another age. What is more, even within the same culture, communication of appreciation, as well as the very understanding of the meaning of appreciation, is a difficult endeavor as we can never be sure that we are meaning the same thing.[107] Words can hardly be of help: if we are not familiar with the game played, we just cannot turn to them, as they are utterly uncharacteristic and unrevealing. This shows in the way we teach and learn aesthetic predicates:

> If you ask yourself how a child learns "beautiful," "fine," etc., you find it learns them roughly as interjections. . . . The word is taught as a substitute for a facial expression or a gesture. . . . What makes the word an interjection of approval? It is the game it appears in, not the form of words. Language is a characteristic part of a large group of activities. . . . We are concentrating, not on the words "good" or "beautiful," which are entirely uncharacteristic, generally just subject and predicate ("This is beautiful"), but on the occasions on which they are said—on the enormously complicated situation in which the aesthetic expression has a place, in which the expression itself has almost a negligible place.[108]

We understand aesthetic expressions, which by themselves are unremarkable placeholders, just because we are familiar with and used to the rules governing (or, better, instituting) "the enormously complicated situation"— that is, the game in which they are employed.

Wittgenstein's view on aesthetic expressions and how they are learned is a prominent example of his general views on teaching and learning. While education as a topic is not directly at the core of Wittgenstein's philosophy (although it is worth noting that he was a schoolteacher for six years, from 1920 to 1926), he provides an outline within the framework of his broader interest in meaning and explanation. The basic idea, already evident in the quoted passage on aesthetic expressions, is that "the teaching of language is not explaining, but training."[109] And, as Hans-Johann Glock puts it, "training does not presuppose understanding, but only patterns of reaction on the part of the trainee."[110] "Training" here translates the German words *abrichten* and *Abrichtung*, which are not commonly employed regarding children education but for the training/drilling of animals for specific abilities or actions. The rather controversial and old-fashioned tone given to Wittgenstein's conception of education by this terminological choice has been diversely interpreted and criticized.[111] Here I can only focus on exploring an ecological approach to Wittgenstein's philosophy of education, as illustrated among others in a short paper by Pierluigi Biancini. The key notion in this ecological approach is exactly that of *Abrichtung*, translated not as "training," however, but as "enskilment," in the footsteps of Ingold:

> We could consider the process of learning as an enskilment in which the practitioners learn not definitions, as supposed by the russellian theory, but also are directly engaged in an interaction with the environment.... Environment that is the range of possible situations in which they *live*—the term *Leben* in Wittgenstein is used as a synonym of activity to which we could give a meaning.... Choosing to translate the German *Abrichtung* with Enskilment we arrive to see two dimensions of learning as strictly interwoven: an ontogenetic dimension of the growing of an organism in an environment, and the ontological commitment of the linguistic practices in building the world. To learn a language means to grow as person and to dwell an environment.[112]

Here learning does not occur through the explanation of definitions of objective (or objectified) external facts but through direct and active engagement. This further implies that meanings are not associated with independently given, objective essences but are constructed and instituted in and through interaction with the environment (in the Wittgensteinian sense as explained by Biancini).

Since meanings cannot be simply pointed at via definitions but need to be learned in practice, the groundwork for education is *Abrichtung*. As we saw with aesthetic expressions, the meaning of words is not typically learned through other words but rather through the dynamics of various and more or less complex situations where the word itself is unremarkable and could be replaced by gestures, interjections, facial expressions. Consequently, we learn a language (and other practices) by being trained/drilled in its usage, with an initial focus on establishing certain patterns of behavior rather than on understanding.[113] Understanding emerges from within the practice itself by following its rules and examples, such as when we learn a game by starting to play it rather than by collecting definitions of all objects involved in it. *Enskilment* can then function as a more up-to-date and charitable rendition of *Abrichtung*, at the same time preserving Wittgenstein's antidualistic intention. Conversely, seen from a Wittgensteinian angle, the concept of "enskilment" gains radicality and complexity, which are often absent from tendentially optimistic formulations of landscape education. Furthermore, such complexity is directly associated with aesthetic expressions and games, paving the way to a privileged role of the aesthetic in representing and unraveling the complexity of landscape education. In the next section, I develop these two points (complexity of education through enskilment and prominence of the aesthetic dimension) in their connection and advance the idea of an aesthetic landscape education.

4.3 Aesthetic education: Skills for our time

The way I am framing landscape education entails a deep, transformative dimension that cannot be pursued through explanations, unlike environmental education. Instead, it requires a practical commitment to institute, linguistically or otherwise, our "environment" (in Wittgenstein's sense) in certain ways, and ourselves within it. Even when compared with successful practices in environmental education, landscape education is a substantially different game to learn and teach. We cannot rely solely on explanations and definitions; we need to transmit a whole new form of life or culture. Following Stickney's comments on Wittgenstein, "trying on worldviews is unlike putting on new glasses or playing dress-up. If the teacher commands, 'Now see the tree like *this*,' there is no guarantee that pupils see the alternate aspect to which the teacher points.... It is not simply a matter of attaching new pictures to the corresponding thing, but of gradually coming through training and enculturation to react differently while seeing."[114] It should be noted that Stickney focuses on Wittgenstein's notion of *seeing* things in a certain way ("see the tree like *this*") based on his thematization of "environmental education," which, from the point of view of my own focus on landscape, appears somewhat limiting. However, I believe that what Stickney claims applies unproblematically to nonvisual actions and reactions covering the more concrete notion of learning landscapes, including hearing, smelling, touching, tasting, feeling, and learning about the history, folklore, and culture of the place.

Briefly, reacting in a new way to our habitat requires being in a new way, which means learning a new way of life. The deeply transformative nature of this task further emphasizes my previous point about the significant difference between the ease and frivolity of occasional pastimes and poses and the upsetting difficulty of adopting a new habit.[115] To quote Wittgenstein again: "An education quite different from ours might also be the foundation of quite different concepts. For here life would run on differently. —What interests us would no longer interest them (i.e., the other people involved). Here different concepts would no longer be unimaginable. In fact, this is the only way in which *essentially* different concepts are imaginable."[116] A different education results in different concepts but most of all in different forms of life. Establishing communication and common interests across resulting groups of people is challenging. Therefore, there is no room for easy optimism about the possibility of establishing a different and "better" way of being (in) our landscapes through transformative teaching without resorting to unrealistic nostalgias and ineffective poses and projections.[117]

While I do not have an easy solution to offer, I want to conclude this topic by making the claim that, if radical change requires truly transformative education, it is what we may call "the aesthetic," if adequately conceived, that has the potential to change not only language and deeds but also the forms of life in which they are embedded. As we saw in Wittgenstein, aesthetic games can lead to extreme divergence and incommunicability because they are a particularly powerful and complex way of establishing and communicating the ever-shifting meanings we associate with our habitats. The complexity inherent in even conceiving a time- and task-adequate notion of landscape education parallels such complexity of the aesthetic dimension.[118] Transformative landscape education should be seen as an example of a broader aesthetic education framework. However, this is not a traditional education focused on the beautiful, artistic, and tasteful. Rather, it involves a comprehensive, flexible, complex knowing-how to map and interpret the spaces we inhabit and to institute/communicate a variety of symbols and meanings within them. Essentially, it is a pragmatic education that imparts a dynamic set of competences conducive to building an "aesthetically" successful habitat without relying on essentialistic or dualistic forms and structures often associated with environmental education. Aesthetic education should not be viewed as a legacy of an old-fashioned humanistic curriculum but rather as an increasingly relevant umbrella term for a diverse range of locally based practices of enskilment. This type of education reflects and systematizes the growing complexity of the reality to which such practices need to apply. This is true not only in light of epochal critical changes such as ecological ones but also in terms of more daily yet equally important challenges. Due to the pervasive nature of the aesthetic as outlined here, the skills needed should be pluralistically conceived but still follow a Deweyan/pragmatist principle of order and rhythm in terms of source and application.

Matteucci provides an outline for such skills:

> Knowing how to manage the complex system of appearance even in the absence of references to deep structures of existence ... is the skill increasingly required of the contemporary human being, and perhaps decisive in general for human beings from the beginning insofar as they are prompted by their own nature to extend their mind, to live in dialogue with something that cannot remain merely "outside." An aesthetic knowledge that, in order to be expressed effectively, must remain operative and thus be entrenched in a field of experience that involves dynamic categories, ready to change on impact with circumstances without stiffening into structures that are too elementary because abstractly atomic.[119]

Even though Matteucci's discourse is not about landscape per se, I believe landscape could very well be a destination of the mind's "extension" and the "experience with" he pleads for. Berleant also proposes a similar idea, although again not specifically related to landscapes, with his "Education as aesthetic."[120] This concept highlights the correspondence between the "aesthetic field" and the educational situation concerning the four main terms respectively involved (art object-educational subject matter or project, artist-scholar or scientist, appreciator-student, performer-teacher). More precisely, the terms involved are "not independent elements cast in various combinations. They are facets of a single total activity" endowed with self-sufficiency and internal criteria of success, conceived, once again, in a Deweyan way in terms of resolution, fulfillment, vitality, creativity, and so on.[121] While critically underscoring, as I did, the difficulty and "rarity" of the occurrences of such successfully accomplished educational situation in today's context, Berleant concludingly asks whether such "aesthetic integration" may "stand as an exemplar of the larger social order," thus connecting education and broad social issues as well as everyday life under the mark of the pervasiveness of a so-conceived aesthetics.[122]

The idea of aesthetic knowledge and education presented here may seem ambitious and warrants a broader discussion addressing conditions for empirical application.[123] Although this is not the place to do so, the conceptual framework outlined—with its emphasis on pragmatism, pluralism, rejection of dualisms, and the lived, aesthetic character of learning (with) landscapes—can hopefully provide plausible coordinates through which these demands can be framed more effectively than traditional options allow. In this spirit, I conclude this chapter with a brief remark on the topic of multidisciplinarity, interdisciplinarity, and transdisciplinarity to try to reconnect, once again, some of the ties I developed in the first, theoretical chapters of this book and that have now come to the fore in the dialogue with more applied aspects of landscape studies.

5. INTERDISCIPLINARY PERSPECTIVES

That a concept as broad, as terminologically blurred and difficult to define, and as historically and culturally branched out as landscape stands at the intersection of several disciplines and approaches and hence requires multi-, inter-, and transdisciplinarity is beyond argument.[124] Several aspects have already spontaneously emerged while addressing many different topics, thus confirming how interdisciplinarity with regard to landscapes is not a specific issue but an overarching one. One may even claim, as a matter of fact, that landscape research *only* exists at the crossing of several borders and through the constant effort of pushing back and relocating those borders. Of course, the interdisciplinary character of landscape research is widely acknowledged

FIGURE 4.10. Landscape and interdisciplinarity. Image from Christine Tudor, "An Approach to Landscape Character Assessment," fig. 1, https://assets.publishing.service.gov.uk/media/5aabd31340f0b64ab4b7576e/landscape-character-assessment.pdf. © Natural England 2014. Used with permission.

in the literature and its further development presented as a desideratum.[125] On this I cannot and will not add anything. Conversely, though, landscape research is also a paradigmatic instance of the pragmatist-aesthetic stance for hybridization (of nature and culture, language and world, human and nonhuman) I have been pursuing here. I want to suggest, therefore, not only that interdisciplinarity is important for the landscape discourse but also that the landscape discourse is important for interdisciplinarity.[126] By structurally transcending essentialistically conceived boundaries and yet constantly working at the provisional fixation, erosion, and relocation of meanings (and, hence, of pragmatically, dynamically constructed boundaries), landscape provides direction and sense for a concrete merging of different practices, theories, and disciplines, offering important methodological clues in this regard. The "integrating" potential of landscape is still, in my opinion, widely underestimated and risks, in fact, being overlooked.[127]

Also in this connection, as I am approaching the end of this long chapter, I would like to suggest that aesthetics should play a leading role in establishing and "popularizing" this potential. Both directions of the connecting link between landscapes and interdisciplinarity are best understood and pursued as being governed by aesthetics as conceived here—that is, as providing a (flexible) principle of sense, order, and experiential consummation.[128] The contribution of aesthetics can prove decisive not only regarding the applied and practical cooperation of landscape-related specializations but also to its theorization. As has been noted, the "pragmatic interdisciplinarity" of landscapes works rather well: "It is the concrete site as an empirical object that guarantees successful communication between the involved disciplines about landscape as a life-worldly object."[129] The theorization of this cooperation through the definition of the main shared concepts and principles, however, is remarkably harder, as we are forced to confront "the reality of the problem of interdisciplinarity[, which] is above all a failure of communication about the differences within an existing unit."[130] Uncritically aiming for unity might remove (or pretend to remove) important differences between disciplines and approaches, thus escaping the real difficulty and undermining the real goal of interdisciplinarity—namely, the translation of concepts from one discipline to the other. Being a pervasive and multiform modality of experience and not a restricted disciplinary subset of it, aesthetics as I have delineated it here can, I believe, contribute remarkably to this essential theoretical work of translation across the disciplines involved in landscape research.[131] Even more than the previous sections of this chapter, the most these cursory remarks on landscape and interdisciplinarity can hope to do is to scratch, not even plow, the ground, showing its fertility for future research. To give more substance and unity to such an attempt, and to the explorations of the whole chapter, the next chapter focuses on a seemingly specific issue, that of landscape character and its assessment, which brings together many of the threads discussed so far.

Chapter Five

BUILDING COMMON GROUND
Landscape Character and Its Assessment

After the broad, multidirectional exploration of the previous chapter, my aim in this chapter is to focus on a specific issue, only touched on in passing earlier—namely, landscape character and its assessment. Not only is this issue central to contemporary landscape research and practice, but it is also emblematic of the strained relationship between aesthetics and landscape studies addressed by this book. Moreover, the issue of landscape character assessment can be seen as a meeting point of several of the rather disparate threads touched upon so far and as a good overall test bed for the framework I am proposing. Focusing on this issue will help to clarify the directions in which such a framework might hope to contribute and, more generally, the potentials (and limitations) of a philosophical approach to pressing issues that may not seem to have much to do with it. The chapter provides, in the first part, a critical examination of the standard framing of the subjectivism versus objectivism dualism in the concept and practice of landscape character and, in the second part, some suggestions for its improvement. After a brief overview of the emergence of the concept, partly in response to the modernist-aestheticist view of landscape, and of the mentioned dualism that this notion harbors, I discuss some main problems associated with the currently dominant "objectivist strain" in the framing of the dualism. Such problems have a common root—namely, a narrow unexamined view of experience and the aesthetic dimension. In the constructive part, I propose to reframe the relationship between subjectivity and objectivity based on the framework elaborated so far and drawing on Georg Simmel's notion of landscape "mood." Finally, I outline some implications and advantages of the suggested alternative over both the objectivist strain in the current discourse and the modernist-aestheticist paradigm.[1]

1. REASONS AND LIMITS OF OBJECTIVISM IN LANDSCAPE CHARACTER ASSESSMENT

The notion of "landscape character" (LC) and the method of "landscape character assessment" (LCA), closely related to the European Landscape Convention's (ELC) definition of landscape, can be seen, among other things, as a part of the attempt to overcome the modernist, aestheticist, elitist landscape paradigm.[2] The marginalization of aesthetics highlighted in chapter 2 is reflected and amplified by the LC concept. The latter aims at taking the control of landscape values and management away from the arbitrary, taste-related, elitist preferences of a few privileged individuals and to formulate criteria that are transparent, accessible, and democratic. Also, as the scholarship reiterates, LC is an egalitarian and pluralistic notion aimed not at hierarchically ordering landscapes as better or worse but at highlighting and valorizing their differences. To accommodate the possibly diverging needs tied to pluralism and transparency and, more in general, to frame a paradigm that is at the same time inclusive and effective, the notion of LC has to work out and implement a "twofold perspective"—that is, a duality of subjective and objective approaches (as well as of qualitative and quantitative methods).[3]

The challenge to keep together this perspective is widely acknowledged in the research.[4] Here I start from the assumption that, while the risks associated with an excess of subjectivism in the LC's twofold perspective are probably more obvious, those tied to an unbalance favoring objectivism are less visible but not less concerning. This assumption is also motivated by a prevalence of approaches favoring objectivism (and quantitative method) in the recent literature.[5] To be clear: my aim is not to oppose to such tendency a subjectivist approach as preferable. On the contrary, my aim is to contribute to their integration and, more precisely, to the overcoming of the very dualism, which hinders the improvement of the LC concept and the LCA practice.[6] Let me begin by reviewing some main problems connected with the objectivist strain.

First, unbalanced objectivism goes to the detriment of lived experience: "Rather than addressing landscape as a lived experience, landscape planners, through LCAs, tend to handle it as an objective unit of analysis, representing a backdrop to predominantly an objective outsiders view; contrasting with the intimate experience of those who inhabit the landscape."[7] If character is an objective essence existing independently of lived experience (essentialism), then the inquirer's personal experience not only does not contribute to its discovery, it actually prevents it by introducing individual, nonquantifiable elements that blur the perspective on the object. The objectivist strain also risks reproducing the primacy of the visual-contemplative or ocularcentrism:[8] if character is an objective, essential state of affairs, then to grasp it we need to give priority to its most objective and stable aspects in the experience we make of it—namely, the visual ones. Only they are relatively stable and accessible to a neutral onlooker, whereas personal immersive and engaged experience and nonvisual sensations vary too much, not only from subject to subject but even for the same subject at different times. Relying on the visual seems, then, more conducive to the aim of a unified, stable, transparent picture of LC.

The essentialism and ocularcentrism that still characterize much of the landscape discourse and practice hinder the much-talked-about (on paper) aim of true interdisciplinarity or even transdisciplinarity: "Contemporary wisdom holds that landscape research requires crossdisciplinary collaborations, and consideration of character has been seen as one way to achieve this, yet character-based methods of landscape assessment incline towards unidisciplinarity."[9] Indeed, there are several different disciplinary approaches to landscape in general, but they tend to remain noncommunicating with each other: "Observing that landscape research is currently dispersed across many domains and its proponents are often divided by disciplinary barriers, the authors indicate the need to enhance integrative approaches between human, social and natural and physical sciences."[10] The dominant approach tends to remain reliant on the skills, methods, and perspectives of landscape architects and geographers, disregarding other disciplines as well as different cultural perspectives.[11] As such, this approach is an obstacle to the advancement of collective, shared goals in an area that is, by its very nature, characterized by the need for active cooperation: "The many disciplines that use landscape as a perspective, a conceptual frame, an analytical tool or an object of study still need to develop a common ground of objectives, approaches and terminology."[12]

This leads us to a practical critique: the "objective outsider perspective results in an entity imposed on the public, representing work by planners for planners. Such a view of landscape echoes the conceptualisation exposed and critiqued by [Denis] Cosgrove . . . over 30 years ago. If planners fail to address landscape as more than just a surface as viewed by outsiders then the nature of what is represented in assessments, and consequently what will inform decision-making, goes unquestioned."[13] That is, the objectivist strain tends to reproduce the traditional top-down elitist model that it had set out to criticize and replace. Whereas traditional top-down imposition was built on political, economic, and cultural hegemony, today's imposition is softer in that it presents itself as scientifically motivated—that is, not as an imposition at all but as an objectively rational decision-making process. Admittedly, the assessment and decision-making process involves, at least nominally, some representative local voices that are called to share or reject it. This, however, does not really address the issue, not only because public involvement tends to happen at the last stage as a mere formal confirmation of a decision already taken but also because, more importantly, it happens through the unquestioning acceptance of already-defined standards, even when it is not treated as a mere formality.[14]

Such essentialist, objectivist concept of LC is reflected in a corresponding conception of the landscape values to be protected and promoted. Accordingly, "the values communicated in these assessments tend to be those of 'objective' outside experts, predominantly based on aesthetics and focusing on the physicality of landscape."[15] Notice how here "aesthetics" has nothing to do with engaged and lived experience but is in fact conceived as resonant with the focus on the physical character of the landscape: as I argue, this is due to a reductionist and narrow concept of aesthetics. The problem raised here is not only a quantitative one that concerns the limited scope of the values at issue. It is also, more importantly, a qualitative one that concerns *how* values are thought of. If values are thought of as objective and such objectivity is not further problematized, then we just need an assessment system that is neutral enough to mirror them. Landscapes, however, are also to be seen as subjective, historical, and social constructs, and so are the values characterizing them. A paradigm unbalanced toward objectivism ignores or conceals the fact that evaluation does not just neutrally mirror some preexisting, independently given values but contributes to construing them. In the terms of a recent proposal, then, the aim is "passing from 'evaluation depending on values' to 'evaluation constructing values.'"[16] In the evaluation process, the construction of value should not be hidden by the search for some pretended objectivity, but it should rather be made explicit and, thus, shared with and partaken of by all involved parties.

As we can see, the main reasons for criticizing an excessive tendency to objectivism are immanent: such tendency, if pushed too far, jeopardizes the very concept and purposes of LC and LCA (as well as the implementation of the ELC's view of landscape). In other words, the issue with the objectivist strain is that it reproduces many of the characteristic weaknesses or unilateralities, criticism of which first led to the emergence of the LC conception. Even the consideration of subjective and experiential aspects envisaged by the standard current LC concept is included only to the extent that they are transparent and, hence, tend to objectivity, as we see better in the next section. Of course, one cannot just oppose a subjectivist strain to the objectivist one as a remedy, as this would simply reverse the problem and in fact render the LC concept unusable. Yet the issue is so deep that it cannot be addressed by making some focused adjustments here and there without reframing the dualism of subjectivity and objectivity inherent in the twofold perspective's challenge. I do not mean to downplay attempts to reform the current paradigm: some of them are indeed praiseworthy in themselves, such as the proposal to integrate LCA with "historical landscape characterisation."[17] My point is that isolated reform attempts might leave the core problems untouched, and they would be more effective if they were rooted in an adequate systematic, philosophical framework that is conceptually alternative and antidualistic. What I propose in the remaining of this chapter, then, is an application of the philosophical framework elaborated in this book to the critique of the roots of the mainstream, reductionist, and dualistic formulation of the twofold perspective, followed by a reframing suggestion.

2. THE NARROWNESS OF EXPERIENCE AND THE DISAPPEARANCE OF AESTHETICS

My claim is that the problems discussed in the previous section share a common root—namely, a philosophically unexamined view of experience. On paper, LC theories and practices follow the recent scholarly and institutional insistence on the need to allow for a broad, holistic concept of experience, not just a visual, detached, and disinterested appreciation of scenic or particularly "valuable" landscapes. As we saw above, in such broad, encompassing sense, experience should not mean just the (most literal) point of *view* of a neutral, abstract subject but, to put it schematically, should (1) factor in all senses (not just sight); (2) be both individual and collective; (3) be present as well as past, including significant historical changes and turning points; (4) be immediate as well as mediated (e.g., through artistic representations of the landscape, local stories and myths, etc.); (5) be cultural and natural; (6) account for expert as well as lay points of view; (7) consider the pleasant, the ordinary, the unpleasant, and the like; and (8) accommodate a plurality of cultural backgrounds, media, and so on. Clearly, keeping all these aspects together while trying to achieve practical aims would be impossible. Still, though, one should at least keep this comprehensive concept of experience in mind as guidance and be aware and explicit about the adopted restrictions to it, something that, as the literature has emphasized, happens only in a rather limited way.

Let us have a closer look at the concept of experience at play in the dominant objectivist strain. To be sure, experience appears in LC literature and guidelines, most notably as the sensible, perceptual aspects to be investigated in the fieldwork stage of the assessment, including "cultural associations" and the experience of the locals. That is, experience features in specific, sectorial roles, well-delimited within the overall framework, and without any claim to a more comprehensive guiding role. This is so because of the dualistic framing of the current LC concept. Instead of aiming at keeping together the potentially infinite aspects of landscape experience, the objectivist paradigm is very keen on separating and compartmentalizing them. In doing so, it in fact ends up bracketing or even removing, against the letter if not the spirit of the LC's notion as such, the lived experience of the subjects inhabiting the landscape. Such lived experience only features insofar as it has a well-framed meaning and a controllable, quantifiable import. While this is an apparently only necessary move within the aimed for LC's "robust, auditable and transparent baseline," such move inevitably leads not only to a quantitative but also to a qualitative reduction of experience.[18] Besides, reducing experience to an abstract, special area of a broader process might suggest, intentionally or not, that the other areas are not experience-regulated or experience-related but somehow have to do with objective facts (and values) that are independent of experience, with problematic implications. In short, while it may be practically effective for some specific goals, there are several reasons to be dissatisfied with such a narrow, unexamined view of experience.

If experience in general has a limited, sectorial role in the objectivist paradigm, this is even more the case for what we may generally refer to as the aesthetic aspects, which, as we abundantly saw, tend to be marginalized in a large part of contemporary landscape research also beyond the issue of landscape character assessment. Aesthetic aspects are held to constitute a subset of or complement to the perceptual/experiential ones to be assessed at the field study stage. Subset or complement: there is indeed an oscillation between them, with the aesthetic dimension featuring sometimes as a piece of the experiential one (together with the perceptual one) and sometimes as something different from but complementary to it (in which case the experiential and the perceptual dimensions seem to become synonyms).[19] This oscillation is symptomatic of an unexamined compartmentalization, tied to a commonsensical employment of both terms, "experience" and "aesthetic." Again, the implications are (1) that the aesthetic dimension only has a specific role within its limited "sector" and, hence, (2) that beyond such restricted sector the LC components have no aesthetic relevance, and vice versa, so that (3) what is aesthetically relevant can be "professionally" controlled, quantified, recorded, and put to practical use. This is explicitly stated, for example, by Tudor, in a passage that should be quoted at length: "Desk based research cannot usually identify aesthetic, perceptual/experiential factors, . . . hence Field Survey is essential. These dimensions of landscape character are as important as the more tangible elements and characteristics that also inform landscape character. All need to be woven into factual, objective, written descriptions of landscape character. [Aesthetic] factors can be recorded in a rigorous and systematic manner using professionally informed judgements. Factors

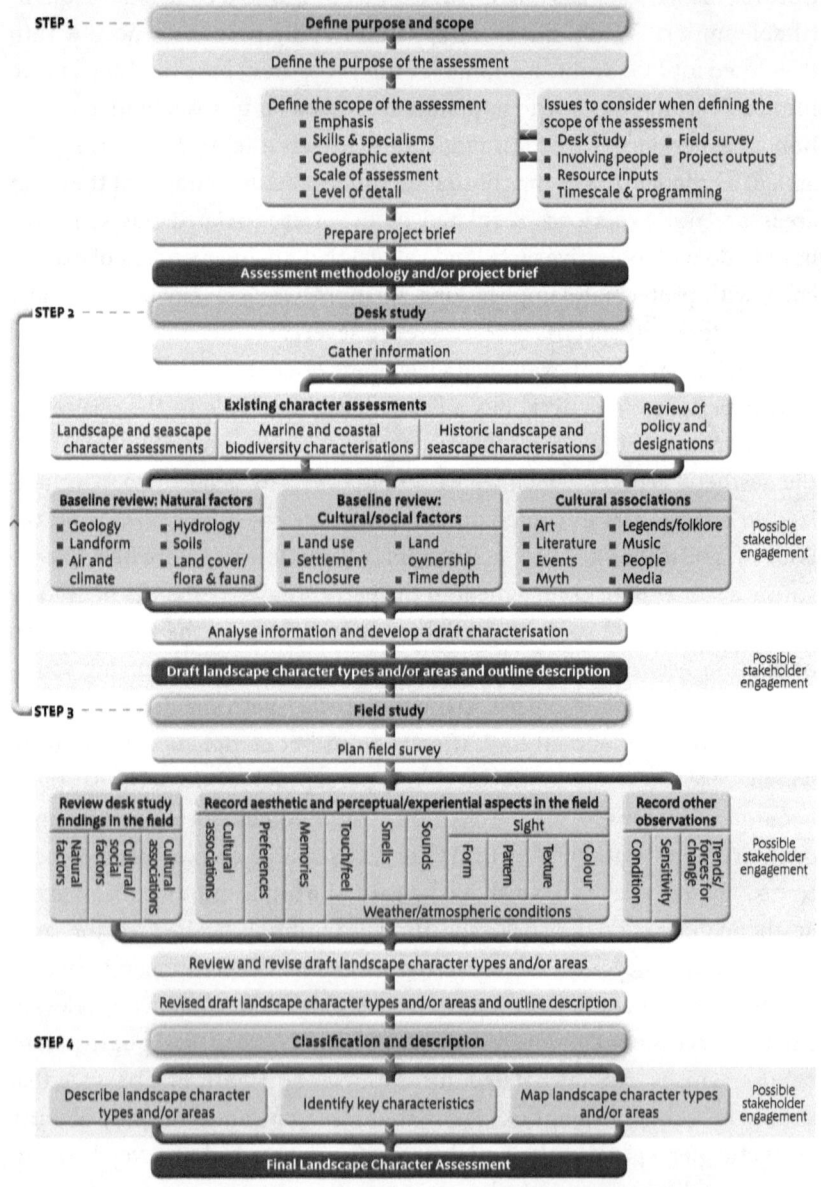

FIGURE 5.1. The process of landscape character assessment. Image from Christine Tudor, "An Approach to Landscape Character Assessment," fig. 2), https://assets.publishing.service.gov.uk/media/5aabd31340f0b64ab4b7576e/landscape-character-assessment.pdf. © Natural England 2014. Used with permission.

that might be considered—along with their associated descriptions—would include scale, enclosure, diversity, texture, form, line, colour, balance, movement and pattern."[20]

While the aesthetic dimension has its own recognized space in this paradigm, this space is restricted by rigid borders: what we can take into account are only objective, rigorous, professional descriptions with a clear hierarchical subordination of the aesthetic-experiential to the objective-scientific. We may wonder, then, what conceptually distinguishes the aesthetic aspects from the natural-objective ones that have been assessed already in the desk study. This distinction ultimately seems to amount to the fact that the "existing character assessments" can be done from a desk by reviewing existing information, while the aesthetic-experiential ones require field work to empirically collect new information. If the latter is objective, rigorous, and professional enough, then we may reasonably surmise that it can be adequately stored and become "existing character assessment" material when a new assessment is made of that landscape. In other words, the aesthetic dimension is only relevant and compelling insofar as we may hope to turn it into a collection of objective facts, ideally independent of experience, sensation, subjective evaluation—that is, if we ultimately strip it of what makes it aesthetic. Such wording may sound provocative, but the next section fleshes out the genuine philosophical point behind the provocation.

In concluding this section it is worth noting that the modernist-aestheticist model and the currently dominant objectivist strain raise similar problems due to the very view of aesthetics that both models deploy, which is the same though they take opposite stances toward it. In both models, experience in general and aesthetic experience in particular are conceived of according to a traditional essentialist model that reduces them to categorized, separable faculties and properties instead of comprehensive, holistic ways of interacting with the environment that are characteristic of the human being. Therefore, actual improvement should come from the application of a different, more up-to-date aesthetic concept, one that can address criticism to the modernist paradigm without relinquishing the decisive role of aesthetics in concrete, lived experience. The second half of this chapter outlines such an alternative concept based on the pragmatist-aesthetic framework elaborated in this book.

3. A PRAGMATIST ALTERNATIVE

The starting idea is that, while for some specific purposes it may be expeditious or necessary to divide the LC and the related assessment methodologies into different steps or aspects or skills, we should keep in mind that such distinctions are pragmatic, not essential. In other words, they serve some specific purpose but do not neutrally reflect a given essence of reality. This also means that they do not portray some independently existing and objectively given character, but they do construct it.[21] In a pragmatist perspective, experience has to do with any and all interactions between the human being and its environment, and aesthetics describes a perfected, successful, and satisfying modality of such interaction. Therefore, every connection and every kind of interaction with the environment, be it in theory, practice, leisure, creativity, and so on, is experiential, and every experience is embryonically and potentially aesthetic.

The proposed view is reflected in a holistic and integrated concept of landscape in general, which in turn can lead to a more balanced account of the values informing LC. Experience is not just a specific faculty or way of seeing the world through which we assess some specific aspects of a landscape, it is instead the totality of our active life, involving us as subjects as well as our environment. Aesthetics, in turn, is not just the umbrella name for specific objects or properties and for our related taste, judgment, and enjoyment; it is a way to describe the successful establishment of a well-balanced, conscious way of being, acting, and dwelling in our landscapes. Accordingly, LC is not a neutral way of referring to more or less objective, independently existing properties but is the balance we strike each time between the different values and perspectives (both subjective and objective) through which we at the same time institute and experience a specific landscape. In other words, any LC is not the objective correlate of a specific, proceduralized mode of knowing consisting of a (fragmented) collection of skills but a living, precarious negotiation reflecting the concretely located multiformity of our experience. Even though we can (and probably cannot avoid to) try to analyze, parcel out, objectify such process for ever-changing purposes, we cannot reduce an LC to the sum total of those parcels and objects: an LC is way more elusive and dynamic. Of course, here one could object that in this way we are just opposing a subjectivist strain to the objectivist one and the LC notion itself becomes so blurred as to be useless, since it can mean everything and nothing. We should not forget, however, that, as we have seen above and as manifested by scholars of different orientations, the current paradigm of LC involves numerous elements of arbitrariness, although often concealed under a pretense of objectivity. The alternative view I propose calls us to be aware of and explicit about the arbitrariness and instability and to be pragmatic and pluralist in our search for principles of order, which have an aesthetic nature, as seen in chapter 2.

To develop this idea, let me briefly return to Simmel's seminal philosophical conception of landscapes as based on "mood" (*Stimmung*). As we saw, Simmel's investigation of the kind of unity giving rise to landscapes follows an aesthetic-pragmatist pattern.[22] Natural objects or phenomena can be gathered into different kinds of unities based on the perspective used or the aim set: "We say that a landscape arises when a range of natural phenomena spread over the surface of the earth is comprehended by a particular kind of unity, one that is distinct from the way this same visual field is encompassed by the causally thinking scholar, the religious sentiments of a worshipper of nature, the teleologically oriented tiller of the soil, or a strategist of war."[23] Thus, landscapes are, first, negatively set apart from other kinds of unities that pursue apparently clearer aims and principles. Then Simmel positively introduces the specific principle of unification for landscapes, which is also the distinctive feature of his philosophy of landscape: "The most important carrier of this unity may well be the 'mood,' as we call it, of a landscape."[24]

Whereas the dominant LC paradigm strives for objectivity and transparency, Simmel's mood places emphasis on elusiveness: "When we refer to the mood of a person, we mean that coherent ensemble that either permanently or temporarily colours the entirety of his or her psychic constituents. . . . In the same way, the mood of a landscape permeates all its separate components, frequently without it being attributable to any one of them. In a way that is difficult to specify, each component partakes in it, but a mood prevails which is neither external to these constituents, nor is it composed of them."[25] As we saw, whereas the dominant paradigm tends to separate LC from the subjectivity of the lived experience, Simmel points to the impossibility to actually distinguish between the unitary perception giving rise to a landscape and the mood we experience with it. The latter is normally taken to be the ensuing specific feeling that follows and is different from the experience of a landscape. For Simmel, asking whether the unitary perception precedes the feeling or vice versa already means introducing undue dualism and fragmentation: experience is always *one*, and the same act underlies the "creation" of the material landscape and our feeling about it. This does not mean erasing the possibility of a distinction in our psychical activity: it is not as if our experience were the undifferentiated product of a single, undivided mental activity. Rather, our perception and our feeling (and, indeed, any other "energy" involved in the act) retain each the specificity of their tonality, yet they utter the same word in unison. And, just like a mood in its concreteness is always *this* mood and no two moods are the same, the same applies to landscapes: "The mood of a landscape pointed to here is one pertaining to *just this* particular landscape and never to any other, even though both may possibly be subsumed under a general concept, such as melancholic. . . . It is only by effacing its immediate and actual character that I can reduce it to general concepts, such as melancholic, cheerful, serious or exciting."[26] Here Simmel explicitly employs the term *character* (*Charakter* in German), noting how using general concepts and abstract categories means, plain and simple, effacing the immediate reality of it. His perspective, hence, runs exactly contrary to the currently dominant LC paradigm. In the next, concluding section I aim to gain more depth by asking how the alternative view outlined here can help reframe the twofold perspective challenge within the LC discourse, making it more consistent with the ELC definition of landscape.

4. BEYOND SUBJECTS AND OBJECTS: REFRAMING THE TWOFOLD PERSPECTIVE CHALLENGE

According to the objectivist LC paradigm, it is taken for granted or predetermined which values or features are to be assessed. There is, of course, space for discussing or negotiating such assessments, but the very "rules" of the game are externally and "professionally" predetermined, and they are not really open for negotiation with the "intimate experience" of the inhabitants.[27] The whole paradigm seems to rely on unquestioned assumptions that, through their claim to objectivity, end up dictating the whole decision-making process. Recall the criticism: "If planners fail to address landscape as more than just a surface as viewed by outsiders then the nature of what is represented in assessments, and consequently what will inform decision-making, goes unquestioned."[28] Compare this with Simmel. For him, the very definition of a landscape is elusive and, we may say, "unprofessional," so much so that it is first given through negation of other approaches (religious, scientific, military . . .) and then based on the notion of "mood," itself obscure and unstable. Landscape character for Simmel is much more of a process, or an atmosphere, or a color shade than an objective fact or collection of facts. It also entails a twofold perspective, but it does so in a pragmatic, antidualistic fashion based on which landscape is a unity in constant becoming, as is the mood generating it or by which it is generated. If we try to put clear-cut, objective tags on it, we lose the very reality and value of what we are looking for—namely, its character.

Let us see some implications. First, the alternative view does not take for granted but problematizes what a landscape is. Accordingly, LC is not an already existing object to be examined, but it requires that all involved parties and stakeholders contribute to its institution through their perception/feeling. Second, this institution does not happen once and for all. Landscape changes with/through the experience we make of it and the definition of its character should account, as far as possible, for psychological and cultural plurality. Third, universalizing abstractions may be necessary at times, but they should not be taken to express the real, living character of a landscape: in fact, they are its opposite. Fourth, landscapes are not the same as artworks but can be explained and, hence, discussed and, hence, their value can be assessed based on a continuist view.[29] Accordingly, it is impossible to set out fixed criteria for landscapes, but this does not result in full-blown subjectivist blurredness and skepticism—no more than it would happen with artworks. There are no essentialistically conceived borders, but borders can be pragmatically and provisionally drawn and shifted at any time based on varying experiences and needs.

The list may go on, but we can establish a general point. Due to a more comprehensive, less compartmentalized concept of experience and aesthetics, the view I am proposing can help reframe and address the shortcomings, both theoretical and practical, outlined above. As we saw, the dominant objectivist paradigm gives aesthetics and experience a secondary, partial role, partly in response to the previously dominating modernist, aestheticist, and elitist paradigm. In contrast with the latter's focus on the "beauty" or "exceptionality" of landscapes and on the "taste" and "aesthetic experience" of the onlooker/user, the currently dominant paradigm ends up neglecting experience and aesthetics, which are taken into consideration only in a parceled-out, abstract way. More precisely, they only matter as long as they can (purportedly) be accounted for in objective, rigorous terms. In this context, both terms are only significant in a superficial way, in the precise sense that only their surface counts, and consequently landscape itself risks to become once again a viewed surface. My alternative concept, instead, fully reclaims the value of aesthetics and experience, yet without falling prey to the critical issues affecting the modernist paradigm. Experience and aesthetics are accordingly not just the subjective counterparts of an already established objectivity to be mirrored in the most neutral and "professional" way possible. Yet they are not the restricted, arbitrary asset of a few privileged subjects who are materially and intellectually able to enjoy beauty either. On the contrary, aesthetics and experience are jointly thematized as the very energies *constructing* meanings in a line of continuity that goes from a selective overview of a place to complex artworks via landscapes. Instead of being only surface, experience and aesthetics are, in fact, "substance," providing a solid yet flexible groundwork for "substantive" landscapes and for an accordingly concrete and encompassing definition of their character.[30]

Thus, the alternative concept is also helpful in a practical sense, as it necessitates a continuous problematization and negotiation of perspectives and values. Accordingly, talking about LC in general does not mean referring to and relying on self-evident, given assumptions but making explicit the process of negotiation through which a specific LC is constructed each time, a process that can be framed via a pragmatist continuistic paradigm. Associating LC with Simmel's idea of "mood" as a unifying principle does not lead to subjectivist relativism as moods themselves can be made explicit, shared, and discussed, thus paving the way to a negotiation between the expectations of the parties involved. Unlike the dominant paradigm, such negotiation would not merely be an abstract formality but the very space in which a specific LC is constructed, and the process of explication of the criteria and values of such construction would lay the conditions for a more pluralist, transparent, and shared decision-making outcome. Therefore, the alternative framework outlined here allows to overcome the juxtaposition of the traditional aestheticist-elitist paradigm and the currently dominant objectivist strain by showing how such juxtaposition is only apparent insofar as it implies the same concept of aesthetics that is embraced by the former and rejected by the latter. By opting for a reconceptualization of the nature and function of experience and aesthetics, my framework eschews the main theoretical and practical problems associated with both views. The next, final chapter does not provide further arguments but three "personal" landscape sketches, which cannot and do not act as "professional" case studies but rather as studies in the aesthetic-artistic sense of "rough casts" of landscapes as experiences, proposing in all briefness some instances of the integrated, antidualistic concept developed here. After that, a succinct conclusion schematically helps to reconnect the main threads.

Chapter Six

LIVED LANDSCAPES
Three Sketches

This final chapter sketches three different readings of landscapes, all of which I personally experienced and lived, for different reasons and in different times. The aim is to provide some concrete, although necessarily cursory, examples of how landscapes can be seen, interpreted, and communicated based on the anti-exceptionalist, pragmatist, aesthetically structured framework I have proposed. It should be clear that I cannot aim to exclusiveness nor to originality per se in the resulting readings: different ones are of course possible, and they can and should in fact integrate and update each other, displaying different ways of drawing borders and finding/instituting meanings and principles of order. It should also be clear that no landscape can adequately be only written or read. Making full sense of the things I will say—that is, experiencing (with) *my* three landscapes, whether following my suggestions or developing different ones—would require a prolonged immersive interaction.

The three landscapes I have chosen are quite different from each other and kept together by the intensely "lived" character of my experiencing (with) them. They differ not only materially and culturally but also, in my reading, in their dominant temporal "tense": not because a specific time can be assigned to each of them but because, in the "palette" of temporal tenses coloring each of them in my experience, a prevalent one can be identified and followed. I have tried in this way to bear witness to my claim about the centrality of temporality and the impossibility to detach it from spatiality and to read landscapes only in terms of the latter. The first landscape is the small region of Valleriana, in Tuscany, Italy. I was there on holiday with my wife and our then six-month old son for the whole of August 2021. Its prevalent temporal tense is the past. The second landscape is the bigger region of Münsterland, in North Rhine-Westphalia, Germany. I lived and worked in its main city, Münster, as a postdoctoral fellow and temporary lecturer at the Department of Philosophy of the local university from January 2011 to July 2013. Its prevalent temporal tense is the present. The third and last landscape is the megacity of Istanbul, Turkey. I lived and worked there as an assistant, then associate professor at the Department of Philosophy of Yeditepe University, one of its many private universities, from August 2013 to August 2016. Its prevalent temporal tense is the future.

1. VALLERIANA: A TUSCAN REVERIE

Valleriana is a small mountainous region consisting of two high valleys (Val di Torbola and Val di Forfora) along the Apennine range, north of Pescia, the municipality in which it is located, in the province of Pistoia, in Tuscany, Italy.[1] The valley is cut through by two main rivers, the Pescia River in Collodi and the Pescia River in Pescia, with their many branches and tributaries. It includes the ten small inhabited *castella*, or fortified hamlets, of Medicina, Pietrabuona, Fibbialla, Aramo, San Quirico, Castelvecchio, Stiappa, Pontito, Sorana, and Vellano, with a total population of about 1,700 (more or less densely distributed, from the 30 residents of Pontito to the 505 of Vellano), located 117 m (at Pietrabuona, the "gate" to the valley) to 745 m above sea level (at Pontito, the remotest village).[2] While the area has been inhabited since the Paleolithic era, the first documentary traces of the existing *castella* date from before the year 1000, with the settlement system consolidated around the twelfth to thirteenth centuries. The region, of great strategic importance, has been the theater of endless battles between the neighboring major centers (most notably, Florence, Pisa, and Lucca) and between their local allies; in fact, there was an eleventh *castella* (Lignana) that was destroyed by the Pisans in 1364. This long and always shifting situation of conflict is still reflected today, among other things, in the complex religious-institutional arrangement, with some of the *castella* belonging to the archdiocese of Lucca and some to the diocese of Pescia. Much more recently, toward the end of World War II, with the Gothic line being right on top of the area and all the intensive resistance activities going on there, the population fell victim to several Nazi-fascist massacres and devastations. Valleriana is also known as Svizzera Pesciatina (Pescia's Switzerland), although there is controversy both on the legitimacy of this toponym and on the extent of its spatial overlapping with the older one.[3] The denomination Svizzera Pesciatina goes back to the Swiss writer, historian, and economist Jean Charles Léonard Simonde de Sismondi, exiled to Pescia, who also offered a description of the area in his 1801 *Tableau de l'agriculture toscane*.

Valleriana attracts a good number of tourists in the summer, although not remotely comparable with that of neighboring areas such as Garfagnana or Lunigiana, not to mention major Tuscan destinations, such as Val d'Orcia or Chianti. Even though easily accessible and close to major centers and attractions, Valleriana is relatively isolated and unknown even in Italy.[4] This fact is associated with its recent depopulation and overall impoverishment but also with its excellent preservation.[5] The landscape, both natural and anthropic, has largely remained the same throughout the centuries. The landscape of Valleriana is characterized by a successful, harmonic, mostly intact interwovenness (one might even say organic co-growth) of natural and anthropic elements. This is instantly apparent in the settlement system of the *castella*, almost magically nestled in the wooded spurs of the Apennines. The forests (80 percent of the territory) and the *castella* (1.3 percent of the territory) are at the same time separated and connected through an impressive, ubiquitous system of terraces (*terrazzamenti* or *ciglionamenti*) built to keep the forests' growth under control and practice agriculture and husbandry. We have, then, a thick wooded plot running along the contours of the valleys, smooth in places, steep in others, and dotted with clearly visible and legible crown-shaped settlement nuclei, presenting themselves as slight, although recognizable, variations of a single, clearly identifiable pattern that brings them together. The woods themselves, constituting the largest share of the area and its most "natural" component, are in fact "cultural" chestnut woods. Chestnut trees used to account for most of the economy and sustenance, both as food (so essential that the trees

LIVED LANDSCAPES

FIGURE 6.1. Pontito, the remotest and least populated of the *castella* of Valleriana, Italy. Photo by Francenanni, August 2018. Reprinted from Wikimedia Commons, https://commons.wikimedia.org/wiki/File:Una_piramide_in_Valleriana,_%22Pontito%22.jpg.

were called "bread trees") and as woodland. At least two other activities need to be mentioned: paper mills and quarries of *pietra serena*, a compact and fairly pliable sandstone with a beautiful grey color and a high frost resistance.

As for papermaking, the history of Valleriana has been revolving around it at least since the fifteenth century, thanks to its favorable hydrography and the abundance of woods and building stone. In fact, Valleriana and the neighboring areas were home to the highest concentration of paper mills in the whole of Italy based on a widespread, small-scale, high-quality production model that has its legacy in today's large and highly automated Paper District in the nearby area of Capannori and in the important Museo della Carta (Museum of Paper) in Pietrabuona. As for the *pietra serena*, it was extensively employed in Tuscan (and especially Florentine) Renaissance architecture and, more interestingly for us, for pretty much every building in Valleriana, from houses to fortifications, from churches to road paving, from the paper mills to the agricultural works, fountains, walls. The extraction of *pietra serena* never reached an industrial level and was mostly carried out without the help of machines from very small, almost invisible quarries—sometimes little more than holes in the ground—thus without significant impact on the natural environment.

Obviously, these three main activities (growing chestnut trees, papermaking, and quarrying) have nowadays dramatically shrunk. Still, the fundamental structure of the landscape has not changed, and most importantly it did not give way to obtrusive forms of degradation. Sure, several of the ancient paper mills are crumbling and inaccessible, and wild woods and undergrowth have reclaimed many previously cultivated or at least controlled areas. But the organization of the landscape, the distinctive interwovenness of the natural and cultural is practically intact. Valleriana offers a perfect, although simple or even humble, example of a cultural landscape. As such, it was already recognized by Sismondi, whose identification of the place with his native Switzerland and whose description of the area revolved around the interaction between human cultivation (in a broad sense) and the territory's potential.[6] This very interaction or synergy is what, according to my previous discussion, should be named "landscape," more specifically a cultural landscape: not because nonanthropized landscapes are not somewhat rooted in cultural habits or points of view themselves but because in this case the cultural aspect is an integral part of the "growth" of the landscape, and vice versa. I dwell a bit longer on the "cultural," mediated character of Sismondi's appreciation and identification, which is exemplificative here of a "successful" interaction and commerce with one's environment (think of Dewey), particularly remarkable if we consider that that environment was indissolubly associated, for him, with the trauma of exile.

From an immediate, environmental point of view, Sismondi's identification seems to rely on quite generic and weak grounds, as Valleriana does not seem to share with Switzerland much more than the wooded mountains, the rivers, and possibly a sense of pleasantness, which is not much if we consider the massive differences in the geology, the wildlife, the climate, and so on. Beside these quite generic, objective grounds, the identification is therefore further pursued on a double imaginative and personal level. On the one hand, once in Tuscany, the author starts affixing the patronymic

"Sismondi" to his surname "Simonde," based on a supposed or real genealogical descent from the ancient Pisan Ghibelline Sismondi family, already mentioned by Dante Alighieri and itself exiled to the Dauphiné. On the other hand, he names his villa in Pescia Valchiusa ("closed valley"), thus connecting the closed valley of Valleriana to his beloved childhood house in the Genevan countryside. The hardship and pain of the exile experience is, in this way, at least partly transformed in the joy and relief of repatriation, even more so because of the tight connection created between the maternal house and land and the new ones.[7] Finally, there is a very material ground for such identification, which concerns Sismondi more as an economist and an intellectual. Sismondi was a sharp critic of the growing capitalist exploitation, which in many places led to a large estate system and caused the removal of small-owners-peasants from their lands as well as the abrupt, traumatic reorganization of the latter. For Sismondi, the small *métayer* of the Pescia region is a positive counterexample, of which he highlights the well-being, the relative independence, the healthy lifestyle, and the deep involvement in the land and its work—just like the Swiss small-owners model.[8] Switzerland and Tuscany are, hence, jointly proposed as a concrete, enlightened alternative of social welfare and harmony to the misery and alienation of, among others, Scotland and Ireland. None of these three factors (generic environmental similarities, personal imaginative projection, and socioeconomic analogies), taken on their own, would make up sufficient grounds for such a strong and active feeling of identification. Their combination and interplay, though, can explain it quite well. Now the point, apart from the individual case, is that there are some specificities to Valleriana that afford this combination and interplay: indeed, here one may speak of particularly favorable "affordances."[9]

The main affordance and characteristic of the place is its legibility in terms of a variety of microcosms constituting at the same time a perfect unity: a habitat with an unmistakable, unique appearance, yet not reducible to a single "meaning." This allows for a peculiar dynamism, both spatial and temporal. The spatial one is given by the ever-changing succession of smooth or steep mountain profiles, thick forests suddenly opening onto broad views, fortified stone villages with their terraces looking like gems magnificently embroidered in the natural texture—rivers, tributaries, waterfalls, small natural pools, roads, bridges, and so on. The temporal one is given by a feeling of completion (of consummation, we may say with Dewey) of a history: the history of the place is there all together, crystallized in a lively, surveyable present. The political, religious, and cultural divisions that for centuries have put the *castella* against each other are not removed from the history and consciousness of the place but concur to its dynamic structure, present yet elusive in the organization of the space, the traditions, the articulation of time. There is (almost) nothing out of place or time: everything contributes to a single, harmonic movement, in which the space reflects the organization of time (hours, seasons, epochs . . .) and the time is filled with the presence and the necessities of the "cultured" space. The ancestral relationship between the human element, the land, the rivers, and the sky looks very natural, itself a product of the environment and at the same time perfectly shaped in such a way that it is virtually impossible to establish hard borders between nature and culture.

Another affordance is given by the widespread feeling of self-sufficiency: not in a closed, exclusive way but rather the healthy relative self-sufficiency of a natural organism in a favorable environment. The economy of Valleriana is (or was) indeed (close to) a self-sufficient one. The main sources of all human life were the woods, the stones, and the waters of the valley in their interplays. Water and stones were employed in the production of paper. The local stone is still the material of almost all constructions, and stonecutting was an ancient, well-established, sometimes all-embracing tradition, often reaching outward.[10] Stonecutters (*scalpellini*) were themselves self-sufficient as they mainly worked right in the quarries and even built their own instruments in a forge inside it. Chestnuts and chestnut trees were (almost) everything and everywhere, constituting most of the environment and most of the inhabitants' concerns and activities:

> Special care was taken of chestnut groves, which were, as early as the Middle Ages, the greatest source of sustenance. Chestnut trees were one of the most ubiquitous plants in the area and covered almost one half of the woods; chestnut growing was of vital importance for these mountains: from the trees, firewood was obtained, as well as their fruits, the chestnuts, which for centuries had been the staple food of these populations. Every person, young or old, worked in the harvesting, so for a month the villages were empty and the *selvi* ["woods"] were full of busy people. The trees were harvested as fast as possible, to prevent chestnuts from freezing. Everything was finished in

LIVED LANDSCAPES

30–40 days. The fruits were used in a multitude of ways. Most of them were dried in the typical *metati* (two-stories stone structures where the chestnuts were dried on slow heat), then reduced to flour in the local mills to produce *farina dolce* ["sweet flour"] or used fresh to make *ballotti* [boiled chestnuts] or roasted into *frugiate*.... The *farina dolce* was used mainly to make *necci*, a kind of flat bread made by placing a flour and water batter between two slabs [*testi*] heated on embers.... Chestnut leaves, first dried then soaked in water, were inserted between the batter and the slab to prevent the *neccio* from burning. With the flour, also *polenta neccia, farinata neccia, frittelle, castagnaccio*, etc. were prepared.[11]

Everything from the tree is used in the process: wood for the fire, the fruits for different products, and even the leaves. But not only are chestnuts vital for humans, it is the other way around too, as Sismondi already noticed: "Every time the terrain is disrupted by the waters, a dry stone wall gets built to hold back the collapse, and every time an old chestnut tree dies, or a space opens in which a new one can be planted, a small terrace is set up ... and

FIGURE 6.2. The traditional (one might say archaic) preparation of *necci*, the chestnut-flour flatbreads typical from Valleriana, Italy. Photo by Anton Francesco Renieri, April 2010. Reprinted from Wikimedia Commons, https://commons.wikimedia.org/wiki/File:Neccio.jpg.

supported through a grassy edge to prevent the sapling from being uprooted by the violence of the rains."[12]

This is a paradigmatic aspect of how nature and culture are inseparable in Valleriana: they constitute an organic, largely self-sufficient, self-structuring, self-developing whole. Each of the microcosms constituting this landscape, a small nucleus grown around a castle or *pieve* (parish church), was itself relatively self-sufficient, and the proportions between the different constituents are harmoniously targeted as much to the well-being of the inhabitants as to the preservation of the landscape. The functioning and endurance of this system is predicated on some simple rules: (1) the concentrated form of settlements, only and always built on the strategic as well as resistant portions of the mountainous area; (2) the microcosm paradigm, with a well-proportioned relationship between built, agricultural, and tree-covered areas; and (3) the accurate, careful control over the use of terrains and hydraulic-agrarian constructions. These basic rules allowed to create and define a "morphological order": not merely fixed quantitative relationships but a ductile yet extremely characteristic and identifiable principle of sense in the institution, disposition, and preservation of the landscape.[13] The observation of the rules grounding this order used to be very strict, while clearly now it is much looser: this loosening can be seen as a premonition of decay but also, perhaps a bit optimistically, as a reminder that even such a functional principle of order is not an a priori law but an attempt at orientation in the realm of contingency (Kant), requiring pragmatic readjustments and relocations (Dewey). As has been said, this landscape is not static but persistent in time, not immutable but self-consistent.[14] It is a complex system based on simple rules, a dynamic homogeneity that emerges perfectly, from a visual point of view, in the high "intervisibility" between the hamlets, originated from historical strategic and defensive needs, which is now no longer suggestive of a latent or open conflict but rather of a continuous interaction, giving meaning, protection, and scenic value to the landscape. I mentioned intervisibility as an affordance but, consistent with the framework so far developed, we should not forget the other senses. The webs connecting the different points of meaning within this landscape are not only visual but also olfactive, auditive, gustative, haptic: different areas are characterized by different smells, sounds, tastes, and materials.[15] The road itself crossing the land points beyond the visual in its recent denomination as a portion of the *Strada dei colori e sapori dell'Appennino pistoiese* ("Road of the colors and flavors of the Pistoia Apennine"). In grasping and describing connections and articulations, synesthetic processes are not just metaphors but seem to be essential constituents, so it would be quite accurate to say, for example, that the reality of this landscape is at the same time sweet and rough, like the chestnut-flour based foods it produces.

Finally, I would like to say something more specific about the aesthetics of Valleriana. Unlike many places we commonly associate with Tuscany, Valleriana does not have outstanding artworks to offer, and even its relatively modest artistic heritage is not really advertised and is in fact quite inaccessible. The *pievi*, the churches, and the *oratori* (oratories) with their beautiful frescos are normally closed and only rarely accessible by appointment with a local warden, who mostly does it on a voluntary, nonprofessional basis. There are no fine arts museums or exhibitions whatsoever: the only museums are the big, but still largely unfinished, paper museum in Pietrabuona and a small, "home-made"—although truly worthwhile—mining and quarry museum in Vellano. Yet the few, hardly accessible artworks "appear as single epiphanies, as first-hand testimonies and living documents of the path made during the centuries by small civic consortia, here more than in other places."[16] They are the somewhat absorbed yet self-aware expressions of a whole millennium-long community life that, helped and at the same time frustrated by its isolation, tries to take care of them without exploiting them, sometimes ignored or even hampered rather than supported by the regional and national authorities. On the other hand, the artworks are often the result of an uprooting insofar as many of them were commissioned by locals who emigrated to bigger and artistically more up-to-date centers in the attempt to make up for a feeling of loss through artistic novelty and to remember their native community while being remembered by it. Therefore, "looking for the masterwork in these lands would be not only useless, but also wrong. It is indeed in the *continuum* between work and territory, between environment, history, and artistic history that the specificity of this portion of Tuscany is qualified."[17]

This also applies to the "natural" beauty. Valleriana is certainly full of natural wonders; it is varied, scenic in some points, intact. Yet, even compared to some nearby areas of Tuscany, it does not offer outstanding or breath-taking views or places. Its landscape is a perfect harmony as a whole and beautiful in its particulars, but it would not be accurate to attribute it a clearly defined and distinctive character of exceptionality. I am suggesting, of course, that the aesthetics of Valleriana is a nonisolationist, nonexceptionalist one. It is, as in the last quote, an aesthetics of the continuity between nature and culture, environment and art, territory and work, the ordinary and the remarkable, the utilitarian and the contemplative, and so on. An aesthetics, in conclusion, that rarely culminates in high peaks but rather innervates and structures, in a harmonic, functional way, a whole landscape and the life within it.

2. HEAVEN OVER MÜNSTERLAND

Münsterland is a region in northwest Westphalia, in the German *Land* of North Rhine-Westphalia, roughly delimited by the Teutoburg Forest to the northeast, by the river Lippe in the south, and by the Dutch border to the northwest, although the borders vary depending on the chosen criterion (geographical, historical, political, etc.).[18] The center of the region is the name-giving city of Münster. The region covers almost 7,000 square kilometers, with a total population of around 2.6 million (Münster itself has a population of approximately 320,000). It is characterized by, among other things, a deeply felt regional identity, of which the prevalence of the Catholic confession and of local forms of Low German language constitute the main pillars. Historically, the area features prominently during the Reformation, especially through the Münster rebellion (1534–35, in German: *Täuferreich von Münster*, "Anabaptist dominion of Münster"), the short-lived, radical communitarian-eschatological Anabaptist rule of the city of Münster following the German Peasants' War. The rebellion and subsequent siege of the city, the repression, and the aftermath were brutal and bloody.[19] The Anabaptist leaders were tortured and executed in the city's marketplace, their mutilated bodies warningly exhibited in iron cages hung from the steeple of the central St. Lambert's Church. The three cages are still there for everybody to see, although the bones are no longer there (apparently the bodies were left to putrefy completely until, centuries later, the last remains fell through the bars of the cages onto the market square). One century later the region was one of the many theaters of the Thirty Years' War, one of the most violent conflicts in European history, which started

FIGURE 6.3. The three Anabaptists' cages on St. Lambert's Church tower, Münster, Germany. Photo by Dietmar Rabich, August 2013. Reprinted from Wikimedia Commons, https://commons.wikimedia.org/wiki/File:M%C3%BCnster,_Lambertikirche_-_2013_-_00368.jpg.

as a religious war and eventually transformed the whole European political and territorial balance. One "half" of the Peace of Westphalia, putting an end to the war and providing the basis for the modern state order and international law, was signed in Münster in 1648 (the other "half" was signed in the nearby city of Osnabrück).[20] Later on, during World War II, Münster was one of the most heavily bombed cities in Germany, with 91 percent of the old city destroyed. Unlike many other German cities, after the war the population urged the reconstruction of the city to prewar conditions.

Today Münsterland is a prosperous, peaceful region. Its economy is mostly based on small enterprises, with the agricultural sector being traditionally strong. Industry and manufacturing mainly revolve around agriculture, with mechanical engineering and food industry being the two

LIVED LANDSCAPES

FIGURE 6.4. *Münsterlander Parklandschaft* with the moated Burg Kakesbeck (*center-bottom left*), Germany. Photo by Günter Seggebäing, June 2014. Reprinted from Wikimedia Commons, https://commons.wikimedia.org/wiki/File:20140601_113908_Parklandschaft_mit_Burg_Kakesbeck,_L%C3%BCdinghausen_(DSC02022).jpg.

biggest sectors. The service sector plays a huge role (88.8 percent of the gross value added) in Münster, a rich administrative and university center. The landscape of Münsterland, almost completely flat, is intensively shaped by agriculture, which is, however, scattered in small-scale plots so that it presents a continuous variation of fields, waters, orchards, meadows, small woods, cottages, and hedgerows, echoing the overall appearance of a park. One speaks, indeed, of the Münsterland park landscape (*Münsterlander Parklandschaft*). The area is punctuated by several moated castles, small villages, and monasteries.[21] Due to the even, parceled distribution of the elements and the absence of striking "interruptions" such as large forests, heights, or lakes, the landscape follows a homogenous, at times monotonous, pattern. Different interests compete over this relatively homogenous landscape: for example, agricultural, industrial, residential, touristic, ecological, energetic. Intensive agriculture and livestock farming have negative effects on water quality and climate and raise growing concerns about their ethics and sustainability, which are hardly compatible with the market demand for lower costs. Further concerns are aroused by the preservation and development of the historical and cultural landscape, partly in view of its growing attraction as a tourist destination. Another issue is the environmental and cultural impact of the vast production of renewable energy (mainly photovoltaic, wind, and biogas). More generally, the challenge is about allowing and managing the landscape's changes as far as they are necessary to maintain and develop its prosperity and integrity while addressing the potentially negative externalities of such changes in terms of environment, climate, biodiversity, historical and cultural heritage, quality of life, and so on. Clearly, this challenge is hardly exclusive to this region, and I am not concerned here with its technicalities.

I would like to make, instead, a few aesthetic-oriented remarks on the connection between this "park landscape," the underlying historical consciousness, and the way this change is being addressed. The overall impression is that of efficient, up-to-date, and rational planning.[22] Virtually all stakeholders are actively involved, and the particular interests of private organizations and individuals and of institutions are framed in a general deliberative discourse, aiming to achieve the most satisfactory balance for everybody.[23] This is also the result of an engaged public opinion in which conservatism and vision, local and global perspective, desire for stability and openness to change are well balanced.[24] There is a well-rooted awareness of the need for smart planning and of its long-term impacts on the continuity with past and present. This affects, first and foremost, the lived "habitat." Shaped and employed mostly based on practical needs and motivations, its appearance is nonetheless aesthetically meaningful (beside being pleasant):

> The concept of "Münsterland park landscape" has become a trademark. We note that this designation means that the landscape looks like a park. The inhabitants and the visitors of this space can identify with this designation. For historical research, however, the partial notion of "park" is misleading because park systems are artifacts produced by designers who carry the fitting job title of garden "architects." This cultural landscape, on the contrary, obtained its appearance from the people who worked it. They acted on practical motives and not with aesthetic intentions, although the result is often a pleasing landscape scenery. Already starting in 1947, the then Office for the Management of the Landscape (Amt für Landespflege) of the Regional Association Westfalen-Lippe (LWL) took care of the organization

of the landscape scenery insofar as it performed the duty of promoting voluntary planting measures. In 1975 a landscape plan was introduced in North Rhine-Westphalia through the landscape law, based on which the landscape scenery could be consciously modulated and designed from a planning perspective on a large scale.[25]

One may indeed surmise that before the implementation of such institutional plan, the aesthetic quality of the landscape was merely the unintentional result of contingent actions aimed at utilitarian goals and had nothing to do with awareness and planning. In an abstract sense, the element of contingency is certainly undeniable, but it does not contradict my point about awareness and planning. On the contrary, it shows how awareness and planning are not, in the case at issue, the result of an external, centralized imposition but rather are the organic, concrete offshoot of a centuries-long process of negotiation and adjustment between the human parties, and between them and their "contingent" environment. In other words, planning is here the continuation, in more (or differently) conscious terms, of processes of organization and sense-making that were already active in the "practical" arrangement of the land. The latter, let us not forget, also included fully or partly nonutilitarian elements, such as places of worship, monuments, and unique architectural highlights.[26] These were, in turn, not external or detached museum pieces but integral parts of the same community life that, partly gradually, partly abruptly, under the push of traumatic events such as World War II, started to require different (more rational? more long term?) planning practices.[27]

The aesthetic dimension, similarly to the Valleriana case, is accordingly not reserved to special, exceptional places but is found instead in the concrete appearance of the historical "work" (the word taken in its broadest sense) of a functioning community, in which the element of conflict and violence is not removed but exposed to the highest visibility in the very center of the present life of that community (St. Lambert Church's iron cages). That *memento*, certainly controversial and for many in bad taste, is not a gruesome and menacing symbol of death or laceration but quite paradoxically seems to become the pulsating core of a search for peaceful coexistence through rational dialogue and the balancing of contrasting instances. Its counterpart is the memory of the epoch-making peace, hosted in the Hall of Peace (Friedenssaal) of the Gothic town hall, just a few steps from

St. Lambert's Church. This peace, furthermore, was not just due to a winner's one-sided imposition but was the complex result of a treaty, partaken (for the standards of the time) by all stakeholders and ensuring to a reasonable extent prosperity and stability through the pursuit and recognition of a principle of autonomy, noninterference, and equality. The combined effect of these two symbols is a prosaic and sober yet positive look at both history and the future: a feeling of self-aware satisfaction that is not an expression of superficiality and disinterest but is connected with engagement and a feeling of responsibility.[28]

Just like the landscape, the external appearance of this attitude of planning reasonableness is flat, prosaic, at times possibly monotonous, but aesthetically meaningful in the organization, mapping, and planning of the habitat. Despite the centrality of religion in both the history and the present of the region, the habitat and the life of Münsterland is characterized by an implicit yet pervasive call to the prosaic immanence of the present as the dimension in which we act and based in which we should address goals and challenges, including the ones connected with transcendence. As a matter of fact, the local "metaphysics" is such that, when locals speak of *Westfälischer Himmel* (Westphalian heaven), the reference is not to any transcendent godly realm but to the sausages arranged in the area in front of the fireplace in traditional local farmhouses. These lacked a chimney, so the area was constantly covered in smoke, and hams and sausages were hung from the ceiling to dry and smoke. When a local looks to the sky, it is not "full of hanging violins" but "full of hanging hams and sausages." The German expression "jemandem hängt der Himmel voller Geigen" ("somebody's heaven is full of violins"), probably coming from late Gothic church vaults that were often painted with angels making music, means that someone is exaggeratedly happy and looking optimistically to the future. A *Westfälischer Himmel*, a look to a heaven full not of violins but of hams and sausages, perfectly sums up the metaphysics of the park landscape Münsterland.[29]

3. *HÜZÜN* AND A PROMISE OF IMMANENCE: CODA IN ISTANBUL

Napoleon reportedly said that "if the earth was a single state, Istanbul would be its capital."[30] Whether Napoleonic or not, the statement is suggestive in many respects. A capital city for 1,600 years and three empires (Roman/Byzantine, Latin, and Ottoman); the biggest and one of the very few cities in the world to extend over two continents; a major crossroads of worlds, peoples, and goods at the intersection of Europe and Asia; one of the largest and most densely populated cities in the world ... there are several reasons, more or less stereotyped, to accept the Napoleonic statement.[31] Its very name, which may trace back to the Greek *eis ten polin* ("to/in the city"), bears a promise of absoluteness. On a more elusive level, Istanbul could be the world capital because it concentrates a whole world of contradictions in its spatiotemporal landscape. Today Istanbul is a megacity with officially around 16 million inhabitants (although the unofficial number would be significantly higher) and is the biggest city of Turkey (although not its capital) as well as "the largest urban agglomeration in both Europe and the centre of the Turkic-speaking region of some 200 million peoples extending from the Aegean Sea to beyond the Caspian."[32] An endless influx of migrants, especially from rural Turkey, as well as of refugees, especially from Syria and Afghanistan, together with its size, the geographical conformation, and the political tensions create a mix that is hard to handle. On the other hand, because of its ancient and rich history, strategic position, young population, and extremely dynamic, mixed present, the city has a unique charm and attractiveness for tourism, business, and so on. These and the other contradictions (economical, political, cultural, architectural, etc.) of the city are shaped in a peculiar kind of transcendence, both spatial and temporal. In Istanbul the feeling of impermanence and precariousness or, more precisely, the feeling that the place or time we are living in is always irremediably behind us is omnipresent. This feeling is spatially and temporally concrete.

The city is ominously threatened by the possibility of heavy disasters, both natural and of human origin: "Earthquake, tsunami, flood, sea level rise," but also increasingly "limited open space, increasing number of people, gigantic urban infrastructure, old urban fabric, official plans' incapability to catch the rapid change of the city, urban expansion to the drinking water basins, buried urban streams, and instantly decided megaprojects."[33] To mention only earthquakes, the Marmara earthquake of 1999 officially caused 18,000 deaths in the area (45,000 according to scholarly estimates[34]), even though the epicenter was seventy kilometers away from Istanbul.³⁵ As for the future, "earthquake researchers predict there is a 95% chance that an earthquake of magnitude 7.0 or stronger will strike the city within the next 70 years. An earthquake of that strength would heavily damage or destroy an estimated 194,000 buildings, according to the latest version of Istanbul's Earthquake Master Plan, published in 2018. That would leave more than 10% of Istanbul's 15 million residents homeless."³⁶ Add overpopulation, old buildings, poor roads and escape plans, and traffic congestion to this, and you have a picture of its vulnerability.³⁷

The feeling of impermanence, however, is not only due to the awareness of natural risks. In Istanbul, a typical form of "habitat," which had to be built to accommodate a massive number of rural migrants in the 1970s, is the *gecekondu*, literally meaning "put up overnight" (normally translated as shack, shanty, or squatter house), conveying precarity in the very word—as well as, of course, in the constructions themselves. In the attempt to erase the *gecekondu* form of habitat from space and time, in recent years Istanbul has undergone a traumatic restructuring process, partly ideologically and politically motivated, with heavy socioeconomic costs.³⁸ Megaprojects

FIGURE 6.5. Savage urbanization in Istanbul, Turkey. Photo by Mostafameraji, March 2020. Reprinted from Wikimedia Commons.

are everywhere, and even the craziest-looking ones tend to become a reality.[39] This contributes to the feeling of spatial contingency: this specific area looks like this today, but tomorrow or in a month it will be unidentifiable. Transformations, both material and ideal, are very rapid in Istanbul and seem to make a stark contrast with the political and moral conservatism of the ruling classes.

The city itself is fast, despite the traffic jams and the huge distances, and it conveys an exhilarating vibe that accelerates and distorts the rhythm of time.[40] There are no empty times and there are no empty spaces in the always-alert concrete jungle. This, on the one hand, can easily lead to a feeling of oppression and airlessness. On the other hand, it also arouses the feeling of transcendence I mentioned. The disproportion between the individual and the city is, from every point of view, so abysmal that individual resilience presupposes a capacity for transcendence. I do not mean escapism, even though that is sometimes part of it. I mean the awareness that this disproportion is the vertigo of a city that, for good or bad, is living in the future rather than in the past or present. To be sure, it is not the utopic future of imaginary futuristic cities but a much more uncertain and messier one where anything can happen, and it will not necessarily be for the better, although the fatalistic *inshallahs* of the Istanbulites try to keep the worse at bay. The city landscape fully interprets and expresses that uncertainty and messiness and enables its inhabitants to see it from a distance and, hence, to transcend it. In this transcendence, in the feeling of impermanence of everything and of a rupture between temporal rhythms, is rooted a peculiarly Istanbulite form of melancholy, which Nobel laureate Orhan Pamuk has captured in the term *hüzün*.[41]

The word comes from the Arabic and is used in the Qur'an, where, as in modern Turkish, it stands for, in its most general sense, the melancholy (we may probably say the "blues") associated with "a feeling of deep spiritual loss," of insuperable distance and separation.[42] However, as Pamuk shows, hüzün negates life as much as it affirms it insofar as it is not the desperate melancholy of individual torment but rather a collective feeling, a deep sadness connected with a hope generated by its being shared. Again, this is also because hüzün is not just an immaterial but a very material, embodied feeling, directly connected with landscape, as the verse of Turkish journalist and writer Ahmet Rasim, used as the epigraph of Pamuk's *Istanbul*, boldly states: "The beauty of a landscape resides in its *hüzün*." Istanbul's landscape is one of impermanence and vulnerability, both of the city and of the people moving through it, and hüzün, I suggest, is connected with a multilayered impossibility to adjust to the present dimension and with being caught up in a permanent transcendence.

This feeling and this state are in turn all too well reflected in a temporal-historical and spatial-transportational disharmony. The relationship of the city with its past is extremely contradictory, and this is even more so for the non-Muslim past and heritage, which cannot be erased or dismissed without destroying the history of the city, yet is in most cases just cynically appropriated and repurposed.[43] On the one hand, chauvinist pride for history and traditions is unmitigated. On the other hand, the spatial traces of that history are, with a few extraordinary and showcased exceptions, often perceived and treated more like a hindrance than a heritage or an asset. Historical palaces are precipitously turned into shiny kitsch shopping malls, entire traditional or multicultural neighborhoods bulldozed and rebuilt to make room for (often unsold) luxury apartments or parking lots, the few parks or forests left are razed to accommodate airports, highways, and bridges. One does not need to be a fanatic of the purist-preservationist point of view or to reject the acknowledgment that traumatic interventions may be sometimes necessary given the exceptional conditions of Istanbul. Still, the rapidity and, one may say, annoyance, with which preoccupations regarding history, heritage, environment, or even public safety are dispensed with in Istanbul, and the way this seems to contrast with a nationalistic and communitarian sense of belonging is truly striking. The material common denominator is probably a strongman, macho-populist conception of politics and society, in which the automatic brutal repression of dissent seems to be the key to success, even when further negotiations are needed.[44] The conflictual, curt, uncompromising handling of urban landscape concerns as well as the crucial importance of politics related to the latter emerged most prominently in the 2013 Gezi Park protests.[45] They started as a peaceful sit-in of environmentalists protesting against the planned conversion of a small, unassuming yet cherished park in the central business and leisure area of Taksim Square and, after violent police repression, turned into a countrywide, weeks-long radical protest that can be considered a turning point in recent Turkish history. The disharmony, the contradictions, the conflict about the temporalized space or spatialized time of Istanbul are, I argue, a symptom of the burden of transcendence, the structurally being out of place and out of time imposed by the city onto its inhabitants and vice versa.[46] The amorphous concrete crawls and expands shapelessly, like an "oil stain" covering everything and leaving no empty space or empty time, as if afraid that emptiness may urge pause, reflection, consideration of the road traveled and the one to come.[47] An empty space or time is necessary to feel and know the landscape in which we are: Istanbul escapes moments and places of emptiness because they seem to draw a line of immanence to its unstopping transcendence and to remind the city of its vulnerabilities.

And still, completion through emptiness finds its way, not so much, I would say, in the pretentious contemplative points of the breath-taking rooftop terraces or a Bosporus *yalı* restaurant or club but rather in the very middle of the sea, the element from which the city seems to retract, scared of the void it represents. The sea, though, gives the city its unique identity, separating not only parts of it but two entire continents, and at the same time connecting them. The connection takes concrete shape in the myriad ferries crossing the strait and constituting a beloved (and efficient) mean of transportation for hundreds of thousands of people every day. And not only transportation because Istanbul ferry trips are also a place for leisure, for art, for socialization, for a break from transcendence. Despite being confined to a relatively small space, unlike other means of transportation, people in ferries can walk around, move from inside to outside or vice versa, order and consume food (mostly toasts or *simit*[48]) and drinks (cold drinks in the summer, *sahlep* in winter, black tea year-round[49]), feed the flocks of noisy seagulls that follow the ship, chat comfortably or just enjoy the wonderful changing views, and even perform/watch little music or theater shows by street artists, or smoke outside (forbidden, of course!). Despite their movement, ferries offer a place of rest and a break as well as probably the best, or at least the most encompassing, view of the urban landscape, not from an artificially separated space and time (such as a rooftop observation deck) but from the very heart of its geography and rhythm. Ferries are probably the only places (or nonplaces) in Istanbul where one can feel synchronized with the city: temporarily spared from its voracious vibe and yet not removed from its movement but fully part of it. They are also one of the few perspectives from which the city jungle looks less menacing and monstrous, and beautiful and reconciled instead; this beauty is accessible

FIGURE 6.6. Istanbul from the ferry, with the bridge connecting Europe (*left*) and Asia (*right*) in the back. Photo by author.

to (almost) everybody, thus temporarily leveling out all socioeconomic inequalities.

For all these reasons, ferries can be seen as the counterpart to, yet not the negation of, the huge "oil stain" concrete sprawl. To the latter they confer organization, tractability, visibility, and unity—in one word: sense. They provide a respite, a promise of immanence, that is not, however, separated from the city's urge of transcendence but deeply entwined with it. Their crossings, leaving white wakes in the highly polluted seawater, are indeed motivated by utilitarian reasons and essential to the city life, yet they act as aesthetic vectors and coordinates of sense in an otherwise illegible, annihilating chaos. A space that is apparently void and only "useful" (for transportation, fishing, military purposes)—that is, a nonplace—becomes a counterpart to the suffocating fullness of space and time of the city, overturning a naive gaze: the unforgiving fullness of the city is devoid of legible meanings and coordinates, which are instead conveyed and fulfilled by a ferry trip through its empty spaces. This is but one of the contradictions of Istanbul's landscape, which is usually amazing and unforgettable for tourists, often harsh yet proudly reclaimed by residents from all walks of life, and certainly unique in its spatially alive combination/contradiction of forgetfulness/exaltation of the past, melancholy/struggle of the present, and hard-edged/shapeless transcendence into the future.

CONCLUSION

"How can an aesthetics of landscape contribute to addressing the environmental crisis? How can 'landscape' help to reorient aesthetics, and how can, vice versa, aesthetics help to reorient landscape studies so that both fields can make meaningful contributions to pressing societal questions by opening new perspectives and inviting new ways of thinking and, ultimately, living?" If this book could even just begin to unravel such questions (in the excellent formulation I have borrowed from an anonymous reviewer) with an original perspective reclaiming the value of the humanities, then it will have served its purpose. This, of course, is for the reader to decide. What I can do in these final lines is to briefly revisit some of the central junctures of the discourse offered with the dual aim of providing a recapitulation and connection of its various threads and of pointing to future research directions, even if only by contrast to what was not done, or only superficially done, in this book.

Let me start backward by asking how the "lived landscapes" of the last chapter relate to those pressing questions. One half of the answer is rather trivial, although not to be disparaged: encouraging dwelling on and elaborating one's own lived landscapes can lead to increased appreciation, sentimental attachment, and awareness and can contribute to more careful and sustainable attitudes and ways of thinking and living. The second half of the answer is less trivial. The sketches I have presented are "wholes" or "units of sense." Each of them is apparently constituted by the assemblage of multiple elements and dimensions, material/immaterial, natural/cultural, aesthetic/utilitarian, individual/collective, synchronic/diachronic, and so on. And yet this terminology is misleading. In fact, in each of them there is no assemblage and no dualism before the whole and the unity. The various elements and dimensions are there, in certain positions and with certain emphases, as knots in a web woven around a chosen principle of meaning and order. Other principles could be chosen by other individuals or by myself at different times. But the point is that when we talk of landscapes, the suggested stratification always comes before the strata and their components. This is what distinguishes "landscape" from "environment" and "territory": in the latter two cases, a complete and adequate enumeration of the elements/layers to be considered—that is, their sum—can be said to constitute the whole that is sought. A landscape simply cannot be described by listing its components, whether material or immaterial: it needs to be *experienced* as a whole. Its unifying principle—call it "sense" or "character" or "atmosphere" or "genius loci" or "mood"—can only be experienced in these constituents, but the latter, in the linguistic game of landscapes, can only be experienced as constituents of a landscape in virtue of its unity. The co-belonging of material setting and interpretation, or of natural elements and spiritual tune, or of the thing and its representation, is what we try to get at when we play the linguistic game of landscapes. My three sketches have, in all brevity, pursued units of meaning rather than focusing on constituents and, thus, hopefully provided a sense of "fulfillment" to the preceding threads.

Chapter 5 critically discusses landscape character as a principle of unity, pointing out the limitations of one-sided objectivism and defending a more complex, holistic view, which also serves as an applied recapitulation of the framework advanced in the book. Chapters 3 and 4, still working backward, provide some broader patterns of development of the framework in close dialogue with more or less pressing critical challenges of our time. Finally, chapters 1 and 2, together with the prologue, design the space, rules, ambitions, and limitations of the theoretical core of the discourse, namely the landscape + aesthetics matrix.

What happens between the introduction and the three sketches, then, is the construction of the theoretical framework and the emergence of some

CONCLUSION

concrete patterns aimed at rearticulating and negotiating the discourses of crisis from which I started. The core idea of this attempt is to reframe the intimate yet controversial relationship between landscape and aesthetics by reframing the two terms of the relationship and vice versa. The search for and institution of principles of unity inherent in landscapes has to do with aesthetics as a modality and vector of human experience in its fullness. The idea of a guiding function of aesthetics pervades my entire argument, from the collocation of landscapes as condensations of (Kantian) habitats; to the defining features of the concept and linguistic game of landscapes, to the (Deweyan) proposal of "landscapes as experience"; to art, interpretation, and "non-aesthetic" matters; to the specific case of landscape character assessment. The idea is that the overarching principle of unity and the holistic character of landscapes are given some definition and structure by being framed aesthetically, whereas different approaches guided by other principles of unity would remain too sectorial, focusing on the constituents as such rather than on the preceding unity, thus failing a full appreciation of the potential of landscapes. Conversely, these aesthetics-led explorations of landscape turn out to be landscape-led explorations of aesthetics, where the central question is what would a philosophical aesthetics look like whose primary concern is landscape as opposed to "traditional" aesthetics, which has largely ignored the concept?

Aesthetics gives *some* definition to landscape. I have proposed some explanations of landscape and related matters, but I have never offered a precise definition, avoiding as much as possible an essentialist approach. I believe that several definitions are possible, depending on the focus or objectives pursued. In any case, any definition of landscape must not only take into account the aesthetic dimension as one of many dimensions but also be able to organize itself around an aesthetic core, even if its concerns are not primarily aesthetic in nature, as it is the case of the European Landscape Convention. The framework I propose fits in quite well with the latter's definition, despite—or perhaps because of—the absence of an engagement with aesthetics in the latter. Of course, the very reference to perception as well as to the interaction between the natural and the human ultimately rests on some assumptions in the domain of aesthetics, so I hope that research such as that undertaken here can be of use in articulating such a complex (despite its brevity and apparent simplicity) definition in order to deal with specific instances, whether theoretical or practical, of

CONCLUSION

the challenges from which I have taken my cue and which are central to the ELC.

Let us then return to those starting crisis discourses. The most general sense I am concerned with is the ecological one, in the multiplicity of its actually and potentially catastrophic implications. Within this argumentatively inescapable framework, I argued that not only a change of paradigm but also a new paradigm for change are needed. I placed the concept of landscape at the center of this new paradigm, with the aim to liberate its full potential, which in my view remains severely underutilized and underappreciated due to a series of limitations or even misunderstandings usually associated with the concept itself. I have therefore redirected the discourses of crisis to landscape itself, making it both the agent and the addressee of that discourse: if landscape is to liberate its potential to deal with ongoing pressing challenges, then it must both operate change and be subject to it. This duplicity calls for a lateral approach to landscape that eschews essentialist definitions and disciplinary reclamations. The proposed alignment with aesthetics should not be seen, then, as a disciplinary reclamation but as a critical, performative move that requires significant shifts within aesthetics itself. To put it bluntly, starting from the marginality of aesthetics in landscape studies and that of landscape in aesthetics, my attempt has been to reclaim the centrality of both terms in their connection. The resulting framework is, to put it again bluntly, the conceptual matrix that this book advances to reframe change, although the term *reframe* inevitably suggests dualism, distance, and ocularcentrism, whereas my framework opts for holism, interaction, and immersion. More precisely, the proposal is to locate the Deweyan interaction of environment and (human) organism in the matrix of landscape + aesthetics, with the resulting focus on the primacy of the interaction rather than the separate terms.

The ecological crisis, then, is not thematized as an independent concept because it is not conceived as an issue to be dealt with in the book but as a term to be negotiated and reframed from within the construction of the proposed matrix rather than being presupposed by it. In fact, following the general pragmatist orientation, such a reframing proposal does not really pursue an essence or a truth (or even several) but a change in our experience, attitudes, and practices. Such a multiplicity of orientations, captured by the intentionally vague term of *engaged ecology* and interweaving the

CONCLUSION

theoretical and the practical, does not only require a change of the respective specific paradigms. Instead, as I have argued, the change of paradigm takes the form of a new paradigm for change that is immersed in and integral to dynamism and impermanence rather than seeking a Cartesian *fundamentum inconcussum*, an unshakable foundation supposedly constituting the "normal," permanent, stable perspective from which the crisis can be addressed as something else, something external. Instead, this new paradigm for change, as a matrix, engenders regional paradigm shifts along multiple patterns that are only selectively addressed in the book. Hence the abandonment of transcendentalism and intentionalism in interpretation; hence the direction for art to be sought in gardening and new forms of mapping rather than (or at least alongside) traditional landscape painting; hence the indivisibility of space and time in landscape; hence the emphasis on conceptual, practical, political and infrastructural ephemerality; hence the postenvironmentalist attempt to move "beyond the modern landscape" and beyond established dichotomies such as migration versus settledness, local versus global, insider versus outsider; hence the outline of a "radical" (if only for its Wittgensteinian tone) pedagogy revolving around enskilment, and of a pragmatic, aesthetically driven interdisciplinarity. Hence, too, the development of a model of landscape character and its assessment that reclaims the role of experience and aesthetics not in spite of but *because of* their instability and inability to make a fully quantifiable, "professional," "auditable" contribution. In short, crisis is not addressed as such because the kind of change I am interested in first requires a new paradigm, that of an engaged ecology, to become visible, both as an overall concept and in its concrete patterns.

As is so often the case, this conclusion might give the impression of a rhetorically closed argument. On the contrary, there is very little in this book that even the most charitable reader, and even by the rather loose standards of the humanities in terms of finished jobs, could regard as finished. In a more classical philosophy book, this would probably have disturbed me in the first place, as the author. Here, however, the openness is not only a sign of the intention to continue this research and the hope to receive challenging input from readers. It is also, and more importantly, a constraint inherent in the subject itself, a constraint I have tried to embrace rather than fight or dominate.

NOTES

PROLOGUE

1. This is just one of the reasons why the main goal of this book is not a historical one, although I will refer to some important classics in the philosophy of landscape.
2. For a broader discussion of the topics addressed in this and the next section, see Alberto L. Siani, "Spazi kantiani," *Aesthetica Preprint* 118 (2021): 177–88.
3. See Hannah Arendt, *Lectures on Kant's Political Philosophy*, ed. Rudolf Beiner (Chicago: University of Chicago Press, 1989), 44. Kant's hometown is a fascinating case study in its own right. Founded by the Teutonic Knights during the Northern Crusades, this medieval city situated on the Baltic Sea later became an important cultural center and port. For a long time, it was the easternmost large city in Germany until World War II, when it suffered heavy bombing and eventually came under Soviet control. Renamed Kaliningrad and following reconstruction efforts, the city is now the administrative center of the namesake Russian exclave. Kaliningrad is strategically located, bordering Lithuania to the north and Poland to the south, and, with a population of almost half a million people, serves as a logistical, military, and economic outpost for Russia.
4. Immanuel Kant, *Critique of Pure Reason*, ed. and trans. Paul Guyer and Allen W. Wood (Cambridge: Cambridge University Press, 1998), 339. For original takes on Kant's sea and navigation metaphors, see also Cinzia Ferrini, "The Land of Truth of the Understanding and the Threatening Waters of Reason: Maritime Sources for a Kantian Metaphor," *Esercizi Filosofici* 8, no. 2 (2013): 53–70; and Alessandra Bonazzi, "Il piano dell'oceano: James Cook e Immanuel Kant," *Semestrale di studi e ricerche di geografia* 30, no. 2 (2018): 55–67.
5. On critically mapping the limits and possibilities of human knowledge, see also Alberto L. Siani, "I limiti dell'umano: Osservazioni su Kant e l'intuizione intellettuale," *Studi Kantiani* 23 (2010): 57–75.

6. Immanuel Kant, *Critique of the Power of Judgment*, ed. Paul Guyer, trans. Paul Guyer and Eric Matthews (Cambridge: Cambridge University Press, 2000), 61. On Kant's consistency, see, e.g., Werner Euler, *Natur und Freiheit: Kommentar zu den Einleitungen in Kants »Kritik der Urteilskraft«* (Hamburg: Meiner, 2018), 402n52. I refer to this commentary for a thorough interpretation of the passages discussed here.
7. Kant, *Critique of the Power of Judgment*, 61.
8. Kant, *Critique of the Power of Judgment*, 61–62.
9. Kant, *Critique of the Power of Judgment*, 62.
10. Kant, *Critique of the Power of Judgment*, 62, trans. modified: I employ *habitat* instead of *residence* following the translation by Rudolf A. Makkreel, "Kant and the Need for Orientational and Contextual Thinking: Applying Reflective Judgement to Aesthetics and to the Comprehension of Human Life," *Kantian Review* 26, no. 1 (2020): 60.
11. Kant, *Critique of the Power of Judgment*, 62.
12. See Makkreel, "Kant and the Need for Orientational and Contextual Thinking," 60.
13. Moved, respectively, by the questions: "What can I know?" (*Critique of Pure Reason*) and "What should I do?" (*Critique of Practical Reason*), to both of which a stable and objective answer can be offered that relates, respectively, to nature and freedom, thus fully covering the two "domains" of philosophy.
14. Leonardo Amoroso, "Kant e il problema di una regola delle regole," *Nuova civiltà delle macchine* 3, no. 3–4 (1985): 7.
15. On the former case: "It turned out, of course, that although we had in mind a tower that would reach the heavens, the supply of materials sufficed only for a dwelling [*Wohnhause*] that was just roomy enough for our business on the plane of experience and high enough to survey it; however, that bold undertaking had to fail from lack of material, not to mention the confusion of languages that unavoidably divided the workers over the plan and dispersed them throughout the world, leaving each to build on his own according to his own design." Kant, *Critique of Pure Reason*, 627. On the latter case: "Skepticism is a resting place for human reason, which can reflect upon its dogmatic peregrination and make a survey of the region in which it finds itself in order to be able to choose its path in the future with greater certainty, but it is not a dwelling-place for permanent residence [*ein Wohnplatz zum beständigen Aufenthalte*]." Kant, *Critique of Pure Reason*, 654.
16. "Kant deploys a formidable effort to go beyond the tautological universality of the 'experience *überhaupt*' thematized by the first *Critique*, without however abandoning the transcendental level: the third *Critique* remains in it by framing the problem of an empirical realm differentiated in itself as the problem of a *system* of the empirical and presenting the *a priori* principle that is the condition of the possibility of this system." Amoroso, "Kant e il problema di una regola delle regole," 7.
17. Makkreel, "Kant and the Need for Orientational and Contextual Thinking," 60.
18. See Amoroso, "Kant e il problema di una regola delle regole," 7.
19. For a broader discussion, see Alberto L. Siani, "Kants ästhetische Urteilskraft als nicht-ästhetisches Wissen und das Ende des modernen Subjekts," in *Ästhetisches*

Wissen, ed. Christoph Asmuth and Peter Remmers (Berlin: De Gruyter, 2015), 95–110.
20. "Domains and habitats are both parts of the territory of human experience and fields can be said to border on its edges. The local region in which we feel at home counts as a habitat. Similarly, what is obscurely felt in inner sense can be regarded as a private habitat. However, not all feelings are so delimited in scope. Indeed, the feelings aroused by beauty can transpose us outside ourselves." Makkreel, "Kant and the Need for Orientational and Contextual Thinking," 62.
21. Makkreel, "Kant and the Need for Orientational and Contextual Thinking," 61.
22. See, e.g., Kant, *Critique of the Power of Judgment*, 57. As we saw, philosophy proper is for Kant either theoretical or practical: only the domains of knowledge and morals are the strictly legitimate spaces of philosophy. In this sense, habitats are, strictly speaking, philosophical nonplaces connecting philosophical places (like a bridge connecting two lands without being a place in either of them). This corresponds to the fact that, whereas the first and the second *Critique* are propaedeutic, respectively, to a metaphysics of nature and a metaphysics of morals—that is, to the doctrinal parts of the system—this is not the case with the third *Critique*, in which "the critique serves instead of theory," and there is no space for a doctrinal-metaphysical counterpart—that is, there is no domain (58).
23. Makkreel, "Kant and the Need for Orientational and Contextual Thinking," 68.
24. The German verb *bilden* makes the point better insofar as it brings together the materiality of building things with the cultural aspect of *forming* or *educating* oneself (thus, *Bildungssystem* is the educational system). *Bilden* is also used in compound words, such as *(sich) einbilden*, that is, "to imagine," as an act that requires a construction-formation (of an image). Note that, in using the English "to build," I have this broader context in mind.
25. The image of the game and, more generally, the conclusion of this prologue are a hint to Wittgenstein, to whom I will return at the end of the next chapter and further ahead.

1. A GAME OF LANDSCAPES

1. For a concise historical and etymological outline, see Marc Antrop, "A Brief History of Landscape Research," in Howard et al., *Routledge Companion to Landscape Studies*, 1–15; and Kenneth R. Olwig, "Recovering the Substantive Nature of Landscape," *Annals of the Association of American Geographers* 86, no. 4 (1996): 630–53. Here I am not considering metaphorical uses of the word, such as "political landscape" and the like, nor the differences with corresponding terms in other languages, beginning with the Romance ones (French: *paysage*; Italian: *paesaggio*; Spanish: *paisaje*, etc.).
2. See, to begin with, Mick Atha, Peter Howard, Ian Thompson, and Emma Waterton, "Introduction. Ways of Knowing and Being with Landscapes: A Beginning," in Howard et al., *Routledge Companion to Landscape Studies*, xix–xxviii; and Gareth Doherty and Charles Waldheim, "Introduction: What Is Landscape?," in *Is Landscape . . . ? Essays on the Identity of Landscape*, ed. Gareth Doherty and Charles Waldheim, 1–8 (London: Routledge, 2016), as well as the very conception

1. A GAME OF LANDSCAPES

and articulation of the latter volume, where each chapter addresses landscapes from the angle of a possible identity with a certain practice or discipline (architecture, history, philosophy, planning, etc.).

3. I want to clarify that the adoption of this strategy does not imply an overall commitment to a pragmatist-Wittgensteinian conception of language, or in general any kind of large-scale commitment to a specific philosophy or theory of language. I am not even interested in arguing that it would be *wrong* to take an essentialist approach to the issue of landscape. I am only proposing that a pragmatist approach is more helpful in elucidating different theoretical needs and elaborating different practical responses based on the specificities of the usage context. For some useful methodological considerations, see Paul M. Keeling, "Does the Idea of Wilderness Need a Defence?," *Environmental Values* 17, no. 4 (2008): 505–19.

4. This expression too is, of course, Wittgensteinian.

5. This is not to say that the words *environment* and *territory* suggest a necessary, mutual material independence of the two entities but only that their use is construed in a semantically dualistic way. Substantially different views of environment (the "major" cognate term to *landscape*) can be and have been put forward that are less reductive and in which the human factor plays a major role, and *landscape*, on the other hand, has often been framed in a dualistic fashion. Moreover, using the terms *dualistic* and *nondualistic* is an oversimplification as most conceptions fall somewhere in between. My point is that, in both research and everyday language, *environment* semantically suggests or allows to conceive of the space and of its inhabitants as mutually independent entities, while *landscape* suggests a positioning beyond dualistic opposition. Just consider how, in common usage, if I use the word *environment* without qualification, I may or may not be including the human element, whereas if I use the word *landscape*, the human involvement is structurally already there. Rather than reforming or integrating the mainstream concept of environment, my effort here is to outline an alternative, landscape-centered concept. This in no way implies that I believe that the mainstream concept of environment cannot or should not be reformed along more complex and nondualistic lines but only that I am pursuing a different angle. It should be clear that whenever I use the term *environment* critically, as a negative counterpart to my own proposal, it is the mainstream, reductive view that I have in mind, not the concept as such.

6. Rosario Assunto, "Paesaggio, ambiente, territorio: un tentativo di precisazione concettuale," *Rassegna di architettura e urbanistica* (1980), 50.

7. Assunto, "Paesaggio, ambiente, territorio," 50.

8. Obviously, Assunto's contribution to the philosophy of landscape is not limited to this short paper and is in many respects pioneering or even visionary. Here I can only refer to his 1973 major work without discussing it: Rosario Assunto, *Il paesaggio e l'estetica* (Palermo: Novecento, 1994). It should be added that Assunto's preoccupation with landscape is not only theoretically motivated but moves from a vehement indignation for the devastation of the Italian landscape in the transition from agrarian to industrial economy, leading him to reclaim the aesthetic and historical value of natural spaces against their reduction to "environment."

1. A GAME OF LANDSCAPES

9. On landscape as a process, practice, and performance, see Atha et al., "Introduction," xxvi. On the temporalization and historization of space, see John B. Jackson, "The Word Itself," in *Discovering the Vernacular Landscape* (New Haven, Conn.: Yale University Press, 1984), 8; and Pierre Bélanger, "Is Landscape Infrastructure?," in Doherty and Waldheim, *Is Landscape . . . ?*, 214. On landscape as a relational concept, see Luisa Bonesio, *Paesaggio, identità e comunità tra locale e globale* (Milano: Mimesis, 2017), 21 (and the critical remarks by Paolo D'Angelo, *Filosofia del paesaggio* [Macerata: Quodlibet, 2014], 125); Gunhild Setten, Katrina Myrvang Brown, and Hilde Nymoen Rørtveit, "Landscape and Social Justice," in Howard et al., *Routledge Companion to Landscape Studies*, 425–26; and Kathryn Moore, "Is Landscape Philosophy?," in Doherty and Waldheim, *Is Landscape . . . ?*, 285–301. On intertwining perceiving and acting, see Atha et al., "Introduction," xxvi. On eroding the difference with the self, see Atha et al., "Introduction," xxv; and Richard Kerridge, "New Directions in the Literary Representation of Landscape," in Howard et al., *Routledge Companion to Landscape Studies*, 253–63. On renouncing ocularcentrism, see Jacky Bowring, "Navigating the Global, the Regional and the Local. Researching Globalization and Landscape," in Howard et al., *Routledge Companion to Landscape Studies*, 300. On pushing the boundaries between nature and culture, see Werner Krauss, "Postenvironmental Landscapes in the Anthropocene," in Howard et al., *Routledge Companion to Landscape Studies*, 62. On rejecting a puristic limitation to few extraordinary places, see D'Angelo, *Filosofia del paesaggio*; and Catharine Ward Thompson, "Landscape Perception and Environmental Psychology," in Howard et al., *Routledge Companion to Landscape Studies*, 19–38.

10. Thus, Assunto already overcomes the purely visual and scenic characterization of landscapes toward a substantive, historical, identity-performing one: "Landscape is not only a representation or perception of a subject facing it, but, way more essentially and primarily, a unitary form of the territory obtained by a culture," and "anticipating, in the Seventies, what would in later years become a critical and theoretical acquisition of planning culture, . . . Assunto operated that fundamental change in the concept of landscape from perception and representation as an aesthetic sight to a community's place of life, that is, as the place of our life: not a subjective image and a sentimental projection, but a complex meaning, guaranteeing memory and identity." Bonesio, *Paesaggio, identità e comunità tra locale e globale*, 100–102.

11. This also means that, unlike the abstract environment, landscape is always a landscape "from here," situated and significant for someone, and not existing as a general term. This has important aesthetic implications, as we will see. For now, we may say that the concept of landscape can be put forward as a bulwark against extremized versions of the "view from nowhere" concept as formulated by Thomas Nagel, *The View from Nowhere* (Oxford: Oxford University Press, 1986). Of course, Nagel's own argument stresses the elements of paradox and irreconcilability between an ideal, fully objective view from nowhere and the fact of our subjective situatedness. I have developed these and related issues by connecting them to a reading of Cormac McCarthy's novels *Suttree* and *The Road* in Alberto L. Siani, "Nowhere Between River and Road: A Nagelian Reading of *Suttree* and *The Road*," in *Philosophical Approaches to Cormac McCarthy. Beyond*

1. A GAME OF LANDSCAPES

Reckoning, ed. Chris Eagle (London: Routledge, 2017), 202–19, to which I refer also for a discussion of the attempt to make sense of our habitats when all meanings are lost.

12. See the definition proposed by Jackson, "The Word Itself," 8, of *landscape* as "a composition of man-made or man-modified spaces to serve as infrastructure or background for our collective existence; and if *background* seems inappropriately modest we should remember that in our modern use of the word it means that which underscores not only our identity and presence, but also our history." I return to this definition in chapter 4.1.4.
13. I return to the problem of relativism in chapter 2.6.
14. Isis Brook, "Aesthetic Appreciation of Landscape," in Howard et al., *Routledge Companion to Landscape Studies*, 40.
15. See the example by Brook, "Aesthetic Appreciation of Landscape," 40.
16. I am leaving aside, for now, historical variability, which would further complicate the matter: "virtual" or "urban" landscapes, for example, are clearly more and more accepted meanings today than they were, say, twenty or thirty years ago, whereas *landscape* in the sense of a painting is certainly less used today than it was in the seventeenth century. Particularly representative of the historical variability of the appreciation of nature in general is the case of the "dramatic changes [that] took place between the end of the seventeenth century and the beginning of the eighteenth century in people's attitudes and their aesthetic taste regarding mountains," which from horrid and unruly desolations came to be appreciated as sublime, romantic, awe-inspiring. Yuriko Saito, "Is There a Correct Aesthetic Appreciation of Nature?," *Journal of Aesthetic Education* 18, no. 4 (1984): 39.
17. Brook, "Aesthetic Appreciation of Landscape," 40. See also Denis Cosgrove, "Modernity, Community and the Landscape Idea," *Journal of Material Culture* 11 (2006): 50: "Landscapes have an unquestionably material presence, yet they come into being only at the moment of their apprehension by an external observer, and thus have a complex poetics and politics. These characteristics make landscape frustrating for those preoccupied with conceptual clarity and definitional exactitude."
18. Besides Kant, here I am drawing also on Kottman's concept of sense-making: "By 'sense-making,' I mean a satisfying explanation of some phenomenon or another, or a way of justifying actions and practices, or giving an account of something or someone." Paul A. Kottman, *Love as Human Freedom* (Stanford, Calif.: Stanford University Press, 2017), 4.
19. This is, of course, just a schematic juxtaposition. On this topic, see Don Gifford, "The Touch of Landscape," in *Landscape, Natural Beauty and the Arts*, ed. Salim Kemal and Ivan Gaskell (Cambridge: Cambridge University Press, 1993), 127–38. See also D'Angelo, *Filosofia del paesaggio*, 30.
20. Brook, "Aesthetic Appreciation of Landscape," 48.
21. I think that, despite the diverging aims, this main feature of landscapes is already present in the poignant definition attributed to Alexander von Humboldt: "Landschaft ist das Totalcharakter einer Erdgegend" ("Landscape is the total character of a region of the earth"). The definition is quoted in Antrop, "A Brief History of Landscape Research," 5, who comments: "This definition implies that regional

1. A GAME OF LANDSCAPES

diversification is expressed by the landscape and that landscape should be considered as a holistic phenomenon that is perceived by humans."

22. I would like to thank Paul Kottman for a stimulating conversation we had in Pisa, among others, about the ultimate "residuality" of nature, both from a Kantian perspective and in culture and arts, especially in the instance of the "stone-letter" of the Japanese drama movie *Departures*. I could not directly include those topics or the movie in this book, but they have stayed at the back of my mind, and I am planning to return to them elsewhere.

23. For an original exploration of "performative landscapes" from the point of view of contemporary art (a topic to which I return in chapter 3), see Peter J. Schneemann, "Performative Landscapes: A Paradigm for Mediating the Ecological Imperative?," in *Landscape and Earth in Early Modernity. Picturing Unruly Nature*, ed. Christine Göttler and Mia Mochizuki (Amsterdam: Amsterdam University Press, 2023), 393–414.

24. See also below, chapter 2, section 5.

25. D'Angelo, *Filosofia del paesaggio*, 125.

26. Including not only the modern scientific worldview but also the very Kantian systematic taxonomy (and philosophical system in general) from which I took my cues.

27. See the first chapter of Nicola Perullo, *Estetica ecologica: Percepire saggio, vivere corrispondente* (Milano: Mimesis, 2019).

28. Alastair Bonnett, *Unruly Places: Lost Spaces, Secret Cities, and Other Inscrutable Geographies* (Boston: Houghton Mifflin Harcourt, 2014), "Bir Tawil." The reference is to Bir Tawil, "a 795-squaremile trapezoid of rocky desert between Sudan and Egypt.... It is not just a no man's land; it is actively spurned. It also appears to be the only place on the planet that is both habitable and unclaimed." In the same book, see also the instance of "Baarle-Nassau and Baarle-Hertog," "two villages that sit within and alongside each other. There are 22 bits of Belgium (Baarle-Hertog, population 2,306) scattered in odd profusion inside the Netherlands, within and around the Dutch town of Baarle-Nassau (population 6,668), and 8 parts of Baarle-Nassau that sit inside these Belgic fragments" and Bonnett's observations on borders as

> bureaucratic fault lines, imperious and unfriendly. It's not surprising that so many look forward to a world without borders. Their existence is routinely critiqued by academic geographers who cast them as hostile acts of exclusion. And yet where, in a borderless world, could we escape to? Where would it be worth going? ... The likelihood of a world without borders is not high, and when we think of that world—a utopia of sameness where there is no possibility of escape—we might begin to wonder if it is an attractive destination. Baarle illustrates how creating places and creating borders are interwoven. It also provides an example of the pleasure of borders, hints at their playful and absurd side, and shows us how, in a topophobic world, the fascination of the border can be rediscovered and humanized.

29. The strength and flexibility of landscapes also lies in their acting as an overarching umbrella concept for other "-scape" terms. Think for example of *cityscape*:

this is not just a neutral connection of the terms *city* and *scape* but a term that semantically functions only through the mediation of the concept of *landscape*.
30. See below, chapter 4, section 1.5.
31. I discuss Wittgenstein only insofar as I think it is conducive to my topic, without any claim to exegetical exhaustivity or depth regarding the controversial themes analyzed.
32. Ludwig Wittgenstein, "Remarks on Frazer's *The Golden Bough*," in *The Mythology in Our Language. Remarks on Frazer's Golden Bough*, ed. Giovanni Da Col and Stephan Palmié, trans. Stephan Palmié (Chicago: HAU Books, 2018), 54.
33. The point about the kind of reasons and explanations we should look for famously underlies Wittgenstein's harsh criticism of Frazer. See Michael Puett, "Wittgenstein on Frazer," in *The Mythology in Our Language. Remarks on Frazer's Golden Bough*, ed. Giovanni Da Col and Stephan Palmié (Chicago: HAU Books, 2018), 145.
34. This seems to be consistent, among others, with the controversial *topos* of the landscapes and nature-hating peasant or shepherd, causing puzzlement and irony in landscapes and nature-seeking artists, from Petrarch to Wilde and Cézanne. People for whom a certain landscape is the place of hard daily work and a source of sustenance, or also just an ordinary prosaic view—that is, people who are less distanced from it are accordingly less likely to appreciate it. I return to this point for a more nuanced discussion at the end of chapter 2 (section 6) as well as in the discussion of the insider/outsider oppositional couple in chapter 4 (section 3.2).
35. See Knut Christian Myhre, "Deep Pragmatism," in *The Mythology in Our Language. Remarks on Frazer's Golden Bough*, ed. Giovanni Da Col and Stephan Palmié (Chicago: HAU Books, 2018), 99.
36. Myhre, "Deep Pragmatism," 99.
37. Ludwig Wittgenstein, *Philosophical Investigations*, ed. Peter Michael Stephan Hacker and Joachim Schulte, trans. Gertrude Elizabeth Margaret Anscombe, Peter Michael Stephan Hacker, and Joachim Schulte (Chichester, UK: Wiley-Blackwell, 2009), 15, 11. "A form of life is a culture or social formation, the totality of communal activities into which language-games are embedded." Hans-Johann Glock, *A Wittgenstein Dictionary* (Chichester, UK: Wiley-Blackwell, 1996), 125.
38. This is, interestingly for us, particularly true of aesthetic expressions: "The words we call expressions of aesthetic judgement play a very complicated role, but a very definite role, in what we call a culture of a period. To describe their use or to describe what you mean by a cultured taste, you have to describe a culture. . . . What we now call a cultured taste perhaps didn't exist in the Middle Ages. An entirely different game is played in different ages. . . . What belongs to a language game is a whole culture." Ludwig Wittgenstein, "Lectures on Aesthetics," in *Lectures and Conversations on Aesthetics, Psychology and Religious Belief*, ed. Cyril Barrett (Berkeley: University of California Press, 1967), 8.
39. Myhre, "Deep Pragmatism," 101. See also Pierluigi Biancini, "Language as Environment: An Ecological Approach to Wittgenstein's Form of Life," in *Papers of the 32nd International Wittgenstein Symposium*, ed. Volker A. Munz, Klaus Puhl,

1. A GAME OF LANDSCAPES

and Joseph Wang (Kirchberg am Wechsel: Austrian Ludwig Wittgenstein Society, 2009), 57: "The general conclusion I would reach is that the term *Lebensform* works in the direction of destroying the dualism language-world."
40. Wittgenstein, *Philosophical Investigations*, 8.
41. A discussion of the relationship between the notion of *niche* and that of *landscape* presented here would take us too far. In principle, *landscape* is a specific "dense" expression or historically given form of condensation of the human niche. In using the latter term, I refer mainly to Giovanni Matteucci, *Estetica e natura umana: La mente estesa tra percezione, emozione ed espressione* (Roma: Carocci, 2019), e.g., 13–14; and Roberta Dreon, *Human Landscapes. Contributions to a Pragmatist Anthropology* (Albany: State University of New York Press, 2022), 88, which derives from pragmatism "a picture of human sensibility as basically rooted in the dependence of organic life on a natural environment, more specifically in the dependence of human life on a highly social and cultural-linguistic environment—an environmental niche both shaping specifically human forms of life and modeled by them in a loop whose starting point cannot be traced." See also Kim Sterelny, "Minds: Extended or Scaffolded?," *Phenomenology and the Cognitive Sciences* 9, no. 4 (2010): 465–81.
42. Quoted in Myhre, "Deep Pragmatism," 101. "In the beginning was the deed" is a quote from Goethe's *Faust*, which stands in ironical opposition to the biblical "in the beginning was the word."
43. Wittgenstein, "Remarks on Frazer's *The Golden Bough*," 66. *Environment* in the last sentence is not to be taken in a merely metaphorical sense: "Wittgenstein's perspicuous survey of language-games delivers a philosophical ethnography of our *form of life*, much needed perspective in environmental education." Jeffrey A. Stickney, "Seeing Trees: Investigating Poetics of Place-Based, Aesthetic Environmental Education with Heidegger and Wittgenstein," *Journal of Philosophy of Education* 54, no. 5 (2020): 1296. In general, see the whole article for a stimulating discussion of the role Wittgenstein's philosophy can play in aesthetic environmental education: I return to this below, chapter 4, sections 4.2–3.
44. See Wittgenstein, *Philosophical Investigations*, 54, 55. See the whole paragraph: "A main source of our failure to understand is that we don't have *an overview* of the use of our words. —Our grammar is deficient in surveyability. A surveyable representation produces precisely that kind of understanding which consists in 'seeing connections.' Hence the importance of finding and inventing *intermediate links*. The concept of a surveyable representation is of fundamental significance for us. It characterizes the way we represent things, how we look at matters."
45. Wittgenstein, *Philosophical Investigations*, 56.
46. Wittgenstein, *Philosophical Investigations*, 57.
47. Wittgenstein, *Philosophical Investigations*, 3 (my emphasis).
48. "Along with Wittgenstein's equation between meaning and use, the result is that words and notions neither refer to nor index objects and practices, but surround, contain, and entail activities that entangle and engage things in specific language-games. Phrased differently, language-games gather up objects in multiple ways . . . and hence involve a plethora of world-relations." Myhre, "Deep Pragmatism," 102.

2. LANDSCAPE AND AESTHETICS

1. See Kenneth R. Olwig, "Recovering the Substantive Nature of Landscape," *Annals of the Association of American Geographers* 86, no. 4 (1996): 630; and Vittoria Di Palma, "Is Landscape Painting?," in *Is Landscape . . . ? Essays on the Identity of Landscape*, ed. Gareth Doherty and Charles Waldheim (London: Routledge, 2016), 48.
2. John B. Jackson, "The Word Itself," in *Discovering the Vernacular Landscape* (New Haven, Conn.: Yale University Press, 1984), 8.
3. Olwig, "Recovering the Substantive Nature of Landscape," 630–31.
4. See Denis Cosgrove, "Prospect, Perspective and the Evolution of the Landscape Idea," *Transactions of the Institute of British Geographers* 10, no. 1 (1985): 45–62.
5. See James Corner, "Eidetic Operations and New Landscapes," in *Recovering Landscape: Essays in Contemporary Landscape Architecture*, ed. James Corner (New York: Princeton Architectural Press, 1999), 152–69.
6. See William J. T. Mitchell, "Imperial Landscape," in *Landscape and Power*, ed. William J. T. Mitchell (Chicago: University of Chicago Press, 2002), 5–34.
7. Mick Atha, Peter Howard, Ian Thompson, and Emma Waterton, "Introduction: Ways of Knowing and Being with Landscapes: A Beginning," in *The Routledge Companion to Landscape Studies*, ed. Peter Howard, Ian Thompson, Emma Waterton, and Mick Atha (London: Routledge, 2019), xxiii–xxviii.
8. On the European Landscape Convention, see, however, chapter 4, section 3.1.
9. On the neglect of natural beauty, see the classic Ronald W. Hepburn, "Contemporary Aesthetics and the Neglect of Natural Beauty," in *British Analytical Philosophy*, ed. Bernard Williams and Alan Montefiore (London: Routledge and Kegan Paul, 1966), 285–310.
10. See Steven C. Bourassa, "Toward a Theory of Landscape Aesthetics," *Landscape and Urban Planning* 15, no. 3-4 (1988): 241–52; and Alberto L. Siani, "Landscape Aesthetics," *International Lexicon of Aesthetics* (Spring 2022), https://lexicon.mimesisjournals.com/international_lexicon_of_aesthetics_item_detail.php?item_id=124.
11. This is evident even by simply googling "landscape" or by searching related pages, groups, or profiles on Facebook, Instagram, and so on.
12. The extent and significance of Kant's theory of aesthetic disinterestedness is of course too broad a topic to be dealt with here.
13. UNESCO, World Heritage Convention (1972), https://whc.unesco.org/en/conventiontext/. See also chapter 4, section 3.1.
14. See Luc Brisson, "Plato's Theory of Sense Perception in the Timaeus: How It Works and What It Means," *Proceedings of the Boston Area Colloquium of Ancient Philosophy* 13, no. 1 (1997): 147–76; and Immanuel Kant, *Critique of the Power of Judgment*, ed. Paul Guyer and Eric Matthews (Cambridge: Cambridge University Press, 2000), 201ff.
15. See Danijela Kambaskovic and Charles T. Wolfe, "The Senses in Philosophy and Science: From the Nobility of Sight to the Materialism of Touch," in *A Cultural History of the Senses in the Renaissance*, ed. Herman Roodenburg (London: Bloomsbury Academic, 2014), 107–25.

2. LANDSCAPE AND AESTHETICS

16. The issue of ocularcentrism, or the privileging of the visual sense, is a complex topic that requires a more extensive discussion of visual culture than what is possible here. At least, it is important to note that criticizing ocularcentrism should not lead to a rejection or devaluation of the increasingly pervasive and influential role of the visual in our lives, which has been amplified by technological advancements. Nor should it lead to the avoidance of uncomfortable visual experiences, that is, to "look away." Such an approach would be simplistic and ultimately counterproductive. Instead, the challenge is to learn to "see better," to develop a more critical and inclusive approach to seeing that acknowledges the limitations of vision, including what is intentionally or unintentionally hidden or obscured. This requires cultivating a more comprehensive and multisensory understanding of experience. For further discussion on these issues, see Alexis L. Boylan, *Visual Culture* (Cambridge, Mass.: MIT Press, 2020), especially chapter 4, which addresses visual environments, landscapes, and the Anthropocene. Additionally, see the remarks on Dewey in section 3, below, and the brief discussion of landscape as a part of visual ideology in chapter 3, section 2.2.
17. There is, so to speak, a midcult of landscapes, which is not to say, of course, that appreciating scenic views is only for the aesthetically incompetent!
18. See also Vera Vicenzotti, "On the Concept of Landscape in Landscape Urbanism," in Howard et al., *Routledge Companion to Landscape Studies*, 572.
19. As previously stated, my critical and constructive approach in this work is broadly informed by pragmatism. However, this is not the appropriate space for an in-depth historical and theoretical exploration of pragmatism and its internal distinctions. In addition to Wittgenstein (to the extent—controversial—that he can be characterized as a pragmatist), Dewey, and to a lesser extent Umberto Eco and Charles Sanders Peirce (discussed in the next chapter), I also draw inspiration from contemporary neopragmatist philosophers such as Arnold Berleant, *Living in the Landscape: Toward an Aesthetics of Environment* (Lawrence: University Press of Kansas, 1997). Berleant's book has been path-breaking in reclaiming the importance of continuity, aesthetic engagement, and the social foundations of experience. While I share many of Berleant's assumptions and objectives as well as the overall sensitivity to the topic, my framework is directly based on Dewey's philosophy both in terms of its fundamental principles and its methodological approach. My goal is, then, to connect these philosophical foundations with a broader, mostly nonphilosophical literature on landscape, a task that Berleant has not pursued to the same extent. This is why my primary philosophical groundwork is Dewey himself, and Berleant remains, despite the proximity, rather in the background. Nevertheless, his book provides an insightful discussion of various topics in this field, some of which I also address in my work.
20. Dewey is among the critics of Kant as an isolationist: see John Dewey, *Art as Experience*, ed. Jo Ann Boydston (Carbondale: Southern Illinois University Press, 1987), 257ff. Here I cannot enter the substance of Dewey's critique. In a sense, I would say that, drawing on both Kant and Dewey, I am interested in developing a point of view on aesthetics that is beyond both Kant's dualism and disinterestedness *and* Dewey's partly superficial criticism, and this point of view emerges in a paradigmatic way through the investigation of landscapes. For a more focused

2. LANDSCAPE AND AESTHETICS

discussion of Dewey in this regard, see Leonardo Amoroso, "L'estetica come filosofia dell'esperienza. Rileggendo Dewey con Garroni," in *Esperienza estetica: A partire da John Dewey*, ed. Luigi Russo (Palermo: Centro internazionale studi di estetica, 2007), 99–109; and Alberto L. Siani, "Continuando un dialogo: Amoroso e la ridefinizione deweyana dell'estetica," in *Ragione estetica ed ermeneutica del senso: Studi in memoria di Leonardo Amoroso*, ed. Alberto L. Siani (Pisa: ETS, 2022), 53–62.

21. Dewey, *Art as Experience*, 9.
22. Dewey, *Art as Experience*, 9.
23. Dewey, *Art as Experience*, 9.
24. Dewey, *Art as Experience*, 9–10.
25. Dewey, *Art as Experience*, 34.
26. See, however, the mountain simile quoted above as well as what Dewey says on natural landscapes in *Art as Experience* (206). It may also be noted that Dewey is one of the very few philosophers to feature more or less regularly in the scholarship on landscape and, more specifically, on landscape aesthetics; see, e.g., Bourassa, "Toward a Theory of Landscape Aesthetics."
27. Dewey, *Art as Experience*, 19.
28. Dewey, *Art as Experience*, 19.
29. Dewey, *Art as Experience*, 28.
30. Dewey, *Art as Experience*, 23.
31. Dewey, *Art as Experience*, 23.
32. Dewey, *Art as Experience*, 28.
33. Dewey, *Art as Experience*, 28.
34. I discuss some aspects related to the necessity of reconciliation between the useful and the aesthetic in the landscape discourse in chapter 4, section 1.4.
35. Dewey, *Art as Experience*, 25.
36. From this point of view, at least, Kant and Dewey share some common aims.
37. Dewey, *Art as Experience*, 25.
38. Dewey's anti-isolationist polemic directly involves social, political, and economic structures. While I cannot give details here, I discuss some related aspects in chapter 4.
39. See also Rita Messori, "Il ritmo performativo del paesaggio," *Studi di estetica* 49/4, no. 3 (2021): 1–16.
40. Dewey himself has an anti-isolationist and synesthetic conception of view and the eye: "While the optical apparatus may be isolated in anatomical dissection, it never *functions* in isolation. It operates in connection with the hand in reaching for things and in exploring their surface, in guiding manipulations of things, in directing locomotion. . . . This factor is so continually and so unfailingly involved in every use of the eyes that the visually experienced quality of lines cannot possibly be referred to the action of the eyes alone." Dewey, *Art as Experience*, 105–6.
41. For a similar approach in which criticism of ocularcentrism and detachment, on the one side, and expansion of the landscape notion beyond the modernist-scenic paradigm, on the other, go hand in hand, compare Berleant's "aesthetics of engagement," in Berleant, *Living in the Landscape*; and Arnold Berleant, "The Art in Knowing a Landscape," *Diogenes* 59, no. 1–2 (2012): 52–62.
42. Dewey, *Art as Experience*, 25.

2. LANDSCAPE AND AESTHETICS

43. See, from another perspective, Isis Brook, "Aesthetic Appreciation of Landscape," in Howard et al., *Routledge Companion to Landscape Studies*, 48:

> Landscape is about wholes and the aesthetic experience of landscapes requires that we consider the place—that vaguely bounded area—as a whole. We might be attracted to detail or particular features, but the feeling of the whole is our focus. Our thoughts can reach further to the context of that landscape in history and in the wider environment through many channels of information. Our thoughts can also sift the emotions, responses, impressions, and institutions that arise in order to arrive at considered aesthetic judgments, which can then be discussed and debated. However, none of this can begin before the experience itself; experience is the bedrock of the aesthetic and without it we just recycle the thoughts of others and never enter the aesthetic field.

44. Dewey, *Art as Experience*, 248–49.
45. Dewey, *Art as Experience*, 9. See also: "Art is a quality of doing and of what is done. Only outwardly, then, can it be designated by a noun substantive. Since it adheres to the manner and content of doing, it is adjectival in nature" (218).
46. Dewey, *Art as Experience*, 70–71.
47. Dewey, *Art as Experience*, 71.
48. Dewey, *Art as Experience*, 71.
49. Indeed, this questioning has been already widely called for, especially in pragmatist theories of interpretations. Just think of, among others, Umberto Eco's concept of "open work," according to which artworks are not complete, static structures but dynamic processes in which meanings are produced through interpretation and fruition, and of course Richard Rorty's rejection of the presence of transcendental meanings and internal coherence in texts: "Given this [i.e., Eco's] picture of texts being made as they are interpreted, I do not see any way to preserve the metaphor of a text's *internal* coherence. I should think that a text just has whatever coherence it happened to acquire during the last roll of the hermeneutic wheel, just as a lump of clay only has whatever coherence it happened to pick up at the last turn of the potter's wheel." Richard Rorty, "The Pragmatist's Progress," in *Interpretation and Overinterpretation*, ed. Umberto Eco and Stefan Collini (Cambridge: Cambridge University Press, 1992), 97. I return to the issue of interpretation and to the pragmatist approach to it in chapter 3, sections 1–2, and to the questioning of our relationship with artworks as prompted by landscapes in chapter 3, sections 3–4.
50. Dewey, *Art as Experience*, 30.
51. Dewey, *Art as Experience*, 29.
52. Dewey, *Art as Experience*, 29.
53. Dewey, *Art as Experience*, 29.
54. Notice, again, the parallel between landscape and artwork.
55. Clearly, in Dewey's conception, it makes no sense to essentialistically define and set apart space from time as they are interwoven in our experience: "Space thus becomes something more than a void in which to roam about, dotted here and there with dangerous things and things that satisfy the appetite. It becomes a comprehensive and enclosed scene within which are ordered the multiplicity of

doings and undergoings in which man engages." Dewey, *Art as Experience*, 29. I return to the issue of spatiality and temporality in chapter 4, section 1.
56. Such aesthetics has many points of contact with the "everyday aesthetics" thematized most notably by Yuriko Saito, *Everyday Aesthetics* (Oxford: Oxford University Press, 2007), but a discussion of them would take us too far. See also Berleant, *Living in the Landscape*.
57. Giovanni Matteucci, "The (Aesthetic) Extended Mind: Aesthetics from Experience-of to Experience-with," *Proceedings of the European Society for Aesthetics* 10 (2018): 406.
58. Matteucci, "The (Aesthetic) Extended Mind," 406. The concept of collusion is central to Matteucci's argument, based on the etymology of the word: from the Latin *cum* (with) + *ludere* (to play). Here think of Wittgenstein's "games."
59. Matteucci, "The (Aesthetic) Extended Mind," 409.
60. Matteucci, "The (Aesthetic) Extended Mind," 409.
61. Matteucci, "The (Aesthetic) Extended Mind," 411.
62. Matteucci, "The (Aesthetic) Extended Mind," 411.
63. Matteucci, "The (Aesthetic) Extended Mind," 412.
64. Matteucci, "The (Aesthetic) Extended Mind," 413. I cannot discuss here the difference between the extended and the scaffolded mind model, although the latter seems more appealing for my framework. On the topic, see Kim Sterelny, "Minds: Extended or Scaffolded?," *Phenomenology and the Cognitive Sciences* 9, no. 4 (2010): 465–81.
65. See Matteucci, "The (Aesthetic) Extended Mind," 419–20:

> However, this does not mean that any definition of these categories is acceptable. A pure relativism that led to believing something like that would be at least unusable. In reality, it is precisely the nature of the operative categories to follow specific polarizations that historically define their margins of effectiveness. "Historically" means, in this case, in relation to certain practices of experience-with that are interrelated in various manners. In short, the area of significance of an operative category can be compared more to a force field than to a static domain. Within it possible discrete positions appear, discontinuous though correlated (even opposing), which continuously redesign the temporary physiognomy of the category itself, still based on a sort of indeterminacy principle that makes some traits salient in certain circumstances to the detriment of others, which in any case may subsequently acquire renewed importance.

66. Denis Cosgrove, "Modernity, Community and the Landscape Idea," *Journal of Material Culture* 11 (2006): 52.
67. For further clarifications on this kind of approach, see Paul M. Keeling, "Does the Idea of Wilderness Need a Defence?," *Environmental Values* 17, no. 4 (2008): 505–19.
68. "Affordance" is a neologism introduced by psychologist James J. Gibson in the framework of his ecological approach to visual perception in connection with the properties of objects making specific actions possible ("affording"). On affordances and landscapes, see Michael Kempf, "From Landscape Affordances to Landscape Connectivity: Contextualizing an Archaeology of Human Ecology,"

2. LANDSCAPE AND AESTHETICS

Archaeological and Anthropological Sciences 12, no. 174 (2020): 174; and see Catharine Ward Thompson, "Landscape Perception and Environmental Psychology," in Howard et al., *Routledge Companion to Landscape Studies*, 20, who speaks of affordances as "cues in the environment which aid perception and facilitate behaviour."

69. I say something more about ethics (and politics) in chapter 4, section 3, although of course the ethics of landscape would deserve its own discussion, which I cannot undertake as such in this book.
70. See section 2, above.
71. In this regard, see Hepburn, "Contemporary Aesthetics and the Neglect of Natural Beauty," 298–99, noticing that aesthetics of nature "is only one of several areas in aesthetics where we have to resist the temptation to work with a single supreme concept and must replace it by a *cluster* of related key concepts."
72. Matteucci, "The (Aesthetic) Extended Mind," 426–27.
73. For a concrete application, see the discussion of Landscape Character Assessment in chapter 6 and in Alberto L. Siani, "Between Professional Objectivity and Simmel's Moods: A Pragmatist-Aesthetic Proposal for Landscape Character," *Landscape Research* 48, no. 4 (2023): 583–93.
74. For a critique of the "coarse applications of old historical materialism to culture" in the landscape discourse, see Paolo D'Angelo, *Il paesaggio: Teorie, storie, luoghi* (Bari-Roma: Laterza, 2021), 39.
75. Augustin Berque, "Beyond the Modern Landscape," *AA Files*, no. 25 (1993): 33. On the controversy, see D'Angelo, *Il paesaggio*, 150–51.
76. This also means without making a false and reductive identification between landscapes and environment—that is, trying to bypass the problem by resorting to an abstract, less problematic term. Here also lies the main problem I see with approaches such as Carlson's cognitivist one; e.g., Allen Carlson, "Appreciation and the Natural Environment," *Journal of Aesthetics and Art Criticism* 37, no. 3 (1979): 267–75. For critical readings, see Yuriko Saito, "Is There a Correct Aesthetic Appreciation of Nature?," *Journal of Aesthetic Education* 18, no. 4 (1984): 35–46; Noël Carroll, "On Being Moved by Nature: Between Religion and Natural History," in *Landscape, Natural Beauty and the Arts*, ed. Salim Kemal and Ivan Gaskell (Cambridge: Cambridge University Press, 1993), 244–66; and Paolo D'Angelo, *Filosofia del paesaggio* (Macerata: Quodlibet, 2014), 130–49. Cognitivism after the model of natural sciences may perhaps make sense for environmental aesthetics but certainly not for landscape aesthetics, and the choice to focus on environmental aesthetics as enabling a cognitivist approach is itself reductive, in my opinion. For similar reasons, also ethological-naturalistic approaches such as Appleton's "prospect-refuge theory" (see, e.g., Jay Appleton, "Prospects and Refuges Re-Visited," *Landscape Journal* 3, no. 2 [1984]: 91–103; and Susan Herrington, "Landscape Design," in Howard et al., *Routledge Companion to Landscape Studies*, 489) or the "savanna hypothesis" (see Kevin Bennett, "Savanna Hypothesis and Landscape Preferences, The," in *Encyclopedia of Evolutionary Psychological Science*, ed. Todd K. Shackelford and Viviana A. Weekes-Shackelford [Cham: Springer International, 2019], 1–4) are of course to be considered in this context but cannot take on an absolute explanatory role.

3. PATTERNS OF ENCOUNTER I

1. For some perspectives on landscape and crisis, see Mick Atha, Peter Howard, Ian Thompson, and Emma Waterton, "Introduction. Ways of Knowing and Being with Landscapes: A Beginning," in *The Routledge Companion to Landscape Studies*, ed. Peter Howard, Ian Thompson, Emma Waterton, and Mick Atha (London: Routledge, 2019), xix–xxviii; Marc Antrop, "A Brief History of Landscape Research," in Howard et al., *Routledge Companion to Landscape Studies*, 8; and Stefania Bonfiglioli, "Sull'attualità del concetto di paesaggio," in *Oltre la convenzione: Pensare, studiare, costruire il paesaggio vent'anni dopo*, ed. Benedetta Castiglioni, Matteo Puttilli, and Marcello Tanca (Firenze: Società di studi geografici, 2021), 38–48.
2. I say something on some on these aspects in the next chapter.
3. For some partly related considerations on the (aesthetic) economics of landscapes, see Colin Price, "Researching the Economics of Landscape," in Howard et al., *Routledge Companion to Landscape Studies*, 387–401.
4. An important concept in this regard it that of "landscape character," on which see chapter 5.
5. Sections 1.1 and 1.2 are a re-elaboration of Alberto L. Siani, "Unifying Art and Nature: Brady and Eco on Interpretation," *Aesthetica Preprint* 114 (2020): 49–58. My thanks go to the publishers and editors of the journal for allowing me to partly reuse the article.
6. "With artworks, it is in some ways easier to differentiate between relevant and irrelevant knowledge because the aesthetic object is fixed by artistic boundaries and conventions.... Aesthetic appreciation of the environment involves interpretation to a greater or lesser degree, depending on several factors: the type of landscape—cultural or natural; the nature of the particular aesthetic object; and the situation of the individual and context of appreciation. With nature, which has no content, the boundaries of interpretation are less clear, and there is more freedom on the part of the interpreter in terms of what sources they draw upon for interpretation." Emily Brady, "Interpreting Environments," *Essays in Philosophy* 3, no. 1 (2002): 62.
7. Roland Barthes, "The Death of the Author," in *Image Music Text*, trans. Stephen Heath (London: Fontana Press, 1977), 142–48.
8. Brady, "Interpreting Environments," 58.
9. Notice that here Brady refers to both cultural and natural spaces, hence her position, while nominally focusing on "environments" is entirely relevant to my discourse. Notice also that her aesthetic differentiation partly stems from the commitment to "a distinction, if not clear-cut, between nature and culture" (Brady, "Interpreting Environments," 57), which is also a distinction I am trying to pragmatistically deflate. For a broader presentation of her point of view on the relationship between art and environment, and between culture and nature, including the issue of interpretation, see also chapter 3 of Emily Brady, *Aesthetics of the Natural Environment* (Edinburgh: Edinburgh University Press, 2003).
10. Stefan Collini, ed., with Umberto Eco, Richard Rorty, Jonathan Culler, and Christine Brook-Rose, *Interpretation and Overinterpretation* (Cambridge: Cambridge University Press, 1992).

3. PATTERNS OF ENCOUNTER I

11. Umberto Eco, "Reply," in *Interpretation and Overinterpretation*, ed. Stefan Collini (Cambridge: Cambridge University Press, 1992), 144. Unless otherwise marked, the emphasis is present in the original quote.
12. Brady, "Interpreting Environments," 64–65.
13. Eco, "Reply," 144.
14. Brady, "Interpreting Environments," 65.
15. Here I cannot delve on Eco's distinction between Peirce's pragmaticism and Rorty's pragmatism.
16. Brady, "Interpreting Environments," 62.
17. I should clarify that I am not arguing for an undifferentiated, monolithic theory of interpretation. I am saying that we should aim for a unitary framework, and that differences are to be made not so much between artworks and natural environments, or between specific artistic forms/types of environments, but, if anything, on a case-by-case basis. For this, Brady's own pluralistic, engaged, and multisensory approach offers excellent clues.
18. Brady, "Interpreting Environments," 61.
19. Brady, "Interpreting Environments," 61.
20. Brady, "Interpreting Environments," 61.
21. Brady, "Interpreting Environments," 61.
22. Brady, "Interpreting Environments," 58.
23. Umberto Eco, "Unlimited Semiosis and Drift: Pragmaticism vs. 'Pragmatism,'" in *The Limits of Interpretation* (Bloomington: Indiana University Press, 1994), 38.
24. Eco, "Unlimited Semiosis and Drift," 39.
25. In Eco, the term *drift* designates the idea, which he criticizes, that interpretation can never reach an end but rather floats endlessly and arbitrarily from meaning to meaning. He distinguishes two forms of drift, the contemporary one, associated with deconstruction, and an earlier one, associated with Hermetism: "Contrary to contemporary theories of drift, . . . Hermetic semiosis does not assert the absence of any univocal universal and transcendental meaning. It assumes that everything can recall everything else provided we can isolate the right rhetorical connection because there is a strong transcendent subject." Eco, "Unlimited Semiosis and Drift," 27.
26. Eco, "Unlimited Semiosis and Drift," 40. This is also the groundwork for Eco's "cultural Darwinism"; see Stefan Collini, "Introduction: Interpretation Terminable and Interminable," in Collini, *Interpretation and Overinterpretation*, 16. Notice how this conjectural notion of truth and community, while being explicitly opposed to Kant's a priori transcendental, has many points of contact with Kant's notion of habitats, as presented in the prologue.
27. Brady, "Interpreting Environments," 62.
28. Eco, "Reply," 147.
29. Eco, "Reply," 149. I think it is safe to say that what Eco asserts here concerning the need for interpretation of sense data in general applies even more so to sense data as objects of aesthetic appreciation.
30. Vittoria Di Palma, "Is Landscape Painting?," in *Is Landscape . . . ? Essays on the Identity of Landscape*, ed. Gareth Doherty and Charles Waldheim (London: Routledge, 2016), 47.
31. Di Palma, "Is Landscape Painting?," 48. This is true at least for the English-speaking context, as the author remarks.

32. "Landscape denotes the external world mediated through subjective human experience.... Landscape is not merely the world we see, it is a construction, a composition of that world." Denis Cosgrove, *Social Formation and Symbolic Landscape* (Madison: University of Wisconsin Press, 1998), 13.
33. Di Palma, "Is Landscape Painting?," 67.
34. Di Palma, "Is Landscape Painting?," 67. A concrete example would be Cézanne's Mont Sainte-Victoire series of oil paintings, whereby a changing understanding of "real" landscape, from detached and static to immersive and dynamic, is reflected in a new approach to painting as much as the other way around (on Cézanne, see, among others, Harriet Hawkins, "Picturing Landscape," in Howard et al., *Routledge Companion to Landscape Studies*, 211; and Augustin Berque, "Beyond the Modern Landscape," *AA Files*, no. 25 [1993]: 35).
35. On Simmel and landscape, see Paolo D'Angelo, *Il paesaggio. Teorie, storie, luoghi* (Bari-Roma: Laterza, 2021), 132–52; on Simmel and pragmatism, see Martin Kusch, "Georg Simmel and Pragmatism," *European Journal of Pragmatism and American Philosophy* 9, no. 1 (2019).
36. Georg Simmel, "The Philosophy of Landscape," trans. Josef Bleicher, *Theory, Culture & Society* 24, no. 7–8 (2007): 23.
37. Simmel, "The Philosophy of Landscape," 23.
38. Simmel, "The Philosophy of Landscape," 23.
39. Simmel, "The Philosophy of Landscape," 23. See also Arnold Berleant, "The Art in Knowing a Landscape," *Diogenes* 59, no. 1–2 (2012): 53: "What a concern with environment shows is that what is most significant is not the *object* of appreciation but the *process* of appreciation, that is, aesthetic experience. Environmental aesthetics thus shifts the focus of aesthetic value from the object, i.e., the work of art, to its perceiver. Nowhere is this clearer than in landscape appreciation, for landscape is both a favorite object for the appreciation of nature and a favorite subject for painters and a frequent subject for poets and novelists." For a specific focus on portraits and on "character," see Erich Hatala Matthes, "Portraits of the Landscape," in *Portraits and Philosophy*, ed. Hans Maes (New York: Routledge, 2020).
40. See the conclusion of chapter 2.
41. Simmel, "The Philosophy of Landscape," 27. On Simmel's core concept of "mood" and for a further development of his conception with an actualizing aim, see chapter 5, section 3.
42. See John Dixon Hunt, "Is Landscape History?," in Doherty and Waldheim, *Is Landscape . . . ?*, 250–51.
43. Simmel, "The Philosophy of Landscape," 29.
44. See Denis Cosgrove, "Prospect, Perspective and the Evolution of the Landscape Idea," *Transactions of the Institute of British Geographers* 10, no. 1 (1985): 46:

> [Landscape] was, and it remains, a visual term, one that arose initially out of renaissance humanism and its particular concepts and constructs of space. Equally, landscape was, over much of its history, closely bound up with the practical appropriation of space.... Its connections were with the survey and mapping of newly-acquired, consolidated and 'improved' commercial estates in the hands of an urban bourgeoisie; with the calculation of distance

3. PATTERNS OF ENCOUNTER I

and trajectory for cannon fire and of defensive fortifications against the new weaponry; and with the projection of the globe and its regions onto map graticules by cosmographers and chorographers, those essential set designers for Europe's entry centre-stage of the world's theatre. In painting and garden design landscape achieved visually and ideologically what survey, map making and ordnance charting achieved practically: the control and domination of space as an absolute, objective entity, its transformation into the property of individual or state.... In the case of landscape the technique was optical, *linear perspective*, but the principles to be learned were identical to those of architecture, survey, map-making and artillery science. The same handbooks taught the practitioners all of these arts.

See also John B. Jackson, "The Word Itself," in *Discovering the Vernacular Landscape* (New Haven, Conn.: Yale University Press, 1984), 4, on "the demise of traditional landscape painting." I return to the topic of landscape and/as ideology among others in chapter 4, section 2.

45. See also Salim Kemal and Ivan Gaskell, "Nature, Fine Arts, and Aesthetics," in *Landscape, Natural Beauty and the Arts*, ed. Salim Kemal and Ivan Gaskell (Cambridge: Cambridge University Press, 1993), 14:

Landscape's beginnings in Dutch painting arise from a particular organization of perceptions that yields a distinctively textured experience. Its mode of seeing is based in the techniques of linear perspective, surveying and mapping, though this is still bound up with an irreducible sense of wonder and awe towards nature that escapes mathematical perspectives. Instead of being simply absorbed into that quantifying organization of land and sight, landscape still represents an escape to the world of nature, where life, body, and soul are in harmony. The landscape provides the most telling arena for action against which to judge the history that human beings construct.

The duplicity, if not ambiguity, of the human relationship/obsession with the visual is also underscored, in the context of the ecological crisis, by Alexis L. Boylan, *Visual Culture* (Cambridge, Mass.: MIT Press, 2020), 19, suggesting that the "loving attention" for the external world and for its inhabitants, amply testified across human history and cultures, "seems at odds with what many have argued is a current inability to speak with visual clarity and power to the *when* of climate change, extinctions, pollution, and the other evidences of environmental devastation. What might it mean if visual culture cannot be mobilized to address the most altering events in the story of humanity?"

46. Rachael Z. DeLue, "Is Landscape Theory?," in Doherty and Waldheim, *Is Landscape . . . ?*, 269.
47. DeLue, "Is Landscape Theory?," 270.
48. DeLue, "Is Landscape Theory?," 273.
49. DeLue, "Is Landscape Theory?," 274.
50. Indeed, the word *theory* comes from the ancient Greek *theoria*, primarily meaning sight or contemplation.
51. DeLue, "Is Landscape Theory?," 275.

3. PATTERNS OF ENCOUNTER I

52. DeLue, "Is Landscape Theory?," 275. The issue of the place of the nonhuman or posthuman is and will be more and more widely discussed in landscape studies, which I cannot do here. See also Alberto L. Siani, "Nowhere Between River and Road: A Nagelian Reading of *Suttree* and *The Road*," in *Philosophical Approaches to Cormac McCarthy: Beyond Reckoning*, ed. Chris Eagle (London: Routledge, 2017), 202–19.
53. That such practices and the motives behind them also have a colonial backside of domination, submission, and appropriation is quite clear and aptly stressed with reference to Bartram by DeLue, "Is Landscape Theory?," 281.
54. A new line of discussion on landscapes as a "contested territory" between geography, aesthetics, and art history should therefore be opened. While I cannot do this here, I want to point out that the centrality and at the same time the controversial character of the link between aesthetics and geography for both terms is attracting growing interest in the literature. See, e.g., Paolo Furia, "Connections Between Geography and Aesthetics," *Aesthetica Preprint* 114 (2020): 35–36:

> Geography is connected to aesthetics in at least two important ways. First, the original and indispensable task of geography, which can be found in its very etymology, is to draw the Earth. The primary tool of geography is the map. However accurate and exact a map may be, it always has a fictive trait which reveals something about the illustrator: her research objectives, the scientific conventions she is adopting, the technological support she uses for observations, her cultural heritage. The cartographic rendering is always also a matter of imagination. . . . Second, geography includes field surveys, first-hand explorations, travels, and qualitative methods. In this sense, aesthetic experiences are at the heart of many geographical inquiries.

55. On the challenge to ocularcentrism, see section 2 in this chapter, and chapter 4, section 1. See also Giovanni Matteucci, *Estetica e natura umana: La mente estesa tra percezione, emozione ed espressione* (Roma: Carocci, 2019); Nicola Perullo, "Feet, Lines, Weather, Labyrinth: The Haptic Engagement as a Suggestion for an Ecological Aesthetics," *Contemporary Aesthetics* 17 (2019); D'Angelo, *Il paesaggio*, 73–90; and Claudio Pogliano, *Senso lato. Il tatto e la cultura occidentale* (Roma: Carocci, 2015).
56. The relationship between photography and environment/landscapes is fundamentally ambiguous. Photography promises belonging, but we value it because it allows distance—that is, nonbelonging. Besides, its "realistic" depiction of wilderness is mostly a widely idealized and artifact one, whereas its depiction of human interaction with nature, while being more "true," can have awkward and displacing effects on our landscape imagery. Radically different approaches are possible, from a purist fixation on the scenic and its "exceptionalist" preservation to the critical choice of banal and apparently uninteresting or even ugly sights. See Robin Kelsey, "Is Landscape Photography?," in Doherty and Waldheim, *Is Landscape . . . ?*, 71–92. For a selective overview of land art, see, among others, Venda Louise Pollock, "Land, Art," in Howard et al., *Routledge Companion to Landscape Studies*, 215–26. Consider also the paradox-inducing

case of *Time Landscape* in New York City, "made" by artist Alan Sonfist, author of the manifesto "Natural Phenomena as Public Monuments" (in Alastair Bonnett, *Unruly Places: Lost Spaces, Secret Cities, and Other Inscrutable Geographies* [Boston: Houghton Mifflin Harcourt, 2014], "Time Landscape"), which I reference again in chapter 4, section 1.3, figure 4.2. On shocking, weird, avant-garde, or disturbing approaches, see the critical remarks by Paolo D'Angelo, *Filosofia del paesaggio* (Macerata: Quodlibet, 2014), 101–2, with which I agree.

57. For a discussion of contemporary art expressions reflecting the need for a shift toward an engaged, critical, nonhierarchical approach and also accounting for related issues of gender, see Peter J. Schneemann, "Performative Landscapes: A Paradigm for Mediating the Ecological Imperative?," in *Landscape and Earth in Early Modernity. Picturing Unruly Nature*, ed. Christine Göttler and Mia Mochizuki (Amsterdam: Amsterdam University Press, 2023), 393–414; e.g., 402: "From the perspective of the ecological discourse and related to the criticism of anthropocentric models, the idea of the landscape as a composition is replaced by an interest in the physicality, sensitiveness, and movement of one's own body. Our position towards the environment is defined in a non-hierarchical way to understand its reality as independent from the human gaze. Explorations into this relationship, in which the agency of reality is maintained, require the element of distance to be overcome." Whereas Schneemann criticizes Simmel's approach in this regard, I tried to show its attractiveness for the development of a new perspective.

58. See D'Angelo, *Filosofia del paesaggio*, 101 and 34, where the author also points out how "the garden ends up somehow occupying the summit of Assunto's research as the ideal aim of landscape." See also D'Angelo, *Il paesaggio*, 5–19; Berque, "Beyond the Modern Landscape," 36 (to which I return in chapter 4, section 2.3): "In the present relation between our society and space and nature, the subject can no longer identify with the environment . . . ; nor, however, can the landscape be treated as a mere object. . . . Today, the subject has something much better to do: he can take the stage both for his own pleasure and for the sake of the beauty of the landscape, while also caring for the environment like a prudent gardener." For an original comparison of environmental art and gardening, see Stephanie Ross, "Gardens, Earthworks, and Environmental Art," in Kemal and Gaskell, *Landscape, Natural Beauty and the Arts*, 158–82.

59. Udo Weilacher, "Is Landscape Gardening?," in Doherty and Waldheim, *Is Landscape . . . ? Essays on the Identity of Landscape*, 108. I refer to this chapter for further observations on gardening and landscape.

60. Di Palma, "Is Landscape Painting?," 48.

61. See also Kemal and Gaskell, "Nature, Fine Arts, and Aesthetics," 3: "Human creation and nature so interpenetrate in our understanding that they apparently preclude the likelihood of producing clear conceptual distinctions."

62. See Gareth Doherty, "Is Landscape Literature?," in Doherty and Waldheim, *Is Landscape . . . ?*, 28–29.

63. Doherty, "Is Landscape Literature?," 26.

64. See sections 1–2, above.

4. PATTERNS OF ENCOUNTER II

1. A possible criticism, especially from a readership with a professional landscape expertise, is that I try to cover too much ground at the expense of depth or application—in other words, that it would have been better to choose fewer topics and develop them in more detail (such criticism was, as a matter of fact, raised by one of the anonymous reviewers of this book). To this I reply, first, that the strategy I have chosen has the advantage of pointing a philosophical or general readership in different directions with which they are not necessarily familiar, without making them inaccessible or less attractive, considering that none of the topics discussed here has received much coverage in more traditional philosophical scholarship. Second, what is lacking here in terms of depth and application may be at least partially made up for in the next chapter, which addresses a rather specific issue (landscape character assessment) from what I hope is an original perspective. The present fourth chapter has the function of probing the ground in several directions, pointing to fertile research areas or ways of framing the crisis discourse differently, or even just highlighting some of the major difficulties involved, rather than delving deeply into them or proposing original solutions.
2. See chapter 2, section 4.
3. This is true also of space more in general in the context of a critical approach to visual culture. See Alexis L. Boylan, *Visual Culture* (Cambridge, Mass.: MIT Press, 2020), 19: "Creating a stable geography, a knowable visual space, mapping time itself have been a fixation in the visual sphere. We think we are mapping a 'where,' but we are really visualizing a 'when.' The ocean, the animals, outer space, all have been drawn and redrawn, imagined, categorized, and visually quantified, often detached from the 'when' and placed in a non-time."
4. David Leatherbarrow, "Is Landscape Architecture?," in *Is Landscape . . . ? Essays on the Identity of Landscape*, ed. Gareth Doherty and Charles Waldheim (London: Routledge, 2016), 330. Of course, speaking of "temporality" in the singular does not mean affirming the existence of a single time or temporal dimension/articulation. As landscape itself reminds us, there are different "times" or time arrangements (seasonal, calendric, historical, mythical, ceremonial, etc.), yet they are not simply juxtaposed to each other: "Time is not one thing *or* another: it is both one thing *and* another. Different times nest within each other and draw meaning from each other." Barbara Bender, "Time and Landscape," *Current Anthropology* 43, no. 4 (2002): 104; see the whole article on the relationship of time and landscape.
5. "Aesthetic appreciation of natural environments, including landscapes, differs from the aesthetic appreciation of works of art as a result of some of the essential properties of nature, including the necessary involvement in nature of the fourth dimension—time—and therefore of change." Catharine Ward Thompson, "Landscape Perception and Environmental Psychology," in *The Routledge Companion to Landscape Studies*, ed. Peter Howard, Ian Thompson, Emma Waterton, and Mick Atha (London: Routledge, 2019), 24.
6. See Emma Waterton, "More-than-Representational Landscapes," in Howard et al., *Routledge Companion to Landscape Studies*, 91–101.

4. PATTERNS OF ENCOUNTER II

7. Waterton, "More-than-Representational Landscapes," 94. On "almost things" and "atmospheres," see, to begin with, Tonino Griffero, "Paesaggi e atmosfere: Ontologia ed esperienza estetica della natura," *Rivista di estetica* 45, no. 29 (2005): 7–40; and Tonino Griffero, *Places, Affordances, Atmospheres. A Pathic Aesthetics* (London: Routledge, 2019).
8. Waterton, "More-than-Representational Landscapes," 95.
9. John Dixon Hunt, "Is Landscape History?," in Doherty and Waldheim, *Is Landscape . . . ?*, 250–51.
10. This is the "dwelling perspective" developed by Tim Ingold in "The Temporality of the Landscape," *World Archaeology* 25, no. 2 (1993): 152, as a concrete alternative to "the sterile opposition between the naturalistic view of the landscape as a neutral, external backdrop to human activities, and the culturalistic view that every landscape is a particular cognitive or symbolic ordering of space." See also Luisa Bonesio, *Paesaggio, identità e comunità tra locale e globale* (Milano: Mimesis, 2017), 100: "Landscape is not just the representation or perception of a subject standing in front of it, but way more essentially and primarily a unitary form of the territory, obtained from the selection and interpretation of natural possibilities by a culture. Historicity of the landscape is not just the banal idea of temporal development, but the identity and mutual identification of place and community."
11. With regard to a closed, reactionary formulation of the relationship between identity and time/history, just think of the Nazi ideology of *Blut und Boden* (blood and soil) and the associated philosophical speculations.
12. On landscape and archaeology and specifically on the notion of palimpsest, see Sam Turner, Lisa-Marie Shillito, and Francesco Carrer, "Landscape Archaeology," in Howard et al., *Routledge Companion to Landscape Studies*, 156; and Gareth Doherty, "Is Landscape Literature?," in *Is Landscape . . . ?*, 29.
13. See Sarah De Nardi and Danielle Drozdzewski, "Landscape and Memory," in Howard et al., *Routledge Companion to Landscape Studies*, 429–39.
14. This is also why, as we will see in section 3.4, below, a right to landscape is something way more complex than a right to environment.
15. James Corner, "Eidetic Operations and New Landscapes," in *Recovering Landscape: Essays in Contemporary Landscape Architecture* (New York: Princeton Architectural Press, 1999), 156.
16. Corner, "Eidetic Operations and New Landscapes," 156–57.
17. William J. T. Mitchell, "Imperial Landscape," in *Landscape and Power*, ed. William J. T. Mitchell (Chicago: University of Chicago Press, 2002), 6, 1.
18. Corner, "Eidetic Operations and New Landscapes," 159.
19. "A landscape is not a natural feature of the environment but a *synthetic* space, a man-made system of spaces superimposed on the face of the land, functioning and evolving not according to natural laws but to serve a community. . . . A landscape is thus a space deliberately created to speed up or slow down the process of nature. . . . It represents man taking upon himself the role of time." John B. Jackson, "The Word Itself," in *Discovering the Vernacular Landscape* (New Haven, Conn.: Yale University Press, 1984), 8.
20. Corner, "Eidetic Operations and New Landscapes," 157. One may add that landscape as such already lends itself to perform such criticism and irony: "Landscapes refuse to be disciplined; they make a mockery of the oppositions that we

create between time (history) and space (geography) or between nature (science) and culture (anthropology)." Bender, "Time and Landscape," 106.
21. Jackson, "The Word Itself," 3.
22. "The idea of conceiving the actual landscape as a projection of landscape painting onto nature started spreading precisely in the early 19th century and completed the process whereby the 'aesthetic' landscape had gradually come to be separated from the agricultural one. The gap thus created between the kind of landscape to be admired, painted and described, and cultivated farmland was destined to remain open for almost two centuries. In fact, judging from the works of some contemporary environmental artists fond of hiking and dizzying heights, we might say that the gap remains open to this day." Paolo D'Angelo, "Agriculture and Landscape. From Cultivated Fields to the Wilderness, and Back," in *Philosophy of Landscape: Think, Walk, Act*, ed. Moirika Reker and Adriana Veríssimo Serrão (Lisbon: Centre for Philosophy at the University of Lisbon, 2019), 249. According to the author, there are three main reasons for this state of affairs: first, the widespread identification of a genuine aesthetic value with extraordinariness; second, the endurance of the conventional opposition between the useful and the beautiful; and third, the disregard for the beauty of a place by the people working in it, as in the case of Cézanne's farmers of Mont Sainte-Victoire.
23. Jackson, "The Word Itself," 8.
24. Jackson, "The Word Itself," 8.
25. See Pierre Bélanger, "Is Landscape Infrastructure?," in Doherty and Waldheim, *Is Landscape . . . ?*, 190–227.
26. Bélanger, "Is Landscape Infrastructure?," 200.
27. There are, of course, numerous examples of this tendency: see, among others, Frederick Steiner, "Is Landscape Planning?," in Doherty and Waldheim, *Is Landscape . . . ?*, 138–61.
28. See Bélanger, "Is Landscape Infrastructure?," 207.
29. See Bélanger, "Is Landscape Infrastructure?," 212.
30. See Hayley Saul and Emma Waterton, "Anthropocene Landscapes," in Howard et al., *Routledge Companion to Landscape Studies*, 139–51.
31. Werner Krauss, "Postenvironmental Landscapes in the Anthropocene," in Howard et al., *Routledge Companion to Landscape Studies*, 62. See also the first thesis in Dipesh Chakrabarty, "The Climate of History: Four Theses," *Critical Inquiry* 35, no. 2 (2009): 197–222. I return to these points below, in section 2.
32. Leatherbarrow, "Is Landscape Architecture?," 334.
33. Leatherbarrow, "Is Landscape Architecture?," 336.
34. Saul and Waterton, "Anthropocene Landscapes," 140.
35. On the World Heritage Convention, see below, section 3.1.
36. Mick Atha, "Ephemeral Landscapes," in Howard et al., *Routledge Companion to Landscape Studies*, 115.
37. Atha, "Ephemeral Landscapes," 117. The author discusses, by way of example, the Kam Tin Jiao Festival in Hong Kong. On festivals, see also Alastair Bonnett, *Unruly Places: Lost Spaces, Secret Cities, and Other Inscrutable Geographies* (Boston: Houghton Mifflin Harcourt, 2014), "Nowhere."
38. Atha, "Ephemeral Landscapes," 124.

4. PATTERNS OF ENCOUNTER II

39. Ingold, "The Temporality of the Landscape," 162. Reframing or explaining landscapes in terms of taskscapes reminds us, "when our surroundings seem to be laid out for our gaze, that our perception of them is not comprehensive, but is a function of the activity we are engaged in, work or leisure. Perception is conditioned by the specialization that a task involves—what the eye of the farmer or police officer picks out, as compared to the birdwatcher or historian—and by the duration of the task, its rhythms and the intervals for vision that it affords." See Richard Kerridge, "New Directions in the Literary Representation of Landscape," in Howard et al., *Routledge Companion to Landscape Studies*, 258.
40. Of course, other authors have opposed this thesis. I cannot enter the controversy here.
41. Georg Simmel, "The Philosophy of Landscape," trans. Josef Bleicher, *Theory, Culture & Society* 24, no. 7–8 (2007): 22.
42. Simmel, "The Philosophy of Landscape," 22.
43. See Joachim Ritter, "Landschaft: Zur Funktion des Ästhetischen in der modernen Gesellschaft," in *Metaphysik und Politik. Studien zu Aristoteles und Hegel* (Frankfurt am Main: Suhrkamp, 2003), 141–90, which also offers a useful history of the concept of landscape.
44. Denis Cosgrove, "Modernity, Community and the Landscape Idea," *Journal of Material Culture* 11 (2006): 57.
45. Bonesio, *Paesaggio, identità e comunità tra locale e globale*, 85.
46. Bonesio, *Paesaggio, identità e comunità tra locale e globale*, 205.
47. See Bonesio, *Paesaggio, identità e comunità tra locale e globale*, 217.
48. Kathryn Moore, "Is Landscape Philosophy?," in Doherty and Waldheim, *Is Landscape . . . ?*, 285–86.
49. Moore, "Is Landscape Philosophy?," 288–90.
50. And also, of course, from the point of view of aesthetics: as we saw above, authors such as John Dewey and Giovanni Matteucci consciously work at the overcoming or deconstruction of typically modernist/cartesian/rationalistic dualisms and ways of thinking in aesthetics. See, in this regard, Giovanni Matteucci, "The (Aesthetic) Extended Mind: Aesthetics from Experience-of to Experience-with," *Proceedings of the European Society for Aesthetics* 10 (2018): 425: "The theories of aesthetic experience mentioned at the beginning of this paper tend, sometimes explicitly sometimes critically, to focus exclusively or as a priority on art experience precisely because they are patterned after the paradigm of experience-of. This reveals how intrinsically 'modern' they are, and therefore how limited is their theoretical validity, which seeks to justify the aesthetic starting from a philosophy of culture or even starting from a cultural ideology."
51. See Nina-Marie Lister, "Is Landscape Ecology?," in Doherty and Waldheim, *Is Landscape . . . ?*, 119.
52. Lister, "Is Landscape Ecology?," 120.
53. Lister, "Is Landscape Ecology?," 125.
54. Lister, "Is Landscape Ecology?," 127.
55. See Krauss, "Postenvironmental Landscapes in the Anthropocene," 62. See the same chapter for an outline of the history and concept of postenvironmentalism.
56. See Krauss, "Postenvironmental Landscapes in the Anthropocene," 65.

57. I take this opportunity to address a more general potential objection to my discourse. The fact that I am not confronting environmental crisis figures in their quantitative objectivity does not mean that I do not take them seriously. On the contrary, it would not be serious for me to claim to have something to say about them. My whole discourse presupposes the acknowledgment of the full extent of the environmental crisis as a hard fact but situates itself on a different level in an attempt to provide an alternative (yet not exclusive) perspective to a reductively environmentalist one.
58. Krauss, "Postenvironmental Landscapes in the Anthropocene," 71.
59. See Ian Thompson, "Landscape and Environmental Ethics," in Howard et al., *Routledge Companion to Landscape Studies*, 559. See also Krauss, "Postenvironmental Landscapes in the Anthropocene," 64, on postenvironmentalism as an alternative to a typical environmentalist view of nature as a separate and victimized entity.
60. Louis F. Cassar, "Landscape and Ecology: The Need for a Holistic Approach to the Conservation of Habitats and Biota," in Howard et al., *Routledge Companion to Landscape Studies*, 478. Of course, speaking of "agency" would require addressing ethical presuppositions and implications, which I cannot do here. For a pragmatistically and pluralistically oriented discussion, see Thompson, "Landscape and Environmental Ethics." From the point of view of education, to which I return in section 4, below, see Heesoon Bai, "A Critical Reflection on Environmental Education During the COVID-19 Pandemic," *Journal of Philosophy of Education* 54, no. 4 (2020): 919–20: "The habit of mind that sees the environment as 'out there,' that our work as environmental educators or activists is to do something *about, to* or *for* the environment, and that other beings have no consciousness, value and agency of their own, is one-piece with the [modern Western] epistemology of dualism. The latter separates mind from matter, inner life from outer environment, what is animate from what is inanimate and so on."
61. Isis Brook, "Aesthetic Appreciation of Landscape," in Howard et al., *Routledge Companion to Landscape Studies*, 47.
62. Krauss, "Postenvironmental Landscapes in the Anthropocene," 70.
63. Another example could be industrial and postindustrial landscapes; see Wolfram Höfer and Vera Vicenzotti, "Post-Industrial Landscapes: Evolving Concepts," in Howard et al., *Routledge Companion to Landscape Studies*, 499–510.
64. Cassar, "Landscape and Ecology," 483.
65. See, among others, Paolo D'Angelo, *Il paesaggio: Teorie, storie, luoghi* (Bari-Roma: Laterza, 2021), 42–45.
66. Steiner, "Is Landscape Planning?," 155. Steiner goes on to state that "the more we involve ecological processes in our plans and designs, the more it is reinforced that, like it or not, we are still part of nature" (159).
67. Augustin Berque, "Beyond the Modern Landscape," *AA Files*, no. 25 (1993): 33–34.
68. Berque, "Beyond the Modern Landscape," 34.
69. Berque, "Beyond the Modern Landscape," 35.
70. Berque, "Beyond the Modern Landscape," 36.
71. Berque, "Beyond the Modern Landscape," 36.
72. Berque, "Beyond the Modern Landscape," 36.

4. PATTERNS OF ENCOUNTER II

73. See Gunhild Setten, Katrina Myrvang Brown, and Hilde Nymoen Rørtveit, "Landscape and Social Justice," in Howard et al., *Routledge Companion to Landscape Studies*, 421.
74. Council of Europe, European Landscape Convention (2000), https://rm.coe.int/16807b6bc7.
75. Graham Fairclough, Ingrid Sarlöv Herlin, and Carys Swanwick, "Landscape Character Assessment. A Global Practice," in Howard et al., *Routledge Companion to Landscape Studies*, 584. See also Kenneth R. Olwig, "The Law of Landscape and the Landscape of Law: The 'Things' That Matter," in Howard et al., *Routledge Companion to Landscape Studies*, 384, about the very recent "shift away from the idea of landscape as an assortment of physical things organised within spatial boundaries, or visually as scenery, that can be categorised and shelved, or mapped in a landscape character assessment, towards an interest in the relationship between justice and landscape understood as the place of a (political) community. . . . This no doubt has much to do with the promulgation of the *European Landscape Convention* and subsequent efforts to put it into practice and expand the ideals of this convention to other parts of the world."
76. UNESCO, World Heritage Convention (1972), https://whc.unesco.org/en/conventiontext/.
77. Fairclough et al., "Landscape Character Assessment," 584. Obviously, here the point is not to criticize the WHC and its specific mission as such but to show instead that a more encompassing and inclusive conception of landscape also calls for different institutional frameworks.
78. The expression "outstanding universal value" recurs throughout the WHC. It may be interesting to remark that, from this point of view, the ELC seems to reflect better some recent changes in our habits, which have been made possible by technological advancement (and the other way around, of course: technological advancement is in turn made necessary by shifting habits). I mean that it is becoming more and more common, for example, to take photos or selfies of, or in, the most ordinary places, not just extraordinary ones. Ordinary places then become just as "meaningful" and share-worthy as the extraordinary ones, or, perhaps more precisely, this distinction collapses altogether as a result of technology allowing us to take as many photos as we want. A photograph is no longer an "extraordinary" medium in itself, something to be set aside for some specific worthy moment and place but becomes the ordinary celebration of ordinariness. To be sure, such a process is not free from concerning prospects either.
79. See chapter 2, section 1.
80. Kenneth R. Olwig, "Recovering the Substantive Nature of Landscape," *Annals of the Association of American Geographers* 86, no. 4 (1996): 630–31.
81. We should also keep in mind that, as we saw above, according to a significant part of the literature, landscapes are intrinsically "problematic" insofar as they are the product of the bourgeois, rationalistic worldview and its attending problematic ramifications: anthropocentrism, eurocentrism, colonialism, domination and control of nature, and the like.
82. Maggie Roe, "Landscape and Participation," in Howard et al., *Routledge Companion to Landscape Studies*, 413.
83. On the wind-turbines diatribe, see section 2.2.

84. Olwig, "The Law of Landscape and the Landscape of Law," 384, focuses on "the rise of New Liberalism, with its emphasis upon the privatisation and enclosure of the landscape as a common good[, which] has led to a revived concern to protect this common landscape ... by the legal means offered, for example, by international conventions such as the *European Landscape Convention*. Future landscape research will likely be dominated by such conflicting ideals concerning the role of landscape as either private property or as a public good, and hence by larger legal questions concerning the right to landscape." In the context of landscape and urbanism research, see also Charles Waldheim, "Is Landscape Urbanism?," in Doherty and Waldheim, *Is Landscape . . . ?*, 164: "The challenges of our present urban conditions ... have more to do with the political failures of a culture that has largely abandoned welfare state expectations of rational planning."
85. For a concrete example, see Denis Byrne, "Reclaiming Landscape: Coastal Reclamations Before and During the Anthropocene," in Howard et al., *Routledge Companion to Landscape Studies*, 277–87, on the coastal reclamation of the Pearl River Delta in China.
86. For an overview on landscapes, globalization, and the local, see Jacky Bowring, "Navigating the Global, the Regional and the Local. Researching Globalization and Landscape," in Howard et al., *Routledge Companion to Landscape Studies*, 299–310.
87. Setten, Brown, and Rørtveit, "Landscape and Social Justice," 423.
88. China is just an example but, of course, a very important one in this regard, given, among others, its economic and political power; the characteristics of its economic transition, land, and population size; and the number of UNESCO-protected sites (currently second only to Italy). On bias in international conventions, see the case of Longjing tea gardens in the context of the World Heritage listing of West Lake, Hangzhou, in Ken Taylor and Qing Xu, "Challenging Landscape Eurocentrism: An Asian Perspective," in Howard et al., *Routledge Companion to Landscape Studies*, 318–20. On non-European states exploiting landscape and heritage, see the Chinese case: Taylor and Xu, "Challenging Landscape Eurocentrism," 315.
89. Taylor and Xu, "Challenging Landscape Eurocentrism," 324.
90. Notice, at a more general level, that none of the categories of involved actors are monolithic either. On the connection between "perceptual lenses" on landscape and factors such as gender, nationality, ethnicity, social status, age, and so on, often working in an exclusionary sense, see Peter Howard, "Perceptual Lenses," in Howard et al., *Routledge Companion to Landscape Studies*, 51–61.
91. Shelley Egoz, "Landscape and Identity in the Century of the Migrant," in Howard et al., *Routledge Companion to Landscape Studies*, 329.
92. Egoz, "Landscape and Identity in the Century of the Migrant," 329–30.
93. Egoz, "Landscape and Identity in the Century of the Migrant," 335.
94. Damian Holmes, "The Increasing Importance of Outdoor Space," *World Landscape Architecture* (blog), January 10, 2021, https://worldlandscapearchitect.com/the-increasing-importance-of-outdoor-space/.
95. For a different perspective, see Bai, "A Critical Reflection on Environmental Education During the COVID-19 Pandemic." A very fruitful interpretive key on the topics of this section (and beyond) is provided by the dialectic between the Italian

concepts of *"spaesamento"* (displacement, uncanniness, bewilderment) and *"appaesamento"* (settling in, acclimatization, territorialization): see Paolo Furia, *Spaesamento: Esperienza estetico-geografica* (Milano: Meltemi, 2023).

96. See Setten, Brown, and Rørtveit, "Landscape and Social Justice," 426–27. Remember here the distinction between *landscape*, *environment*, and *territory*. We use the first term in contexts in which we want to underline not so much the characteristics of a space (as in *environment*), nor the dependence of that space on a human practice, legislation, or jurisdiction (as in *territory*) but rather some relational property, or fact, or phenomenon, taking place between human agency and a space.

97. For a broader discussion of landscape education, see Alberto L. Siani, "Landscape Education, Enskilment, and Aesthetics: Complex Skills for Our Time," *Contemporary Aesthetics* (forthcoming).

98. Brian Wattchow and Alex Prins, "Learning a Landscape. Enskilment, Pedagogy and a Sense of Place," in Howard et al., *Routledge Companion to Landscape Studies*, 105.

99. Wattchow and Prins, "Learning a Landscape," 103.

100. Wattchow and Prins, "Learning a Landscape," 108–9. See the original formulation of enskilment by Tim Ingold, *The Perception of the Environment: Essays on Livelihood, Dwelling and Skill* (London: Routledge, 2000), 416: "'Understanding in practice'... is a process of *enskilment*, in which learning is inseparable from doing, and in which both are embedded in the context of a practical engagement in the world—that is, in dwelling."

101. Wattchow and Prins, "Learning a Landscape," 106.

102. Jeffrey A. Stickney, "Seeing Trees: Investigating Poetics of Place-Based, Aesthetic Environmental Education with Heidegger and Wittgenstein," *Journal of Philosophy of Education* 54, no. 5 (2020): 1279.

103. See Emily Brady, *Aesthetics of the Natural Environment* (Edinburgh: Edinburgh University Press, 2003), 216–17; and Stickney, "Seeing Trees," 1281–90. On the plural character of the appreciation of nature, see also Yuriko Saito, "Is There a Correct Aesthetic Appreciation of Nature?," *Journal of Aesthetic Education* 18, no. 4 (1984): 35–46.

104. It is important to clarify that while this should not be taken in the mere sense of a humanizing of nature, it should not exclude it either but rather should combine it with its counterpart, the naturizing of the human being: "To be 'one' with nature [is] to realize vividly one's place in the landscape, as a form among its forms. And this is not to have nature's 'foreignness' or otherness overcome, but in contrast, to allow that otherness free play in the modifying of one's everyday sense of one's own being." Ronald W. Hepburn, "Contemporary Aesthetics and the Neglect of Natural Beauty," in *British Analytical Philosophy*, ed. Bernard Williams and Alan Montefiore (London: Routledge and Kegan Paul, 1966), 297. See also Hepburn's dichotomy of serious and trivial: Ronald W. Hepburn, "Trivial and Serious in Aesthetic Appreciation of Nature," in *Landscape, Natural Beauty and the Arts*, ed. Salim Kemal and Ivan Gaskell (Cambridge: Cambridge University Press, 1993), 65–80.

105. In this sense, and paraphrasing Matteucci's talk of "experience-with" rather than "experience-of" (see Matteucci, "The (Aesthetic) Extended Mind," to which I

return in the conclusion), it may also be convenient to speak of "learning through (or with) landscapes" rather than "learning landscapes."

106. Ludwig Wittgenstein, "Lectures on Aesthetics," in *Lectures and Conversations on Aesthetics, Psychology and Religious Belief*, ed. Cyril Barrett (Berkeley: University of California Press, 1967), 9.

107. On the meaning of appreciation: "It is not only difficult to describe what appreciation consists in, but impossible. To describe what it consists in we would have to describe the whole environment." Wittgenstein, "Lectures on Aesthetics," 7. See also: "There are lots of people, well-offish, who have been to good schools, who can afford to travel about and see the Louvre, etc., and who know a lot about and can talk fluently about dozens of painters. There is another person who has seen very few paintings, but who looks intensely at one or two paintings which make a profound impression on him. Another person who is broad, neither deep nor wide. Another person who is very narrow, concentrated and circumscribed. Are these different kinds of appreciation? They may all be called 'appreciation.'" Wittgenstein, "Lectures on Aesthetics," 9.

108. Wittgenstein, "Lectures on Aesthetics," 2.

109. Ludwig Wittgenstein, *Philosophical Investigations*, ed. Peter Michael Stephan Hacker and Joachim Schulte, trans. Gertrude Elizabeth Margaret Anscombe, Peter Michael Stephan Hacker, and Joachim Schulte (Chichester, UK: Wiley-Blackwell, 2009), 7.

110. Hans-Johann Glock, *A Wittgenstein Dictionary* (Chichester, UK: Wiley-Blackwell, 1996), 112.

111. Apparently, Wittgenstein's own methods as a schoolteacher in rural Austria were, to say the least, rough even for the standards of the time.

112. Pierluigi Biancini, "Language as Environment: An Ecological Approach to Wittgenstein's Form of Life," in *Papers of the 32nd International Wittgenstein Symposium*, ed. Volker A. Munz, Klaus Puhl, and Joseph Wang (Kirchberg am Wechsel: Austrian Ludwig Wittgenstein Society, 2009), 75.

113. The process seems alarmingly akin to a conception of education as behavioristic conditioning, or even animal taming, and certain Wittgensteinian expressions do not contribute to dispel this impression. Once again, the point here is not to evaluate Wittgenstein's theory of education as such.

114. Stickney, "Seeing Trees," 1293.

115. I cannot pursue here an autonomous investigation of the concept of "habit" in its relationship to "habitat," "inhabiting," and so on. I can only say that in this context, habits are public, social facts, "second natures" for which we do not normally seek foundation and justification, insofar as the community acts as an implicit guarantor. Habits and communities are constantly, jointly changing: the establishment of a different habit means having a different community, and vice versa. See also the discussion of "habit" in Eco in chapter 3, section 1.2.

116. Quoted in Stickney, "Seeing Trees," 1297.

117. On this difficulty, see Claudia Ruitenberg, "The Cruel Optimism of Transformative Environmental Education," *Journal of Philosophy of Education* 54, no. 4 (08): 832–37.

118. On the topic of the public and performative dimension of aesthetic appreciation, Brady also provides valuable insights in her *Aesthetics of the Natural*

Environment (218). The notion of a broadly conceived "aesthetic" as paradigmatic or even foundational is not unique to Wittgenstein. Just recall how, in Kant, the aesthetic judgment grounds and shows the possibility of meaningful communication and publicity within the domain of empirical contingency and, in Dewey, aesthetic experience shapes and guides our interactions with the environment we live in.

119. Matteucci, "The (Aesthetic) Extended Mind," 427.
120. Arnold Berleant, *Living in the Landscape: Toward an Aesthetics of Environment* (Lawrence: University Press of Kansas, 1997), chap. 8.
121. Berleant, *Living in the Landscape*, 131.
122. Berleant, *Living in the Landscape*, 132, 134.
123. A central issue here is that of the institutionalization of such a "curriculum," only part of which can be entrusted, in my opinion, to schools, with the proviso that this should not lead to a "bookish," compartmentalized reduction of it.
124. Here, of course, one should more carefully distinguish between the three concepts and their meanings for *landscapes*. I employ *interdisciplinarity*, being the intermediate and more widespread one, as an umbrella concept here.
125. See Mick Atha et al., "Introduction. Ways of Knowing and Being with Landscapes: A Beginning," in Howard et al., *Routledge Companion to Landscape Studies*, xix–xxviii; and Gareth Doherty and Charles Waldheim, "Introduction: What Is Landscape?," in *Is Landscape . . . ?*, 1–8.
126. See also, from another perspective, Paolo Furia, "Connections Between Geography and Aesthetics," *Aesthetica Preprint* 114 (2020): 42: "Even though aesthetic ideas help to develop deeper insights into geographical concepts such as place, aesthetic appreciation as such is also useful in geographical knowledge. This is clearly evidenced by the fact that geography shares one of its core concepts with the history of art: landscape. Along with geography and art history, in recent years the theoretical discourses on landscape have increased their presence in the domains of architectural studies, planning, juridical studies, physical and cultural anthropology, psychology, economy, demography, not to mention geology, geomorphology, and pedology."
127. See Fairclough, Herlin, and Swanwick, "Landscape Character Assessment," 584:

> The argument that 'landscape' is a way of living together in the world, much more than a simple view or prospect (which is what the *Oxford English Dictionary* continues to suggest) does not however seem to have made much headway in public discourse or political debates. It may perhaps be that despite becoming such a prevalent and widely used term, landscape's moment is passing and the role of being the integrating concept that grand challenges demand is passing to other concepts, such as ecosystems or environmental humanities. This would be unfortunate, because . . . it is really only landscape . . . that covers all disciplines and brings together both people and place.

128. See also Lister, "Is Landscape Ecology?," 132: "Emerging approaches to landscape design in the context of resilience tend to reflect the characteristics of the ecological paradigm shifts that have laid its foundation: they are often interdisciplinary, integrating landscape, architecture, engineering and ecology specifically, and art

and science more broadly. These are not easy marriages... but they reveal the free-form dance that is the relationship between landscape and ecology."
129. Vera Vicenzotti, "On the Concept of Landscape in Landscape Urbanism," in Howard et al., *Routledge Companion to Landscape Studies*, 571.
130. Ulrich Eisel and Heather Nicholas, "About Dealing with the Impossible: An Account of Experience in Landscape Planning Courses," *European Journal of Education* 27, no. 3 (1992): 240.
131. On the importance of aesthetics in defusing tensions within landscape theory and practice, see Vicenzotti, "On the Concept of Landscape in Landscape Urbanism," 572.

5. BUILDING COMMON GROUND

1. This chapter is a reduced, re-elaborated version of Alberto L. Siani, "Between Professional Objectivity and Simmel's Moods: A Pragmatist-Aesthetic Proposal for Landscape Character," *Landscape Research* 48, no. 4 (2023): 583–93. My thanks go to the publishers and editors of the journal for allowing me to partly reuse the article.
2. The standard definition of landscape character is "a distinct, recognisable and consistent pattern of elements in the landscape that makes one landscape different from another, rather than better or worse." Christine Tudor, "An Approach to Landscape Character Assessment," Natural England (2014), 54, https://assets.publishing.service.gov.uk/government/uploads/system/uploads/attachment_data/file/691184/landscape-character-assessment.pdf. See also the definition by Graham Fairclough, Ingrid Sarlöv Herlin, and Carys Swanwick, "Landscape Character Assessment. A Global Practice," in *The Routledge Companion to Landscape Studies*, ed. Peter Howard, Ian Thompson, Emma Waterton, and Mick Atha (London: Routledge, 2019), 577, as "the distinct and recognisable combination of elements that occurs consistently in a particular area of land, and is perceived by humans as landscape." A landscape character assessment is "the process of identifying and describing variation in the character of the landscape. It seeks to identify and explain the unique combination of elements and features (characteristics) that make landscapes distinctive." Tudor, "An Approach to Landscape Character Assessment," 54. The ELC's definition of landscape, to recall, is "an area, as perceived by people, whose character is the result of the action and interaction of natural and/or human factors."
3. I borrow "twofold perspective," which appears throughout the chapter, from Theano S. Terkenli, Aikaterini Gkoltsiou, and Dimitris Kavroudakis, "The Interplay of Objectivity and Subjectivity in Landscape Character Assessment: Qualitative and Quantitative Approaches and Challenges," *Land* 10, no. 1: 53 (2021): 3.
4. See Terkenli et al., "The Interplay of Objectivity and Subjectivity"; Christopher Tilley, "Introduction: Identity, Place, Landscape and Heritage," *Journal of Material Culture* 11, no. 1–2 (2006): 7–32; and Meryem Atik, Rabia Canay Işıklı, Veli Ortaçeşme, and Emrah Yıldırım, "Exploring a Combination of Objective and Subjective Assessment in Landscape Classification: Side Case from Turkey," *Applied Geography* 83 (2017): 130–40.

5. See the meta-analysis in Terkenli et al., "The Interplay of Objectivity and Subjectivity," 12–16.
6. I should also clarify at the outset that, given my philosophical approach and scope, I do not pursue specific case studies or local practices (for which, see Graham Fairclough, Ingrid Sarlöv Herlin, and Carys Swanwick, eds., *Routledge Handbook of Landscape Character Assessment: Current Approaches to Characterisation and Assessment* [London: Routledge, 2018]) but an encompassing conceptual critique that may then be reframed on a case-by-case basis.
7. Andrew Butler, "Dynamics of Integrating Landscape Values in Landscape Character Assessment: The Hidden Dominance of the Objective Outsider," *Landscape Research* 41, no. 2 (2016): 249.
8. See Butler, "Dynamics of Integrating Landscape Values."
9. Graham Fairclough and Pete Herring, "Lens, Mirror, Window: Interactions Between Historic Landscape Characterisation and Landscape Character Assessment," *Landscape Research* 41, no. 2 (2016): 186.
10. European Science Foundation and COST, "Landscape in a Changing World: Bridging Divides, Integrating Disciplines, Serving Society" (2010), 1, http://archives.esf.org/hosting-experts/scientific-review-groups/humanities-hum/strategic-activities/esf-cost-synergy-initiatives/landscape-in-a-changing-world.html.
11. See Fairclough and Herring, "Lens, Mirror, Window."
12. European Science Foundation and COST, "Landscape in a Changing World," 6.
13. Butler, "Dynamics of Integrating Landscape Values," 249.
14. See Andrew Butler and Ulla Berglund, "Landscape Character Assessment as an Approach to Understanding Public Interests within the European Landscape Convention," *Landscape Research* 39, no. 3 (2014): 219–36.
15. Butler, "Dynamics of Integrating Landscape Values," 239. See also Grazia Brunetta and Angioletta Voghera, "Evaluating Landscape for Shared Values: Tools, Principles, and Methods," *Landscape Research* 33, no. 1 (2008): 71–87.
16. Brunetta and Voghera, "Evaluating Landscape for Shared Values," 72.
17. See Fairclough and Herring, "Lens, Mirror, Window."
18. Tudor, "An Approach to Landscape Character Assessment," 6.
19. This oscillation is visible in Tudor, "An Approach to Landscape Character Assessment."
20. Tudor, "An Approach to Landscape Character Assessment," 42.
21. See Brunetta and Voghera, "Evaluating Landscape for Shared Values."
22. See chapter 3, section 2.1.
23. Georg Simmel, "The Philosophy of Landscape," trans. Josef Bleicher, *Theory, Culture & Society* 24, no. 7–8 (2007): 26.
24. Simmel, "The Philosophy of Landscape," 26.
25. Simmel, "The Philosophy of Landscape," 26.
26. Simmel, "The Philosophy of Landscape," 28.
27. Butler, "Dynamics of Integrating Landscape Values," 249.
28. Butler, "Dynamics of Integrating Landscape Values," 249.
29. See chapter 3, section 2.1.
30. The implicit reference for the notion of "substantive landscapes" is Kenneth R. Olwig, "Recovering the Substantive Nature of Landscape," *Annals of the Association of*

American Geographers 86, no. 4 (1996): 630–53. For a convincing defense of the co-implication between a rich, nonsuperficial understanding of "character" and the employment of a plurality of aesthetic categories not reducible to the "scenic," and for an application of this connection to issues of environmental conservation, see Emily Brady, "Aesthetic Character and Aesthetic Integrity in Environmental Conservation," *Environmental Ethics* 24 (2002): 75–91.

6. LIVED LANDSCAPES

1. I want to thank Çiğdem Oğuz for her suggestions on this section.
2. Information received in October 2021 from the Municipality of Pescia. I take this occasion to warn that some of the numbers and data in this whole chapter may not be up to date or double checked; given the aim of these sketches, strict quantitative precision is not a must.
3. The origin of the toponym Valleriana is unclear and undocumented. The most credited origins are "Valle di Rii" (valley of rivers) or the Latin Vallis Arriani (valley of Arrianus).
4. This, of course, is also due to transport. The construction of the winding, narrow road system, where the roads are often not wide enough for two vehicles, connecting the *castella* between them and with the neighboring regions, did not start until the 1930s and was completed in the 1970s. Public transportation is practically nonexistent.
5. To be precise, thanks mostly to a relatively flourishing tourism, the area cannot be called poor. However, there are evident signs of "impoverishment" in a more general sense: the local schools, post offices, shops, bars, and so on have all closed down in the last years. In the hamlets, one cannot even buy bread or other basic goods, which are only sold by a single small food van driving through the area once in the morning, five times a week in the tourist season (I have no information about the cold season). The feeling one sometimes has in Valleriana of abandonment and loneliness, but without degradation and desolation, can be said to be peculiar to the place and to play a role in its aesthetics.
6. He speaks of "several villages nestled like eagle's nests among the rocks or in the steep mounds' slopes and the houses backed against each other that seem to cover them, animate the landscape and confer it the most romantic overview." Quoted in Cristina Scaletti, "Presentazioni," in *Dalla Valleriana alla Svizzera Pesciatina*, ed. Regione Toscana (Pisa: Pacini, 2012), 7.
7. See Francesca Sofia, "Sismondi e la Svizzera Pesciatina," in *Dalla Valleriana alla Svizzera Pesciatina*, 38–39.
8. See Sofia, "Sismondi e la Svizzera Pesciatina," 39–40.
9. For this concept, see chapter 2, section 6.
10. In Vellano alone, the "stonecutters' town," there were around three hundred stonecutters and fifty quarries. In the first half of the twentieth century, many local stonecutters moved not only to Florence or Milan but even as far as Germany, Romania, France, Spain, and the United States.
11. Davide Trane and Mauro Agostini, "Vita nelle 'Castella' e antichi mestieri," in *Dalla Valleriana alla Svizzera Pesciatina*, 64. As often happens, chestnut flour

from those areas is nowadays a relatively rare, sought after, and expensive delicacy.

12. Quoted in Ilaria Tabarrani, "Struttura del paesaggio," in *Dalla Valleriana alla Svizzera Pesciatina*, 71.
13. On these rules, see Tabarrani, "Struttura del paesaggio," 72.
14. Trane and Agostini, "Vita nelle 'Castella' e antichi mestieri," 69.
15. Regarding tastes, most notably, one should mention the famous—relatively to the mini scale of its production—Sorana bean: a small, white, tender bean grown on the rocky terrains of a couple river bights and traditionally cooked in the *gozzo*, a special glass flask. Local olive oil and honey are also widely appreciated.
16. Emanuele Pellegrini, "Beni artistici e architettonici," in *Dalla Valleriana alla Svizzera Pesciatina*, 49.
17. Pellegrini, "Beni artistici e architettonici," 49.
18. I want to thank Peter Borgmann for his suggestions on this section.
19. The historical novel by Luther Blissett offers a good, although fictionalized, account of these events. Luther Blissett, Q, trans. Shaun Whiteside (London: Heinemann, 2003).
20. One speaks of "Westphalian sovereignty" or "Westphalian state system," a

    > term used in international relations, supposedly arising from the Treaties of Westphalia in 1648 which ended the Thirty Years War. It is generally held to mean a system of states or international society comprising sovereign state entities possessing the monopoly of force within their mutually recognized territories. Relations between states are conducted by means of formal diplomatic ties between heads of state and governments, and international law consists of treaties made (and broken) by those sovereign entities. The term implies a separation of the domestic and international spheres, such that states may not legitimately intervene in the domestic affairs of another, whether in the pursuit of self-interest or by appeal to a higher notion of sovereignty, be it religion, ideology, or other supranational ideal. In this sense the term differentiates the "modern" state system from earlier models, such as the Holy Roman Empire or the Ottoman Empire.

    Richard Coggins, "Westphalian State System," in *The Concise Oxford Dictionary of Politics*, ed. Iain McLean and Alistair McMillan (Oxford: Oxford University Press, 2009).

21. The combination of flatness, pleasant nature, excellent infrastructure, and concentration of historical sights (it has been called the Land of Hundred Castles) makes it an ideal place for outdoor leisure or tourist activities such as cycling and horse-riding. Münsterland hosts one of the last herds of wild horses in Europe, and Münster is considered to be a bicycle capital.
22. Of course, I do not mean to imply that the situation is unproblematic or that the problems are easy to solve, especially if we talk of reconciling environmental protection, ethical concerns, and intensive farming in its current form.
23. See SALBES, "Case Study Münsterland, Germany," 2019, 1–2, https://salbes.eu/wp-content/uploads/2019/08/Factsheet_casestudy_Muensterland_12Juni2019_fin.pdf:

6. LIVED LANDSCAPES

The requested stakeholder network consists of all regional relevant actors. The main project partner of the case study region is the cultural landscape association Stiftung Westfälische Kulturlandschaft, a foundation of the Farmers Association for the promotion of the rural areas. The network covers a broad range of regional relevant thematic fields (e.g., agriculture, nature conservation, regional development) and of the hierarchical levels, agencies, land managers (e.g., farmers, planners, nature conservation managers and others), foundations (e.g., cultural landscape associations) and associations (e.g., farmers associations), and NGOs, like NABU, BUND on county and federal state level, departments of administration (agricultural agencies, nature conservancy authorities, agencies for regional development on county and federal state level), local and regional politicians. The stakeholders have a growing interest in innovative, farm-viable, regional-adapted and production-integrated and accompanying solutions, support of green infrastructure to reduce or stop the ongoing habitat and species decline under current and foreseeable future conditions.

24. The local constituency is traditionally moderate, with a strong environmentalist connotation, and scarce support for radical parties, both Left and Right.
25. Landschaftsverband Westfalen-Lippe, "Erhaltende Kulturlandschaftsentwicklung im Münsterland" (2012), 15, https://www.lwl.org/302a-download/PDF/kultur landschaft/KuLaReg_Muensterland_Broschuere.pdf.
26. Such as the moated castle of Vischering.
27. Keep in mind the date of 1947, mentioned in the quote above.
28. According to a 2020 survey, 82 percent of *Münsterländer* see themselves living in Münsterland in the future, and 96 percent think that it is a good place to live. Münsterland, "Münsterland 2020 Brand Study" (2020), https://www.muenster land.com/en/munsterland-e.v/munsterland-brand/brand-study/.
29. In the same spirit, one could also make reference to *Himmel und Erde* (Heaven and Earth), a term not designating ultimate metaphysical matters but a wildly popular local dish mostly associated with the Rhineland but also very popular in Münsterland consisting of black pudding, fried onions, apple mousse (from "heaven"), and mashed potatoes (from "earth").
30. I want to thank Çiğdem Oğuz for her suggestions on this section.
31. On the history of the city, with a special focus on monuments and places, see the classic by John Freely: *Istanbul: The Imperial City* (London: Penguin, 1998).
32. John Lovering and Hade Türkmen, "Bulldozer Neo-Liberalism in Istanbul: The State-Led Construction of Property Markets, and the Displacement of the Urban Poor," *International Planning Studies* 16, no. 1 (2011): 73.
33. Fatma Ayçim Türer Başkaya, "Revealing Landscape Planning Strategies for Disaster-Prone Coastal Urban Environments: The Case of Istanbul Megacity," in *Sea Level Rise and Coastal Infrastructure*, ed. Yuanzhi Zhang, Yijun Hou, and Xiaomei Yang (IntechOpen, 2018), 2–3.
34. See Vasile I. Marza, "On the Death Toll of the 1999 Izmit (Turkey) Major Earthquake," 2004, https://web.archive.org/web/20080409044047/http:/www.esc-web.org/papers /potsdam_2004/ss_1_marza.pdf.

6. LIVED LANDSCAPES

35. For some important observations on the disruptive connections between landscape and earthquake (although in the context of small Italian villages), see Paolo D'Angelo, *Il paesaggio: Teorie, storie, luoghi* (Bari-Roma: Laterza, 2021), 23–36.
36. Tessa Fox, "Can Istanbul Stand up to the Next Big Earthquake?," *Reuters*, December 8, 2020.
37. Istanbul consistently ranks among the most congested cities in the world. I come back to transportation in the conclusion.
38. See Melih Yeşilbağ, "Statecraft on Cement: The Politics of Land-Based Accumulation in Erdoğan's Turkey," *Urban Studies* 59, no. 13 (2021); and Lovering and Türkmen, "Bulldozer Neo-Liberalism in Istanbul," 82. The ambition is to rebuild almost one half of the city.
39. Such as Kanal Istanbul, a planned waterway strongly promoted by President Recep Tayyip Erdoğan and connecting the Black Sea with the Marmara Sea, transforming the European side of Istanbul into a huge island. The project also includes the construction of new ports, transportation hubs, artificial islands, and luxury residential areas.
40. For an "anthropology" of Istanbul traffic, which was ranked as a bigger problem than crime or the cost of living, see Berna Yazıcı, "Towards an Anthropology of Traffic: A Ride Through Class Hierarchies on Istanbul's Roadways," *Ethnos* 78, no. 4 (2013): 515–42.
41. See Orhan Pamuk, *Istanbul: Memories and the City*, trans. M. Freely (London: Faber & Faber, 1995); and Orhan Pamuk, "Hüzün—Melancholy—Tristesse of Istanbul," in *Other Cities, Other Worlds: Urban Imaginaries in a Globalizing Age*, ed. Andreas Huyssen (Durham, N.C.: Duke University Press, 2008), 289–306. For a discussion, see Banu Helvacıoğlu, "Melancholy and 'Hüzün' in Orhan Pamuk's 'Istanbul,'" *Mosaic: An Interdisciplinary Critical Journal* 46, no. 2 (2013): 163–78. Pamuk's comprehensive reading of Istanbul in terms of melancholy was the main ground for the award of the Nobel Prize in 2006 (from the motivation: Pamuk "in the quest for the melancholic soul of his native city has discovered new symbols for the clash and interlacing of cultures"). We may add that associated with this feeling, there is a typically Turkish form of humor: bitter, absurdist, emancipatory, and oddly political and apolitical at the same time.
42. Pamuk, "Hüzün—Melancholy—Tristesse of Istanbul," 289.
43. The most obvious example of this complex relationship with the non-Muslim past is the city's most iconic monument, Hagia Sophia. Built in 537 as the patriarchal cathedral of Constantinople, for almost a thousand years the world's largest cathedral and center of the Eastern Orthodox Church, it was converted to a mosque after the fall of the city to the Ottomans in 1453, turned into a museum in 1935 by the secular Republic of Turkey, and controversially redesignated as a mosque in 2020 by President Erdoğan. But of course there are myriads other fascinating minor examples, such as the Barnathan Apartments, a monumental, beautiful palace in the Galata district built in the nineteenth century by a Jewish family that had arrived to Istanbul in 1492 fleeing the Spanish Inquisition; the palace was then divided among tenants of different ethnic origin after World War I, partly left to abandonment and decay, and currently being rebuilt as a

6. LIVED LANDSCAPES

luxury suites complex. On Barnathan Apartments and for a general reconstruction of these dynamics of change, see Çiğdem Oğuz, *Barnathan Apartments* (Istanbul: Global Basım Yayın, 2016).

44. Even from the point of view of the political or sociological theoretical framing, the situation is confusing, to say the least. The widespread use of categories such as "authoritarian neoliberalism" or "bulldozer neoliberalism" (Lovering and Türkmen, "Bulldozer Neo-Liberalism in Istanbul") is, in my opinion, confusing and ideological in the Turkish context. Turkish politics and economy are in fact markedly centralistic and dirigiste, with very little free-market competition and private businesses often working by dint of personal connections, corruption, or political kinship. Even the category of (re)Islamization seems to me quite generic and not particularly fertile. Despite these perplexities and since I cannot pursue these topics here, I refer to Lovering and Türkmen, "Bulldozer Neo-Liberalism in Istanbul," for a good discussion of specific case studies, showing the many difficulties of categorizing Turkish politics into received concepts as well as, more specifically, the dynamics of conflict outlined here.

45. Although its roots are obviously much older and have to do again with structural historical contradictions, between attempts of modernization and conservatism, Westernization and (neo)Ottomanism, multicultural heritage and nationalistic pushes (Istanbul's imperial cosmopolitanism was in fact despised as corrupt by the secular, Western-oriented but nationalist movement led by Mustafa Kemal Atatürk, who founded the republic), global orientation and localism. See Efsun Güney Ekenyazıcı, "A Study on the Effect of Transportation Systems to the Evolution of the City Image—The Case of Istanbul," *Megaron* 7, no. 1 (2012): 91–107.

46. From this point of view, hüzün and active conflict are to be considered as the two sides of the same coin and are as a matter of fact often found in combination.

47. On "oil stain," see Güney Ekenyazıcı, "A Study on the Effect of Transportation Systems," 92: "After 1970's, the city started to expand in every direction together with the boom of fast and unplanned urbanization, drifting apart from its identity as a city of waterfronts that it preserved for years and taking the identity of a city inland.... With the unplanned sprawl of urban macroform, there occurred an organic character ... likened to 'oil stains.'" On empty space and empty time, Güney Ekenyazıcı writes: "Losing almost all its green areas, the city was disguised to the character of an 'oversized industrial city' with gecekondu, dolmuş, and handseller (işporta) phenomenons, all of which form a texture without any empty spaces." Güney Ekenyazıcı, "A Study on the Effect of Transportation Systems," 98.

48. *Simit* is a ring-shaped, sesame-crusted bread.

49. *Sahlep* is a hot, condensed milk–based drink infused with an orchid tuber's flour and garnished with cinnamon.

BIBLIOGRAPHY

Note: If not indicated otherwise, translations are the author's.

Amoroso, Leonardo. "Kant e il problema di una regola delle regole." *Nuova civiltà delle macchine* 3, no. 3–4 (1985): 5–8.
———. "L'estetica come filosofia dell'esperienza. Rileggendo Dewey con Garroni." In *Esperienza estetica: A partire da John Dewey*, ed. Luigi Russo, 99–109. Palermo: Centro internazionale studi di estetica, 2007.
Antrop, Marc. "A Brief History of Landscape Research." In Howard et al., *The Routledge Companion to Landscape Studies*, 1–15.
Appleton, Jay. "Prospects and Refuges Re-Visited." *Landscape Journal* 3, no. 2 (1984): 91–103.
Arendt, Hannah. *Lectures on Kant's Political Philosophy*. Ed. Rudolf Beiner. Chicago: University of Chicago Press, 1989.
Assunto, Rosario. *Il paesaggio e l'estetica*. Palermo: Novecento, 1994.
———. "Paesaggio, ambiente, territorio: Un tentativo di precisazione concettuale." *Rassegna di architettura e urbanistica* (1980): 49–51.
Atha, Mick. "Ephemeral Landscapes." In Howard et al., *Routledge Companion to Landscape Studies*, 113–26.
Atha, Mick, Peter Howard, Ian Thompson, and Emma Waterton. "Introduction. Ways of Knowing and Being with Landscapes: A Beginning." In Howard et al., *Routledge Companion to Landscape Studies*, xix–xxviii.
Atik, Meryem, Rabia Canay Işıklı, Veli Ortaçeşme, and Emrah Yıldırım. "Exploring a Combination of Objective and Subjective Assessment in Landscape Classification: Side Case from Turkey." *Applied Geography* 83 (2017): 130–40. https://doi.org/10.1016/j.apgeog.2017.04.004.

BIBLIOGRAPHY

Bai, Heesoon. "A Critical Reflection on Environmental Education During the COVID-19 Pandemic." *Journal of Philosophy of Education* 54, no. 4 (2020): 916–26. https://doi.org/10.1111/1467-9752.12472.

Barthes, Roland. "The Death of the Author." In *Image Music Text*, trans. Stephen Heath, 142–48. London: Fontana, 1977.

Başkaya, Fatma Ayçim Türer. "Revealing Landscape Planning Strategies for Disaster-Prone Coastal Urban Environments: The Case of Istanbul Megacity." In *Sea Level Rise and Coastal Infrastructure*, ed. Yuanzhi Zhang, Yijun Hou, and Xiaomei Yang. IntechOpen, 2018. https://doi.org/10.5772/intechopen.73567.

Bélanger, Pierre. "Is Landscape Infrastructure?" In Doherty and Waldheim, *Is Landscape . . . ?*, 190–227.

Bender, Barbara. "Time and Landscape." *Current Anthropology* 43, no. 4 (2002): 103–12. https://doi.org/10.1086/339561.

Bennett, Kevin. "Savanna Hypothesis and Landscape Preferences, The." In *Encyclopedia of Evolutionary Psychological Science*, ed. Todd K. Shackelford and Viviana A. Weekes-Shackelford, 1–4. Cham: Springer International, 2019. https://doi.org/10.1007/978-3-319-16999-6_3726-1.

Berleant, Arnold. "The Art in Knowing a Landscape." *Diogenes* 59, no. 1–2 (2012): 52–62.

———. *Living in the Landscape: Toward an Aesthetics of Environment*. Lawrence: University Press of Kansas, 1997.

Berque, Augustin. "Beyond the Modern Landscape." *AA Files*, no. 25 (1993): 33–37.

Biancini, Pierluigi. "Language as Environment: An Ecological Approach to Wittgenstein's Form of Life." In *Papers of the 32nd International Wittgenstein Symposium*, ed. Volker A. Munz, Klaus Puhl, and Joseph Wang, 56–58. Kirchberg am Wechsel: Austrian Ludwig Wittgenstein Society, 2009.

Blissett, Luther. *Q*. Trans. Shaun Whiteside. London: Heinemann, 2003.

Bonazzi, Alessandra. "Il piano dell'oceano: James Cook e Immanuel Kant." *Semestrale di studi e ricerche di geografia* 30, no. 2 (2018): 55–67. https://doi.org/10.13133/1125-5218.14947.

Bonesio, Luisa. *Paesaggio, identità e comunità tra locale e globale*. Milano: Mimesis, 2017.

Bonfiglioli, Stefania. "Sull'attualità del concetto di paesaggio." In *Oltre la convenzione: Pensare, studiare, costruire il paesaggio vent'anni dopo*, ed. Benedetta Castiglioni, Matteo Puttilli, and Marcello Tanca, 38–48. Firenze: Società di studi geografici, 2021.

Bonnett, Alastair. *Unruly Places: Lost Spaces, Secret Cities, and Other Inscrutable Geographies*. Boston: Houghton Mifflin Harcourt, 2014.

Bourassa, Steven C. "Toward a Theory of Landscape Aesthetics." *Landscape and Urban Planning* 15, no. 3–4 (1988): 241–52. https://doi.org/10.1016/0169-2046(88)90048-5.

Bowring, Jacky. "Navigating the Global, the Regional and the Local: Researching Globalization and Landscape." In Howard et al., *Routledge Companion to Landscape Studies*, 299–310.

Boylan, Alexis L. *Visual Culture*. Cambridge, Mass.: MIT Press, 2020.

Brady, Emily. "Aesthetic Character and Aesthetic Integrity in Environmental Conservation." *Environmental Ethics* 24 (2002): 75–91. https://doi.org/10.5840/enviroethics200224142.

———. *Aesthetics of the Natural Environment*. Edinburgh: Edinburgh University Press, 2003.

BIBLIOGRAPHY

———. "Interpreting Environments." *Essays in Philosophy* 3, no. 1 (2002): 57–67.
Brisson, Luc. "Plato's Theory of Sense Perception in the Timaeus: How It Works and What It Means." *Proceedings of the Boston Area Colloquium of Ancient Philosophy* 13, no. 1 (1997): 147–76.
Brook, Isis. "Aesthetic Appreciation of Landscape." In Howard et al., *Routledge Companion to Landscape Studies*, 39–50.
Brunetta, Grazia, and Angioletta Voghera. "Evaluating Landscape for Shared Values: Tools, Principles, and Methods." *Landscape Research* 33, no. 1 (2008): 71–87. https://doi.org/10.1080/01426390701773839.
Butler, Andrew. "Dynamics of Integrating Landscape Values in Landscape Character Assessment: The Hidden Dominance of the Objective Outsider." *Landscape Research* 41, no. 2 (2016): 239–52. https://doi.org/10.1080/01426397.2015.1135315.
Butler, Andrew, and Ulla Berglund. "Landscape Character Assessment as an Approach to Understanding Public Interests within the European Landscape Convention." *Landscape Research* 39, no. 3 (2014): 219–36. https://doi.org/10.1080/01426397.2012.716404.
Byrne, Denis. "Reclaiming Landscape: Coastal Reclamations Before and During the Anthropocene." In Howard et al., *Routledge Companion to Landscape Studies*, 277–87.
Carlson, Allen. "Appreciation and the Natural Environment." *Journal of Aesthetics and Art Criticism* 37, no. 3 (1979): 267–75. https://doi.org/10.2307/430781.
Carroll, Noël. "On Being Moved by Nature: Between Religion and Natural History." In Kemal and Gaskell, *Landscape, Natural Beauty and the Arts*, 244–66.
Cassar, Louis F. "Landscape and Ecology: The Need for a Holistic Approach to the Conservation of Habitats and Biota." In Howard et al., *Routledge Companion to Landscape Studies*, 476–86.
Chakrabarty, Dipesh. "The Climate of History: Four Theses." *Critical Inquiry* 35, no. 2 (2009): 197–222. https://doi.org/10.1086/596640.
Coggins, Richard. "Westphalian State System." In *The Concise Oxford Dictionary of Politics*, ed. Iain McLean and Alistair McMillan. Oxford: Oxford University Press, 2009. https://www.oxfordreference.com/display/10.1093/acref/9780199207800.001.0001/acref-9780199207800-e-1467.
Collini, Stefan. "Introduction: Interpretation Terminable and Interminable." In Eco and Collini, *Interpretation and Overinterpretation*, 1–22.
Corner, James. "Eidetic Operations and New Landscapes." In *Recovering Landscape: Essays in Contemporary Landscape Architecture*, ed. James Corner, 152–69. New York: Princeton Architectural Press, 1999.
Cosgrove, Denis. "Modernity, Community and the Landscape Idea." *Journal of Material Culture* 11 (2006): 49–66. https://doi.org/10.1177/1359183506062992.
———. "Prospect, Perspective and the Evolution of the Landscape Idea." *Transactions of the Institute of British Geographers* 10, no. 1 (1985): 45–62. https://doi.org/10.2307/622249.
———. *Social Formation and Symbolic Landscape*. Madison: University of Wisconsin Press, 1998.
Dalla Valleriana alla Svizzera Pesciatina, ed. Regione Toscana. Pisa: Pacini, 2012.
D'Angelo, Paolo. "Agriculture and Landscape: From Cultivated Fields to the Wilderness, and Back." In *Philosophy of Landscape: Think, Walk, Act*, ed. Moirika Reker

and Adriana Veríssimo Serrão, 241–56. Lisbon: Centre for Philosophy at the University of Lisbon, 2019.
———. *Filosofia del paesaggio*. Macerata: Quodlibet, 2014.
———. *Il paesaggio: Teorie, storie, luoghi*. Bari-Roma: Laterza, 2021.
De Nardi, Sarah, and Danielle Drozdzewski. "Landscape and Memory." In Howard et al., *Routledge Companion to Landscape Studies*, 429–39.
DeLue, Rachael Z. "Is Landscape Theory?" In Doherty and Waldheim, *Is Landscape . . . ?*, 261–84.
Dewey, John. *Art as Experience*. Ed. Jo Ann Boydston. Carbondale: Southern Illinois University Press, 1987.
Di Palma, Vittoria. "Is Landscape Painting?" In Doherty and Waldheim, *Is Landscape . . . ?*, 44–70.
Doherty, Gareth. "Is Landscape Literature?" In Doherty and Waldheim, *Is Landscape . . . ?*, 13–43.
Doherty, Gareth, and Charles Waldheim. "Introduction: What Is Landscape?" In Doherty and Waldheim, *Is Landscape . . . ?*, 1–8.
———, eds. *Is Landscape . . . ? Essays on the Identity of Landscape*. London: Routledge, 2016.
Dreon, Roberta. *Human Landscapes: Contributions to a Pragmatist Anthropology*. Albany: State University of New York Press, 2022.
Eco, Umberto. "Reply." In Eco and Collini, *Interpretation and Overinterpretation*, 139–51.
———. "Unlimited Semiosis and Drift: Pragmaticism vs. 'Pragmatism.'" In *The Limits of Interpretation*, 23–43. Bloomington: Indiana University Press, 1994.
Eco, Umberto, and Stefan Collini, eds. *Interpretation and Overinterpretation*. Cambridge: Cambridge University Press, 1992.
Egoz, Shelley. "Landscape and Identity in the Century of the Migrant." In Howard et al., eds., *Routledge Companion to Landscape Studies*, 329–40.
Eisel, Ulrich, and Heather Nicholas. "About Dealing with the Impossible: An Account of Experience in Landscape Planning Courses." *European Journal of Education* 27, no. 3 (1992): 239–55. https://doi.org/10.2307/1503452.
Euler, Werner. *Natur und Freiheit: Kommentar zu den Einleitungen in Kants "Kritik der Urteilskraft."* Hamburg: Meiner, 2018.
European Science Foundation and COST. *Landscape in a Changing World: Bridging Divides, Integrating Disciplines, Serving Society* (2010). http://archives.esf.org/hosting-experts/scientific-review-groups/humanities-hum/strategic-activities/esf-cost-synergy-initiatives/landscape-in-a-changing-world.html.
Fairclough, Graham, Ingrid Sarlöv Herlin, and Carys Swanwick, eds. *Routledge Handbook of Landscape Character Assessment: Current Approaches to Characterisation and Assessment*. London: Routledge, 2018.
———. "Landscape Character Assessment. A Global Practice." In Howard et al., *Routledge Companion to Landscape Studies*, 576–88.
Fairclough, Graham, and Pete Herring. "Lens, Mirror, Window: Interactions Between Historic Landscape Characterisation and Landscape Character Assessment." *Landscape Research* 41, no. 2 (2016): 186–98. https://doi.org/10.1080/01426397.2015.1135318.

Ferrini, Cinzia. "The Land of Truth of the Understanding and the Threatening Waters of Reason: Maritime Sources for a Kantian Metaphor." *Esercizi Filosofici* 8, no. 2 (2013): 53–70.

Fox, Tessa. "Can Istanbul Stand up to the Next Big Earthquake?" Reuters, December 8, 2020. https://www.reuters.com/article/turkey-cities-disaster-trfn-idUSKBN28 I1MH.

Freely, John. *Istanbul: The Imperial City*. London: Penguin, 1998.

Furia, Paolo. "Connections Between Geography and Aesthetics." *Aesthetica Preprint* 114 (2020): 35–48.

———. *Spaesamento: Esperienza estetico-geografica*. Milano: Meltemi, 2023.

Gifford, Don. "The Touch of Landscape." In Kemal and Gaskell, *Landscape, Natural Beauty and the Arts*, 127–38.

Glock, Hans-Johann. *A Wittgenstein Dictionary*. Chichester, UK: Wiley-Blackwell, 1996.

Griffero, Tonino. "Paesaggi e atmosfere: Ontologia ed esperienza estetica della natura." *Rivista di estetica* 45, no. 29 (2005): 7–40.

———. *Places, Affordances, Atmospheres: A Pathic Aesthetics*. London: Routledge, 2019.

Güney Ekenyazıcı, Efsun. "A Study on the Effect of Transportation Systems to the Evolution of the City Image—The Case of Istanbul." *Megaron* 7, no. 1 (2012): 91–107.

Hawkins, Harriet. "Picturing Landscape." In Howard et al., *Routledge Companion to Landscape Studies*, 206–14.

Helvacıoğlu, Banu. "Melancholy and 'Hüzün' in Orhan Pamuk's 'Istanbul.'" *Mosaic: An Interdisciplinary Critical Journal* 46, no. 2 (2013): 163–78.

Hepburn, Ronald W. "Contemporary Aesthetics and the Neglect of Natural Beauty." In *British Analytical Philosophy*, ed. Bernard Williams and Alan Montefiore, 285–310. London: Routledge and Kegan Paul, 1966.

———. "Trivial and Serious in Aesthetic Appreciation of Nature." In Kemal and Gaskell, *Landscape, Natural Beauty and the Arts*, 65–80.

Herrington, Susan. "Landscape Design." In Howard et al., *Routledge Companion to Landscape Studies*, 487–98.

Höfer, Wolfram, and Vera Vicenzotti. "Post-Industrial Landscapes: Evolving Concepts." In Howard et al., *Routledge Companion to Landscape Studies*, 499–510.

Holmes, Damian. "The Increasing Importance of Outdoor Space." *World Landscape Architecture* (blog), January 10, 2021. https://worldlandscapearchitect.com/the-increasing-importance-of-outdoor-space/.

Howard, Peter. "Perceptual Lenses." In Howard et al., *Routledge Companion to Landscape Studies*, 51–61.

Howard, Peter, Ian Thompson, Emma Waterton, and Mick Atha, eds. *The Routledge Companion to Landscape Studies*. London: Routledge, 2019.

Hunt, John Dixon. "Is Landscape History?" In Doherty and Waldheim, *Is Landscape . . . ?*, 247–60.

Ingold, Tim. *The Perception of the Environment. Essays on Livelihood, Dwelling and Skill*. London: Routledge, 2000.

———. "The Temporality of the Landscape." *World Archaeology* 25, no. 2 (1993): 152–74.

Jackson, John B. "The Word Itself." In *Discovering the Vernacular Landscape*, 3–8. New Haven, Conn.: Yale University Press, 1984.

Kambaskovic, Danijela, and Charles T. Wolfe. "The Senses in Philosophy and Science: From the Nobility of Sight to the Materialism of Touch." In *A Cultural History of the Senses in the Renaissance*, ed. Herman Roodenburg, 107–25. London: Bloomsbury Academic, 2014.

Kant, Immanuel. *Critique of the Power of Judgment*. Ed. Paul Guyer. Trans. Paul Guyer and Eric Matthews. Cambridge: Cambridge University Press, 2000.

———. *Critique of Pure Reason*. Ed. and trans. Paul Guyer and Allen W. Wood. Cambridge: Cambridge University Press, 1998.

Keeling, Paul M. "Does the Idea of Wilderness Need a Defence?" *Environmental Values* 17, no. 4 (2008): 505–19. https://doi.org/10.3197/096327108X368511.

Kelsey, Robin. "Is Landscape Photography?" In *Doherty and Waldheim, Is Landscape . . . ?*, 71–92.

Kemal, Salim, and Ivan Gaskell, eds. *Landscape, Natural Beauty and the Arts*. Cambridge: Cambridge University Press, 1993.

———. "Nature, Fine Arts, and Aesthetics." In Kemal and Gaskell, *Landscape, Natural Beauty and the Arts*, 1–42.

Kempf, Michael. "From Landscape Affordances to Landscape Connectivity: Contextualizing an Archaeology of Human Ecology." *Archaeological and Anthropological Sciences* 12, no. 174 (2020): 174. https://doi.org/10.1007/s12520-020-01157-4.

Kerridge, Richard. "New Directions in the Literary Representation of Landscape." In Howard et al., *Routledge Companion to Landscape Studies*, 253–63.

Kottman, Paul A. *Love as Human Freedom*. Stanford, Calif.: Stanford University Press, 2017.

Krauss, Werner. "Postenvironmental Landscapes in the Anthropocene." In Howard et al., *Routledge Companion to Landscape Studies*, 62–73.

Kusch, Martin. "Georg Simmel and Pragmatism." *European Journal of Pragmatism and American Philosophy* 9, no. 1 (2019). https://doi.org/10.4000/ejpap.1490.

Leatherbarrow, David. "Is Landscape Architecture?" In Doherty and Waldheim, *Is Landscape . . . ?*, 327–37.

Lister, Nina-Marie. "Is Landscape Ecology?" In Doherty and Waldheim, *Is Landscape . . . ?*, 115–37.

Lovering, John, and Hade Türkmen. "Bulldozer Neo-Liberalism in Istanbul: The State-Led Construction of Property Markets, and the Displacement of the Urban Poor." *International Planning Studies* 16, no. 1 (2011): 73–96. https://doi.org/10.1080/13563475.2011.552477.

Landschaftsverband Westfalen-Lippe. "Erhaltende Kulturlandschaftsentwicklung im Münsterland" (2012). https://www.lwl.org/302a-download/PDF/kulturlandschaft/KuLaReg_Muensterland_Broschuere.pdf.

Makkreel, Rudolf A. "Kant and the Need for Orientational and Contextual Thinking: Applying Reflective Judgement to Aesthetics and to the Comprehension of Human Life." *Kantian Review* 26, no. 1 (2020): 53–78. https://doi.org/10.1017/S136941542000031X.

Marza, Vasile I. *On the Death Toll of the 1999 Izmit (Turkey) Major Earthquake* (2004). https://web.archive.org/web/20080409044047/http://www.esc-web.org/papers/potsdam_2004/ss_1_marza.pdf.

Matteucci, Giovanni. "The (Aesthetic) Extended Mind: Aesthetics from Experience-of to Experience-with." *Proceedings of the European Society for Aesthetics* 10 (2018): 401–29.

———. *Estetica e natura umana: La mente estesa tra percezione, emozione ed espressione.* Roma: Carocci, 2019.
Matthes, Erich Hatala. "Portraits of the Landscape." In *Portraits and Philosophy*, ed. Hans Maes. New York: Routledge, 2020.
Messori, Rita. "Il ritmo performativo del paesaggio." *Studi di estetica* 49/4, no. 3 (2021): 1–16. https://doi.org/10.7413/18258646174.
Mitchell, William J. T. "Imperial Landscape." In *Landscape and Power*, ed. William J. T. Mitchell, 5–34. Chicago: University of Chicago Press, 2002.
Moore, Kathryn. "Is Landscape Philosophy?" In Doherty and Waldheim, *Is Landscape . . . ?*, 285–301.
Myhre, Knut Christian. "Deep Pragmatism." In *The Mythology in Our Language: Remarks on Frazer's Golden Bough*, ed. Giovanni Da Col and Stephan Palmié, 95–113. Chicago: HAU Books, 2018.
Nagel, Thomas. *The View from Nowhere*. Oxford: Oxford University Press, 1986.
Oğuz, Çiğdem. *Barnathan Apartments*. Istanbul: Global Basım Yayın, 2016.
Olwig, Kenneth R. "The Law of Landscape and the Landscape of Law: The 'Things' That Matter." In Howard et al., *Routledge Companion to Landscape Studies*, 377–86.
———. "Recovering the Substantive Nature of Landscape." *Annals of the Association of American Geographers* 86, no. 4 (1996): 630–53. https://doi.org/10.1111/j.1467-8306.1996.tb01770.x.
Pamuk, Orhan. "Hüzün—Melancholy—Tristesse of Istanbul." In *Other Cities, Other Worlds: Urban Imaginaries in a Globalizing Age*, ed. Andreas Huyssen, 289–306. Durham, N.C.: Duke University Press, 2008. https://doi.org/10.1515/9780822389361-014.
Pellegrini, Emanuele. "Beni artistici e architettonici." In *Dalla Valleriana alla Svizzera Pesciatina*, 47–52.
Perullo, Nicola. *Estetica ecologica: Percepire saggio, vivere corrispondente*. Milano: Mimesis, 2019.
———. "Feet, Lines, Weather, Labyrinth: The Haptic Engagement as a Suggestion for an Ecological Aesthetics." *Contemporary Aesthetics* 17 (2019). https://digitalcommons.risd.edu/liberalarts_contempaesthetics/vol17/iss1/16.
Pogliano, Claudio. *Senso lato: Il tatto e la cultura occidentale*. Roma: Carocci, 2015.
Pollock, Venda Louise. "Land, Art." In Howard et al., *Routledge Companion to Landscape Studies*, 215–26.
Price, Colin. "Researching the Economics of Landscape." In Howard et al., *Routledge Companion to Landscape Studies*, 387–401.
Puett, Michael. "Wittgenstein on Frazer." In *The Mythology in Our Language: Remarks on Frazer's Golden Bough*, ed. Giovanni Da Col and Stephan Palmié, 137–53. Chicago: HAU Books, 2018.
Ritter, Joachim. "Landschaft: Zur Funktion des Ästhetischen in der modernen Gesellschaft." In *Metaphysik und Politik: Studien zu Aristoteles und Hegel*, 141–90. Frankfurt am Main: Suhrkamp, 2003.
Roe, Maggie. "Landscape and Participation." In Howard et al., *Routledge Companion to Landscape Studies*, 402–17.
Rorty, Richard. "The Pragmatist's Progress." In Eco and Collini, *Interpretation and Overinterpretation*, 89–108.
Ross, Stephanie. "Gardens, Earthworks, and Environmental Art." In Kemal and Gaskell, *Landscape, Natural Beauty and the Arts*, 158–82.

Ruitenberg, Claudia. "The Cruel Optimism of Transformative Environmental Education." *Journal of Philosophy of Education* 54, no. 4 (August 2020): 832–37. https://doi.org/10.1111/1467-9752.12468.

Saito, Yuriko. *Everyday Aesthetics*. Oxford: Oxford University Press, 2007.

———. "Is There a Correct Aesthetic Appreciation of Nature?" *Journal of Aesthetic Education* 18, no. 4 (1984): 35–46. https://doi.org/10.2307/3332625.

Saul, Hayley, and Emma Waterton. "Anthropocene Landscapes." In Howard et al., *Routledge Companion to Landscape Studies*, 139–51.

Scaletti, Cristina. "Presentazioni." In *Dalla Valleriana alla Svizzera Pesciatina*, 7.

Schneemann, Peter J. "Performative Landscapes: A Paradigm for Mediating the Ecological Imperative?" In *Landscape and Earth in Early Modernity. Picturing Unruly Nature*, ed. Christine Göttler and Mia Mochizuki, 393–414. Amsterdam: Amsterdam University Press, 2023. https://doi.org/10.1515/9789048552153-014.

Setten, Gunhild, Katrina Myrvang Brown, and Hilde Nymoen Rørtveit. "Landscape and Social Justice." In Howard et al., *Routledge Companion to Landscape Studies*, 418–28.

Siani, Alberto L. "Between Professional Objectivity and Simmel's Moods: A Pragmatist-Aesthetic Proposal for Landscape Character." *Landscape Research* 48, no. 4 (2023): 583–593. https://doi.org/10.1080/01426397.2023.2172145.

———. "Continuando un dialogo: Amoroso e la ridefinizione deweyana dell'estetica." In *Ragione estetica ed ermeneutica del senso: Studi in memoria di Leonardo Amoroso*, ed. Alberto L. Siani, 53–62. Pisa: ETS, 2022.

———. "I limiti dell'umano: osservazioni su Kant e l'intuizione intellettuale." *Studi Kantiani* 23 (2010): 57–75. https://doi.org/10.1400/159718.

———. "Kants ästhetische Urteilskraft als nicht-ästhetisches Wissen und das Ende des modernen Subjekts." In *Ästhetisches Wissen*, ed. Christoph Asmuth and Peter Remmers, 95–110. Berlin: De Gruyter, 2015. https://doi.org/10.1515/9783110346244-006.

———. "Landscape Aesthetics." *International Lexicon of Aesthetics* (Spring 2022), https://doi.org/10.7413/18258630126.

———. "Landscape Education, Enskilment, and Aesthetics. Complex Skills for Our Time." *Contemporary Aesthetics* (forthcoming).

———. "Nowhere Between River and Road: A Nagelian Reading of *Suttree* and *The Road*." In *Philosophical Approaches to Cormac McCarthy. Beyond Reckoning*, ed. Chris Eagle, 202–19. London: Routledge, 2017.

———. "Spazi kantiani." *Aesthetica Preprint* 118 (2021): 177–88.

———. "Unifying Art and Nature: Brady and Eco on Interpretation." *Aesthetica Preprint* 114 (2020): 49–58.

Simmel, Georg. "The Philosophy of Landscape." Trans. Josef Bleicher. *Theory, Culture & Society* 24, no. 7–8 (2007): 20–29. https://doi.org/10.1177/0263276407084465.

Sofia, Francesca. "Sismondi e la Svizzera Pesciatina." In *Dalla Valleriana alla Svizzera Pesciatina*, 37–40.

Steiner, Frederick. "Is Landscape Planning?" In Doherty and Waldheim, *Is Landscape . . . ?*, 138–61.

Sterelny, Kim. "Minds: Extended or Scaffolded?" *Phenomenology and the Cognitive Sciences* 9, no. 4 (2010): 465–81. https://doi.org/10.1007/s11097-010-9174-y.

Stickney, Jeffrey A. "Seeing Trees: Investigating Poetics of Place-Based, Aesthetic Environmental Education with Heidegger and Wittgenstein." *Journal of Philosophy of Education* 54, no. 5 (2020): 1278–1305. https://doi.org/10.1111/1467-9752.12491.

BIBLIOGRAPHY

Tabarrani, Ilaria. "Struttura del paesaggio." In *Dalla Valleriana alla Svizzera Pesciatina*, 69–72.
Taylor, Ken, and Qing Xu. "Challenging Landscape Eurocentrism. An Asian Perspective." In Howard et al., *Routledge Companion to Landscape Studies*, 311–28.
Terkenli, Theano S., Aikaterini Gkoltsiou, and Dimitris Kavroudakis. "The Interplay of Objectivity and Subjectivity in Landscape Character Assessment: Qualitative and Quantitative Approaches and Challenges." *Land* 10, no. 1: 53 (2021): 1–19. https://doi.org/10.3390/land10010053.
Thompson, Catharine Ward. "Landscape Perception and Environmental Psychology," in Howard et al., *Routledge Companion to Landscape Studies*, 19–38.
Thompson, Ian. "Landscape and Environmental Ethics." In Howard et al., *Routledge Companion to Landscape Studies*, 552–64.
Tilley, Christopher. "Introduction: Identity, Place, Landscape and Heritage." *Journal of Material Culture* 11, no. 1–2 (2006): 7–32. https://doi.org/10.1177/1359183506062990.
Trane, Davide, and Mauro Agostini. "Vita nelle 'Castella' e antichi mestieri." In *Dalla Valleriana alla Svizzera Pesciatina*, 61–68.
Tudor, Christine. "An Approach to Landscape Character Assessment." Natural England, 2014. https://assets.publishing.service.gov.uk/government/uploads/system/uploads/attachment_data/file/691184/landscape-character-assessment.pdf.
Turner, Sam, Lisa-Marie Shillito, and Francesco Carrer. "Landscape Archaeology." In Howard et al., *Routledge Companion to Landscape Studies*, 155–65.
Vicenzotti, Vera. "On the Concept of Landscape in Landscape Urbanism." In Howard et al., *Routledge Companion to Landscape Studies*, 565–75.
Waldheim, Charles. "Is Landscape Urbanism?" In Doherty and Waldheim, *Is Landscape . . . ?*, 162–89.
Waterton, Emma. "More-than-Representational Landscapes." In Howard et al., *Routledge Companion to Landscape Studies*, 91–101.
Wattchow, Brian, and Alex Prins. "Learning a Landscape: Enskilment, Pedagogy and a Sense of Place." In Howard et al., *Routledge Companion to Landscape Studies*, 102–12.
Weilacher, Udo. "Is Landscape Gardening?" In *Doherty and Waldheim, Is Landscape . . . ?*, 93–114.
Wittgenstein, Ludwig. "Lectures on Aesthetics." In *Lectures and Conversations on Aesthetics, Psychology and Religious Belief*, ed. Cyril Barrett, 1–40. Berkeley: University of California Press, 1967.
——. *Philosophical Investigations*. Ed. Peter Michael Stephan Hacker and Joachim Schulte. Trans. Gertrude Elizabeth Margaret Anscombe, Peter Michael Stephan Hacker, and Joachim Schulte. Chichester, UK: Wiley-Blackwell, 2009.
——. "Remarks on Frazer's *The Golden Bough*." In *The Mythology in Our Language: Remarks on Frazer's Golden Bough*, ed. Giovanni Da Col and Stephan Palmié, trans. Stephan Palmié, 29–75. Chicago: HAU Books, 2018.
Yazıcı, Berna. "Towards an Anthropology of Traffic: A Ride Through Class Hierarchies on Istanbul's Roadways." *Ethnos* 78, no. 4 (2013): 515–42. https://doi.org/10.1080/00141844.2012.714395.
Yeşilbağ, Melih. "Statecraft on Cement: The Politics of Land-Based Accumulation in Erdoğan's Turkey." *Urban Studies* 59, no. 13 (2021). https://doi.org/10.1177/00420980211044044.

INDEX

Abrichtung. See training
adaptability, to change, 89, 111
aesthetics. *See specific topics*
aesthetics crisis, xx, xxii–xxiii, 33–35
affordances, 56; environment relation to, 180n68; of Valleriana, 143–44
agriculture, in Münsterland, 150
ameliorism, 41
Anabaptists, 148
"Angeli" neighborhood, Sicily, Italy, *19*
animals, 43
Anthropocene, 92; cultural ecology and, 92; epistemologies for, 91
antisensualism, 43
Appleton, Jay, 181n76
appreciation: of environment, 184n39, 188n5; meaning of, 196n107; temporality of, 85–86
archaeological-agricultural landscape, *87*
art: chaos relation to, 76; Dewey and, 40–41, 45; environment relation to, 80, 148, 182n9, 183n17; as experience, 48; interpretation of, 64–65, 67–68, 72; landscape, 108; landscapes compared to, 45–46, 47, 48–50, 76; natural beauty compared to, 41; nature relation to, 73, 80, 82; "open work" and, 179n49; postmodernism in, 101; sense and, 76; in Valleriana, 147
Art as Experience (Dewey), 40
artistic boundaries, 182n6
artistic intention, 65
Assunto, Rosario, 18, 19–20, 25, 77; on culture, 171n10; on landscape devastation, 170n8
author: death of, 64; intention of, 65–66

Baarle-Hertog, Belgium, 173n28
Baarle-Nassau, Netherlands, 173n28
background, 90; identity and, 172n12
Bacon, Francis, *Novum Organum* of, 6
Barnathan Apartments, in Istanbul, Turkey, 203n43
Barthes, Roland, 64
Bartram, William, 78, 79
Bathers, Mont Sainte-Victoire in the Background (painting), *75*

INDEX

beauty, xxii–xxiii, 10–11; aesthetics and, 35; isolationist aesthetics relation to, 37–38; Kant and, 9; of landscapes, 60, 64; natural, *10*, 41, 100, 147–48; subjectivity of, 9

behavioristic conditioning, education as, 196n113

Bélanger, Pierre, 90

Berchtesgaden, Germany, Bavarian Alps, *34*

Berleant, Arnold, 119–20; pragmatism and, 177n19

Berque, Augustin, 58, 100, 102

Biancini, Pierluigi, 116

Bicycle Wheel (Duchamp), 49

bilden, 169n24

Bir Tawil, 173n28

Blacklick Woods Metro Park, Ohio, *63*

Bonesio, Luisa, 96

Borbone Royal Palace, Caserta, Italy, *81*

borders: Belgium and Netherlands, *27*; dualism relation to, 31; as exclusion, 173n28; landscape research and, 120–21; meaning and, 26, 138; reality relation to, 26–27

boundaries, 6, 57, 91; of interpretation, 182n6; in LCA, 193n75

Brady, Emily, 64–65, 72; Eco compared to, 66, 67, 69–70; on interpretation, 67–68, 182n9; on landscapes, 69

Brillo Box (Warhol), 49

Brook, Isis, 179n43

Café in Baarle-Nassau, Netherlands, *27*

Campo (artificial lake), *36*

Canadian Museum of Human Rights, Winnipeg, *110*

Carlson, Allen, 181n76

Cartesian dualism, 26, 96, 102

Caserta, Italy, Borbone Royal Palace, *81*

castella, 139–40; Pontito, *141*

certainty, 90

Cézanne, Paul, 184n34

change: adaptability to, 89, 111; climate, 89–90, 91; education for, 118–19; by humans, 98; in landscape, 85; in nature, 188n5

chaos, 7–8, 26; art relation to, 76; contingency and, 44, 45; habitat and, 7; in Istanbul, 159

character, 134; essentialist conception of, 125

chestnut trees, in Valleriana, 144–45, *146*

China, 58, 59; Hangzhou, *108*; UNESCO protected sites in, 194n88

cityscape, 173n29

civil engineering, landscape architecture relation to, 90

civilizations: landscape and, 58–59; environment relation to, 101

climate change, 91; habitat and, 89–90

coastal landscape, 99

cognitivism, 181n76

collective experience, 103–4

collusion, with environment, 53, 54, 56

colonialism, 88; domination and, 186n53

commodification, 39

common good, private good *versus*, 107

communication, 47; judgment and, 196n118; of meaning, 47

community, 66; habit and, 196n115; identity of, 189n10; interpretation and, 66, 69–70; landscape relation to, 86, 171n10; participation in, 106; truth and, 69, 183n26

conflict, 204n46; removal of, 34, 88, 104

consummation: continuity relation to, 43; Dewey and, 43; of experience, 54, 85, 99; order as, 49

contingency: chaos and, 44, 45; determinacy dualism with, 30; Kant and, 7; order and, 23, 25

continuity, 41; art and, 45; between art and landscapes, 76; consummation relation to, 43; education relation to, 114; experience and, 80, 82; humans and, 44

Corner, James, 34; on landscapes, 87

Cosgrove, Denis, 33, 54–55; on humanism, 184n44; on planners, 126; on tradition, 95

COVID-19 pandemic, xix; lockdowns and, 110–11

INDEX

crisis: aesthetics, x, xxii–xxiii; ecological, 164–65; environmental, xx, xxv, 62, 83, 161, 192n57; of the humanities, xx
crisis discourse, xix, xxvii–xxviii; aesthetics in, xxiv; environment in, xxiii; landscapes in, xxv
critical pluralism, 66
Critique of Pure Reason (Kant), 168n15
Critique of the Power of Judgment (Kant), 5, 7, 9, 169n22
Cueva de las Manos, Argentina, *12*
Culler, Jonathan, 65
cultivation, 142
cultural ecology, Anthropocene and, 92
cultural pluralism, 68
culture, 11, 115; biology dualism with, 30; as habitat, 13; interpretation by, 189n10; judgment relation to, 174n38; landscape and, 16, 29, 104, 171n10; life as, 174n37; local, 113; nature and, 20, 91, 93, 100, 144, 146, 148, 182n9, 189n20; visual, 185n45

D'Angelo, Paolo, 190n22
Dante Alighieri, 143
deceit, 88
DeLue, Rachael Z., 78, 79
democracy, 108
democratization, 36
departmental library's garden, spring morning, *2*
Departures (movie), 173n22
deregulation policies, 107
design, 97; in gardening, 184n44; urban, 91
determinacy, contingency dualism with, 30
determinism, 97
Dewey, John, 40–41, 46, 50, 52, 53, 84; on art, 47–48; on consummation, 43; on environment, 42; on experience, 86, 196n118; on Kant, 177n20; pragmatism and, 177n19; on space, 179n55; on visual experience, 178n40
disinterestedness, 37
displacement, 109, 110

ditio. See domain
diversity, landscape and, 104
division, of responsibilities, 104
dogmatism, 4, 8, 26, 168n15; continuity relation to, 44
Dolly Sods Wilderness near Davis, West Virginia, *24*
domain (*ditio*), 5, 169n20; habitat compared to, 23, 25
domicilium. See habitat
domination, 96; colonialism and, 186n53; of space, 184n44
drift, of interpretation, 69, 183n25
dualism, 104; art and nature, 80; biology and culture, 30; borders relation to, 31; Cartesian, 26; in environmental humanities, xxi–xxii, xxv; environment and the human, xxi–xxii, 17–18, 42, 52, 98, 170n5, 192n60; essentialist, 42; in habitat, 11; and intellectualism, 43; landscape relation to, 17, 22; matter *versus* content/function, 19–20; nature and freedom, 23, 30; of subjectivity and objectivity, 123–24, 127; of utilitarian and aesthetic, 35, 58, 100, 162
Duchamp, Marcel, 49
dwelling perspective, 189n10
dynamic ecosystem model, in ecology, 97
dynamism, 165

Earth, *102*
earthquakes, 154–55
Eastern Orthodox Church, 203n43
Eaucourt-sur-Somme, France, *99*
Eco, Umberto, 65; Brady compared to, 66, 67, 69–70; on drift of interpretation, 183n25; on interpretation, 71, 72; pragmatism and, 177n19; on sense data, 183n29
ecological crisis, 164–65
ecology, xxv, 80; cultural, 92; dynamic ecosystem model in, 97; engaged, xxv, 164–65; environmentalism compared to, 98; landscape relation to, 197n128

education, 112; aesthetic, 119–20; as behavioristic conditioning, 196n113; for change, 118–19; continuity relation to, 114; engagement in, 113, 116; environmental, 117, 118, 175n43, 192n60; knowledge and, 120; language and, 116, 117
"Education as Aesthetic" (Berleant), 119–20
Eiderstedt, North Frisia, Germany, 15
Ekenyazıcı, Güney, 204n47
ELC. *See* European Landscape Convention
elitism, 124; objectivity and, 126
empirical place, 1–2
engagement: and aesthetics, xxiii, 37, 177n19, 178n41; in ecology, xxv, 164–65; in education, 113, 116
enskilment, 112, 113, 116, 195n100; education and, 119; as training, 117
environment, 17, 21, 72; affordances relation to, 180n68; appreciation of, 184n39, 188n5; art relation to, 80, 148, 182n9, 183n17; civilizations relation to, 101; collusion with, 53, 54, 56; in crisis discourse, xxiii; experience relation to, xxiv, 45–46, 47, 52, 196n118; habitat relation to, 86, 87; humans relation to, 42–43, 58, 101, 132, 164; interpretation of, 64, 67, 68; knowledge of, 112; landscape compared to, xxvi, 17–18, 86, 100–101, 162, 170n5, 171n11; language relation to, 29; meaning and, 51, 116; natural space and, 170n8; photography relation to, 186n56; pragmatism and, 175n41; protection of, 114; reality of, 187n57; society relation to, 187n58; temporality of, 93; territory compared to, 17–18, 19, 195n96
environmental crisis, xx, xxv, 62, 83, 161, 192n57
environmental education, 112, 118, 192n60; landscape education compared to, 117
environmental humanities, xx–xxii, xxiii–xxiv, 62; dualism in, xxv

environmentalism, 97, 100; ecology compared to, 98; postmodernism and, 96
environmental pessimism, 98
ephemerality: experience and, 94; sense-making process and, 93
epistemologies, for Anthropocene, 91
Erdoğan, Recep Tayyip, 203n39, 203n43
essence, of landscape, 15–16
essentialism: in interpretation, 68, 71–72; and landscape, 16, 125
essentialist dualism, 26, 42, 111, 131
ethics, 181n69
Eurocentrism, 108, 109
Europe, 58, 59; Council of (*See* European Landscape Convention)
European Landscape Convention (ELC), 35, 103–4, 109, 124, 163–64; LC discourse of, 134; WHC compared to, 105–6
everyday aesthetics, 180n56
exceptionalism, 38–39, 96
exclusion, borders as, 173n28
experience, 138–39; aesthetics relation to, xxvii, 126, 135–37; art as, 48; collective, 103–4; consummation of, 43, 54, 99; continuity and, 80, 82; Dewey on, 40–42, 44–45; environment relation to, xxiv, 45–46, 47, 52, 196n118; ephemerality and, 94; fetishization of, 88; interdisciplinarity and, 122; isolationist aesthetics relation to, 41; landscape relation to, 19, 47–48, 63, 162, 184n32; LC and, 128–29, 131, 165; meaning and, 76, 136; ocularcentrism relation to, 177n16; order and, 53; pragmatism on, 132; of space, 77; as spatiotemporal continuum, 84; temporality of, 86; thoughts and, 179n43; time relation to, 51, 84–85; unity and, 163; visual, 178n40
expert discourse: isolationist aesthetics in, 37, 40; on landscapes, 36; on LC, 126
exploitation: touristic, 105, 107
expression, 47–48; aesthetic, 115–16

INDEX

facts: experience and, 129; LC and, 131, 135; meaning relation to, 102–3
fear, of illusion, 4
Feld. See field
ferries, in Istanbul, 158–160
fetishization, 39; of experience, 88; of wilderness, 80
field (*Feld*), 5; territory compared to, 7
field work, 131
finality, art and, 49
flag, of Kaliningrad, 8
"form of life" (*Lebensform*), 28; as culture, 174n37
Frazer, James George, 29
freedom, 7, 168n13; habitat and, 8; in interpretation, 182n6; landscapes relation to, 25–26; in nature, 9, 11; nature dualism with, 23, 26, 30

gardening: art of, 80, 165; design in, 184n44; guerrilla, *81*
Garden of contemplation, Canadian Museum of Human Rights, Winnipeg, Canada, *110*
geography, 186n54; aesthetic appreciation and, 197n126; time relation to, 188n3
German Peasants' War, 148
Gezi Park protests, in Istanbul, 157–58
Gibson, James J., 180n68
globalist views, of landscapes, 107–8
Glock, Hans-Johann, 116
Great-Alachua Savana, East Florida, The (drawing), 78, *79*
growth, experience and, 51
guerrilla gardening, *81*

habit, 69, 71; habitat relation to, 196n115
habitat, as *domicilium* or *Aufenthalt* (Kant), xxvi, 5–6, 57, 163, 169n20; chaos and, 7; climate change and, 89–90; domain compared to, 5–7, 23, 25; environment relation to, 86, 87; freedom and, 8; habit relation to, 196n115; humans relation to, 11, 12–13; of Istanbul, 155; Kant on, 7, 11, 16, 22, 23, 25, 183n26; landscape compared to, 16; landscape relation to, 23, 26, 104; language-game compared to, 31; lockdowns and, 111; meaning and, 64, 93, 112, 171n11; of Münsterland, 153; order in, 9, 14; philosophy and, 169n22; provisional, 103; truth and, 183n26
Hagia Sophia, in Istanbul, Turkey, 203n43
Hamlet (play), 51
Hangzhou, China, Longjing tea district, *108*
Hartshorne, Richard, 33
Harvesters, The (painting), *94*
hearing, 38
Hepburn, Ronald W., 176n9
Hermetism, 183n25
hierarchies, 57, 124
historicity, of landscapes, 86, 87
holism, 47, 132
human gaze, 187n57
humanism: in interpretation, 68; space and, 184n44
humanities, environmental, xx–xxii, xxiii–xxiv, xxv, 62
humanities crisis, xx–xxi, xxv, 62
human rights, landscape as, 109, 110–11
humans: change by, 98; continuity and, 44; environment relation to, 42–43, 58, 101, 132, 164; habitat relation to, 11, 12–13; isolationist aesthetics relation to, 45; landscape relation to, 15, 23, 26, 78, 111–12, 172n21; nature relation to, 95, 96, 195n104; sense-making process and, 16; space relation to, 25
Humboldt, Alexander von, 172n21
Husband Hill, Mars, 67
hüzün (melancholy), 156–57, 203n41, 204n46
hybridization, 97–98, 121
hyperacceleration, 93

identity: background and, 172n12; of community, 189n10; landscape and, 86–87, 104, 109, 110, 171n10
illusion, truth *versus*, 4

INDEX

imagination: landscape and, 78; maps and, 186n54; meaning relation to, 10–11
immanence, 153, 158–59
imperialism, 34, 88
impermanence, 165
impoverishment, 200n5
industrialism, 96
infrastructure, 90, 172n12; landscape and, 90–91
Ingold, Tim, 94, 116; on dwelling perspective, 189n10
innocence: of landscapes, 88; loss of, 34, 88
insiders, outsiders *versus*, 107, 174n34
intellectualism, dualism in, 43
intelligence, senses relation to, 96
intention, of author, 65–66
interdisciplinarity, 100, 120, 121–22, 197n124; landscape and, *121*; in landscape research, 125
interpretation, 64; of art, 64–65, 67–68, 72; boundaries of, 182n6; and community, 70; by culture, 189n10; drift of, 69, 183n25; of environment, 64, 67, 68; of literary texts, 65–66; of meaning, 71, 179n49; of nature, 64, 72; of sense data, 183n29
Interpreting Environments (Brady), 64–65
Is Landscape …? Essays on the Identity of Landscape (Doherty and Waldheim), 169n2
isolationist aesthetics, 37–38, 43, 57; in art, 41; beauty relation to, 37–38; in expert discourse, 37, 40; humans relation to, 45; modernism in, 96; natural beauty and, 100; ocularcentrism in, 39
Istanbul, Turkey, 139, 153, *159*; ferries in, 158, 159–60; Gezi Park protests in, 156–57; Hagia Sophia in, 203n43; *hüzün* and, 156–57, 203n41, 204n46; Kanal, 203n9; Marmara earthquake in, 154–55; megaprojects in, 155, 156, 203n39; transportation in, 203n37; urbanization in, *155*, 204n47

Jackson, John B., 33, 90
judgment, 12–13; communication and, 196n118; culture relation to, 174n38; of taste, 9, 10
justice, 106, 108, 111

Kaliningrad, Russia, 3, 5, 167n3; flag of, *8*
Kant, Immanuel, xxvi, 38, 61, 102–3, 168n16; on beauty, 9–10; *Critique of Pure Reason* of, 168n15; *Critique of the Power of Judgment* of, 5, 7, 9, 169n22; Dewey critiquing, 177n20; on habitat, 7, 11, 16, 22, 23, 25, 183n26; on imagination, 10; isolationist aesthetics relation to, 37; on judgment, 196n118; "land of truth" of, 3–4
Kneiphof island, *4*, 5
knowledge: boundaries of, 6; of environment, 112; pleasure and, 70
Königsberg, Germany, 3, *4*, 167n3
Kottman, Paul A., 172n18

land art, 80, 186n56
"land of truth," Kant and, 3–4
Landscape and Bamboo (painting), 50
landscape architecture, civil engineering relation to, 90
landscape character (LC), 123–24, 198n2; aesthetics and, 126, 129, 131, 135–36; ELC discourse of, 134; experience and, 128–29, 131, 165; facts and, 135; landscape research and, 123; mood and, 136; objectivity and, 125, 126–27, 132–33, 134; unity and, 162; values and, 132
landscape character assessment (LCA), 124, *130*, 198n2; boundaries in, 193n75; objectivity and, 125, 127; planners and, 134–35
landscape civilizations, 58, 59
landscape education, 118–19; environmental education compared to, 117

INDEX

landscape performances, 32
landscape research, 61, 122, 125; aesthetics in, 33, 35–36; borders and, 120, 121; experience in, 129; interdisciplinarity in, 120, 125; LC and, 123; postenvironmentalism and, 97; private good and, 194n84
landscapes. *See specific topics*
Landscape with Two Peasant Girls and a Rainbow (painting), 60
Landscape with Windmills and Christ as Good Shepherd (print), 55
language: education and, 116, 117; environment relation to, 29; "form of life" relation to, 29, 114–15; landscapes relation to, 82; philosophy and, 30–31, 170n3
language-game (*Sprachspiel*), 28, 29, 32, 77–78; culture and, 174n38; "form of life" and, 175n43; habitat compared to, 31; landscapes compared to, 31; meaning and, 175n48; order and, 55
lay discourse: on landscapes, 36; ocularcentrism in, 38, 39
LC. *See* landscape character
LCA. *See* landscape character assessment
Lebensform. *See* "form of life"
"Lectures on Aesthetics" (Wittgenstein), 115
legislative power, 5, 6
legitimacy crisis, of the humanities, xx, 62
life, 41, 43; community and, 171n10; in environment, 42; experience relation to, 132
linear perspective, 33, 184n44; in landscape painting, 185n45
literary texts: interpretation of, 65–66; landscapes compared to, 82
lived landscapes, 161–62. *See also* Istanbul, Turkey; Münsterland, North Rhine-Westphalia, Germany; Valleriana, Tuscany, Italy
local culture, 113
localist views, of landscapes, 107–8

lockdowns, and COVID-19, 110–11
Longjing tea district, Hangzhou, China, 108

maps, 71, 91, 184n44; imagination and, 186n54; time relation to, 188n3
Market Outside Tripoli's Walls, Castle and Cemetery on the Right (photo), 59
Marmara earthquake, 154–55
Mars, Husband Hill, 67
matter *versus* content/function dualism, 19–20
Matteucci, Giovanni, 52–53, 119; on extended mind and the aesthetic, 57; on relativism, 180n65
McCarthy, Cormac, 171n11
meaning: of aesthetics, 37; of appreciation, 196n107; borders and, 26, 138; communication of, 47; environment and, 51, 116; experience and, 76, 136; facts relation to, 102–3; habitat and, 64, 93, 112, 171n11; imagination relation to, 10–11; interpretation of, 64, 71, 179n49; landscapes and, 63, 69; language-game and, 175n48; in literary texts, 65–66; purpose and, 69
megaprojects, in Istanbul, 155, 156; Kanal Istanbul, 203n39
melancholy. *See hüzün*
migration, 110; to Istanbul, 154, 155; safety and, 109
mind, landscapes relation to, 53, 57
Mitchell, William J.T., 34, 88
modernism, 98; in isolationist aesthetics, 96, 191n50; and landscape character, 124, 131; and landscapes, 57–58, 102; pastism relation to, 97
modernity: and landscapes, 95–97; nature in, 95–96; as utopia, 101
monism, 66
Mont Sainte-Victoire (painting), 75, 184n34
mood (*Stimmung*), 124; in landscape, 77–78, 134; LC and, 136; unity and, 133
Moore, Kathryn, 96
more-than-representational, landscapes, 85

INDEX

Münsterland, North Rhine-Westphalia, Germany, 139; agriculture in, 150; Münster, 148, 150; park landscape in, 151–52; St. Lambert's Church, 148, *149*, 152–53; Thirty Years' War in, 148, 149; tourism in, 201n21
Münsterlander Parklandschaft, 150, *150*
Museo della Carta (Museum of Paper), in Valleriana, 141

Nagel, Thomas, 171n11
Napoleon, 153–54
natural beauty, *10*, 176n9; art compared to, xxii–xxiii, 35, 41; isolationist aesthetics and, 100; of Valleriana, 147–48
naturalism, 181n76, 189n10
naturalization, of power dynamics, 88
nature, 7, 168n13; aesthetics and, 38, 181n71; appreciation of, 184n39; art relation to, 73, 80, 82; culture and, 20, 91, 93, 100, 144, 146, 148, 182n9, 189n20; freedom dualism with, 23, 30; freedom in, 9, 11; humans relation to, 95, 96, 195n104; interpretation of, 64, 72; landscapes relation to, 25, 189n19; in modernity, 95–96; peasants relation to, 59–60, 61, 174n34; photography of, 186n56; pleasure and, 68; realism and, 71; representation of, 73; residuality of, 173n22; respect for, 70; time relation to, 188n5
Nauviale, Aveyron, France, *24*
Nazis, 140
necci, *145*
niche, 175n41
nomadism, 109
Novum Organum (Bacon), 6

objectivism, 124–25, 127
objectivity, 7; elitism and, 126; experience and, 129; in judgment, 9; LC and, 125, 126–27, 132–33, 134; in sight, 38; subjectivity relation to, 123–24, 127; values and, 127
ocularcentrism, 20, 78, 80, 84; experience relation to, 177n16; in lay discourse, 38, 39; objectivity and, 125

Olwig, Kenneth, 33, 107, 193n75, 194n84; "Recovering the Substantive Nature of Landscapes" of, 106
"open work," art and, 179n49
Orange Skies at Ladram Bay, The (photo), 39
order, 133; as consummation, 49; experience and, 53; freedom and, 11; in habitat, 9, 14; language-game and, 55; of space, 189n10; as a unifying concept, 76
ordinariness, 37–39, 45, 105; photography and, 193n78
outsiders, insiders *versus*, 107, 174n34

"Paesaggio, ambiente, territorio" (Assunto), 18
paintings: appreciation of, 85, 196n107; landscapes in, 2, 14, 73, 74, 77, 184n34, 185n45, 190n22. *See also* art
palimpsest, 86
Pamuk, Orhan, 156, 203n41
paper mills, in Valleriana, 141–42
park landscape, in Münsterland, 151–52
participation, 47, 104, 106
pastism, modernism relation to, 97
peasants, 59–60, 61, 174n34
Peirce, Charles Sanders, 66, 69; pragmatism and, 177n19
perception, 77–78, 103, 105, 133–34; of landscape, 171n10; taskscape and, 190n39
performative configurations, landscapes as, 25, 49, 94, 173n23
perspective: dwelling, 189n10; linear, 33, 184n44, 185n45
Pescia River, 139
pessimism, environmental, 98
Philosophical Investigations (Wittgenstein), 31
philosophy, xxviii, 3; boundaries in, 6; crisis relation to, 83; habitat and, 169n22; language and, 30–31, 170n3
photography: environment relation to, 186n56; landscapes in, 2; ordinariness and, 193n78
pietra serena quarries, 141–42

INDEX

planners, 126; LCA and, 134–35; of Münsterland park landscape, 151–52
planning, 100, 104
Plato, *Timaeus* of, 38
pleasure, 34; knowledge and, 70; nature and, 68
pluralism: critical, 66; cultural, 68; in interpretation, 65; in landscape theory, xxiii, 16, 54, 56–57; LC and, 124
political landscape, 169n1
politics: of landscapes, 103–5, 106, 111–12; in Turkey, 204n44
Pontito, Valleriana, *141*
postenvironmentalism, 97
posthumanism, 79, 85, 114
postmodernism: in art, 101; environmentalism and, 96
power dynamics, naturalization of, 88
pragmatism, xxv, 16, 170n3, 175n41, 177n19; Dewey and, 41; interpretation and, 72, 179n49; landscape character and, 132
private good: common good *versus*, 107; landscape research and, 194n84
privatization, 107
process, landscape as, 20
prospect-refuge theory, 181n76
protected sites, of UNESCO, 194n88
protection, 105; of environment, 114
provisional habitats, 103
public participation, 108
public transportation, 200n4
Pueblo Indian pottery, 44
purpose, meaning and, 69
purposiveness *(Zweckmäßigkeit)*, 7, 11

quarries, *pietra serena*, 141–42

Rasim, Ahmet, 156–57
rationalism, 96
realism: in interpretation, 71–72; nature and, 71
reality, borders relation to, 26–27
reciprocity, 52
reconciliation, xxi–xxii, 46, 102–3

"Recovering the Substantive Nature of Landscapes" (Olwig), 106
relativism, 21, 53–54, 56, 66, 69, 136, 180n65
"Remarks on Frazer's *The Golden Bough*" (Wittgenstein), 28
representation: and experience, 42; of landscape, 171n10; of nature, 73
res cogitans, 26
res extensa, 26
residuality, of nature, 173n22
respect, for nature, 70
responsibilities, division of, 104
Ritter, Joachim, 95
Road, The (McCarthy), 171n11
romantic aestheticism, 37
rootedness, 109
Rorty, Richard, 65, 70
rose, 9; natural beauty of, *10*
Routledge Companion to Landscape Studies (Howard et al.), 34

safety, 90; migration and, 109
Saito, Yuriko, 180n56
scalpellini. *See* stonecutters
scenery: landscape as, 14; territory *versus*, 106
seasons, 1–2
security, 90
sense data, interpretation of, 183n29
sense-making process: aesthetics in, 99; ephemerality and, 93; Kottman on, 172n18; landscape and, 16, 25
senses, 128; intelligence relation to, 96. *See also* ocularcentrism
separation, in isolationist aesthetics, 39
sight, 38. *See also* ocularcentrism
Simmel, Georg, 74, 76, 95; LC and, 135; on mood, 124, 133–34
Sismondi, Jean Charles Léonard Simonde de, 140, 142–43
skepticism, 4, 8, 26, 168n15; continuity relation to, 44
society, environment relation to, 187n58
solipsism, 69
Sonfist, Alan, 89, 186n56

space: domination of, 184n44; experience of, 77; habitat as, 44; humanism and, 184n44; humans relation to, 25; interpretation of, 119; landscape relation to, 20–21, 23, 26; order of, 189n10; synthetic, 189n19; time relation to, 84, 88, 179n55, 189n20

spatiality, 50; temporality relation to, 139

spatiotemporal continuum, experience as, 84

Sprachspiel. See language-game

stability, 90; beauty relation to, 9

Stickney, Jeffrey, 117–18

Stiftung Westfälische Kulturlandschaft, 201n23

Stimmung. See mood

St. Lambert's Church, Münster, 148, *149*, 152–53

stonecutters (*scalpellini*), 144, 200n10

subjectivity, 7; of beauty, 9; objectivity relation to, 123–24, 127

subject-object paradigm, 79

substantive landscape. *See* Olwig, Kenneth

Surf-swimming, Hawaii (illustration), *113*

Suttree (McCarthy), 171n11

Svizzera Pesciatina, 140

Switzerland, 142, 143

synthetic space, 189n19

Tableau de l'agriculture toscane (Sismondi), 140

Tanner Lectures. *See* Eco

taskscape, 94; perception and, 190n39

taste, judgment of, 9, 10

Tempest, The (painting), *74*

temporality, 84, 188n4; of environment, 93; of landscapes, 86, 87–88; spatiality relation to, 139

territory: as *Boden* (in Kant), 5; borders relation to, 26; environment compared to, 17–18, 19, 195n96; of experience, 9; field compared to, 7; landscape as, 14; landscape compared to, xxvi, 17–19, 21, 162, 170n5; scenery *versus*, 106

Teutoburg Forest, 148

Thirty Years' War: in Münsterland, 148, 149; Treaties of Westphalia and, 201n20

thoughts, experience and, 179n43

Timaeus (Plato), 38

time, 188n4; experience relation to, 51, 84–85; geography relation to, 188n3; landscapes relation to, 87–88; nature relation to, 188n5; space relation to, 84, 88, 179n55, 189n20

Time Landscape (land artwork), 89, 186n56

tourism: in Münsterland, 201n21; in Valleriana, 200n5

touristic exploitation, 105, 107

tradition, 95

training (*Abrichtung*), 116; education and, 117

transcendence, 156, 157–58

transdisciplinarity, 100, 120, 121

transparency, LC and, 124, 133

transportation: in Istanbul, 203n37; public, 200n4

Treaties of Westphalia, 201n20

Tree of Jesse, Wells Cathedral, England, *71*

truth: illusion *versus*, 3–4; interpretation and, 69, 183n26

Tudor, Christine, 129, 131

Turkey: politics in, 204n44. *See also* Istanbul, Turkey

Tuscany, Italy. *See* Valleriana, Tuscany, Italy

two-world hypothesis, 91

UNESCO: protected sites of, 194n88; WHC of, 93, 105, 193nn77–78

unifying concept, order as, 76

unity, 76, 122; experience and, 163; humans and, 28–29; LC and, 162; mood and, 133

urban design, 91

urbanization, in Istanbul, *155*, 204n47

urban landscapes, 22, 157, 158, 172n16

utopia, modernity as, 101

INDEX

Valleriana, Tuscany, Italy, 139–40, 200n3; affordances of, 143–44; chestnut trees in, 144–45, 146; natural beauty of, 147–48; *pietra serena* quarries in, 141–42; Pontito, *141*; tourism in, 200n5
values, 126; experience and, 129; LC and, 132; objectivity and, 127
Vang Vieng, Laos, *46*
virtual landscapes, 172n16
visual culture, 185n45
visual experience, 178n40

Warhol, Andy, 49
weather conditions, 1–2
Wells Cathedral, England, Tree of Jesse, *71*
Westphalian heaven (*Westfälischer Himmel*), 153
West Virginia, Davis, *24*
WHC. *See* World Heritage Convention

wilderness, 23; fetishization of, 80; as landscape, 48, 49; in photography, 186n56
wind turbines, 98, 99, *99–100*
Winnipeg, Canada, *110*
Wittgenstein, Ludwig, xxvii, 30, 56, 169n25; on aesthetic expressions, 114–15; "Lectures on Aesthetics" of, 115; *Philosophical Investigations* of, 31; pragmatism and, 177n19; "Remarks on Frazer's *The Golden Bough*" of, 28; Stickney on, 117–18. *See also* "form of life"; language-game
Wittgenstein's Cabin 11 (visual artwork), 30
World Heritage Convention (WHC), 93, 193nn77–78; ELC compared to, 105–6
World War II, 149

Zweckmäßigkeit. See purposiveness

GPSR Authorized Representative: Easy Access System Europe, Mustamäe tee
50, 10621 Tallinn, Estonia, gpsr.requests@easproject.com

www.ingramcontent.com/pod-product-compliance
Lightning Source LLC
Chambersburg PA
CBHW022049290426
44109CB00014B/1030